Gregory Mason

ARROWS OF LONGING

ARROWS OF LONGING

SWALLOW PRESS

The Correspondence

between Anaïs Nin

and Felix Pollak

1952–1976

Edited by Gregory H. Mason

OHIO UNIVERSITY PRESS / ATHENS

Swallow Press/Ohio University Press, Athens, Ohio 45701
© 1998 by the Anaïs Nin Trust
Printed in the United States of America
All rights reserved. Published 1998

Swallow Press/Ohio University Press books are printed on acid-free paper ⊗ ™

05 04 03 02 01 00 99 98   5 4 3 2 1

Library of Congress Cataloging-in-Publication Data
Nin, Anaïs, 1903–1977.
    Arrows of longing : the correspondence between Anaïs Nin and Felix
Pollak, 1952–1979 / edited by Gregory H. Mason.
        p.   cm.
    Includes bibliographical references (p.   ) and index.
    ISBN 0-8040-1006-4 (cloth : alk. paper). — ISBN 0-8040-1007-2
pbk. : alk. paper)
        1. Nin, Anaïs, 1903–1977—Correspondence. 2. Women authors,
American—20th century—Correspondence. 3. Pollak, Felix—
Correspondence. 4. Poets, American—20th century—Correspondence.
5. Librarians—United States—Correspondence. I. Pollak, Felix.
II. Mason, George Henry. III. Title.
PS3527.I865Z495   1998
818'.5209—dc21
    [B]   97-46482
                                                            CIP

CONTENTS

Contents

ACKNOWLEDGMENTS

I owe a debt of gratitude to several people who have encouraged and helped me in various ways to get this book completed. In Madison, Wisconsin, Sara Pollak helped me at every stage to access the Felix Pollak Archives and to understand better both Felix Pollak the artist and Felix Pollak the man. Likewise in Madison, Klaus Berghahn and especially Reinhold Grimm eagerly supported this project and helped me to see the importance of Felix Pollak in the context of contemporary Austrian letters. My thanks go also to John Tedeschi, Robin Rider and the Special Collections staff at the University of Wisconsin–Madison for their friendly help and cooperation. In Madison, last but by no means least, my thanks go to Richard Vowles for his rare friendship and warm hospitality. In Los Angeles, I am particularly grateful to Rupert Pole, who encouraged me from the very start in this project when I approached him as a complete stranger, and who generously made the Anaïs Nin Archives available to me. Thanks also go to Charlotte Brown and the Special Collections staff of the University Research Library at the University of California at Los Angeles. The material in this book is published by courtesy of the Department of Special Collections, General Library System, University of Wisconsin–Madison, and by the Department of Special Collections, University Research Library, University of California at Los Angeles. Again, I was extended every courtesy and cooperation during my visit. In all matters pertaining to Anaïs Nin, I am especially indebted to Gunther Stuhlmann who has become a kind of mentor for me in this project, and who has repeatedly and generously drawn on his unique knowledge of Anaïs Nin's life and work to help me prepare this volume. And for help in the final editing stages, I owe special thanks to Nancy Basmajian of Ohio University Press, whose expertise, patience, and good humor kept the project on track while her author roamed from Minnesota to Osaka, Japan and back.

In Saint Peter, I wish to thank Gustavus Adolphus College for the sabbatical leave of 1994–95 which enabled me to gather and collate the essential primary materials, and especially Dean Elizabeth Baer, who has taken a personal interest in my work. At Gustavus, I am also thankful to my colleagues, particularly John Rezmerski, Philip Bryant and Joyce Sutphen, for their interest and support, to Janet Fredlund and Janine Genelin who cheerfully helped me to transcribe the original letters, and to Joyce Hiscock and Bruce Aarsvold who saw me safely through the electronic transcription. Closer to home, I would like to thank Claire, Ross, and Nicholas for cheering me on and for putting up with me when I had to "check out" for long periods of time, and most of all Ruth for her nonstop love and support.

INTRODUCTION

The Correspondence between Anaïs Nin and Felix Pollak

Although Felix Pollak and Anaïs Nin met only once in 1955, they wrote to each other often between 1952 and 1976 and became close friends, exchanging over two hundred letters and postcards. They shared an intense but little-known literary friendship, corresponding at length on a range of topics concerning their work as writers, their shared experiences as exiles from Europe, and the joys and frustrations of their personal lives. The letters and cards that make up this volume reveal the empathic and generous side of Anaïs Nin, attested to by her friends but not often otherwise available in published form. They also introduce the Austro-American poet Felix Pollak, who at times used the pseudonym Felix Anselm, to a deservedly wider international readership.

The biographical outlines of Anaïs Nin's life are now quite widely known. Born in 1903 in Paris to Cuban parents of Catalan lineage on her father's side, and Danish and French lineage on her mother's, Anaïs Nin emigrated with her mother and two younger brothers to the United States in 1914. Her father, Joaquín Nin, a renowned pianist and composer, had abandoned the family shortly before, and Anaïs grew up in New York with her mother, Rosa, and her brothers, Thorvald and Joaquín. In 1923 she married the young New York bank trainee Hugo Guiler. The following year, Guiler was assigned to Paris, and the couple took up residence there for fifteen years, returning to New York in 1939. Beginning in 1948, Anaïs Nin divided her time between life with Hugo Guiler in New York and life with Rupert Pole in California. With the exception of some brief visits to

Europe, Nin remained henceforth in the United States, in New York and, increasingly, in California until her death early in 1977.

All of Anaïs Nin's writings grew out of diaries that she began keeping at the age of eleven on her ocean voyage to New York. She continued writing these diaries, some eighty handwritten volumes, throughout her life. While living in Paris, New York, and Los Angeles, Nin sought out and became a magnet for many writers and artists, including Antonin Artaud, Henry Miller, Lawrence Durrell, and Gore Vidal. She also underwent psychoanalysis with René Allendy and then Otto Rank, whose patient, lover, and professional associate she briefly became. These figures all pass through the pages of Nin's diaries, captured by her sharp and delicate observations. A unique and tireless record of her search for personal identity and fulfillment, Nin's diaries present, in her words, "a woman's journey of self-discovery."

This theme also informs Nin's short fiction, novels, and criticism, beginning with her prose poem, *The House of Incest* (1936). Her short stories are principally collected in *Under a Glass Bell* (1947) and *Collages* (1964). Her ambitious "continuous novel," comprising five interconnected works, *Ladders to Fire* (1946), *Children of the Albatross* (1947), *The Four-Chambered Heart* (1950), *A Spy in the House of Love* (1954), and *Solar Barque* (1958), appeared under the collective title *Cities of the Interior* (1959). Beyond this, Nin authored *D. H. Lawrence: An Unprofessional Study* (1932) and essays in which she laid out her artistic credo, broadly following C. G. Jung's dictum: "From the dream proceed outward."

This impressive career by no means appeared so successful midstream. Success eluded Anaïs Nin for most of her life, and it was only through a courageous and at times obsessive determination that she continued her work as a writer. In desperation, she established her own printing press to publish and distribute her writings. She even resorted to writing pornography briefly in order to support her other writing. Eventually, with the publication of her diaries, Anaïs Nin's unique vision, gifts, and determination were vindicated by international acclaim. Anaïs Nin became a celebrity, admired both for her extraordinary writings and for the inspirational example of her life as an undaunted pioneering spirit.

Felix Pollak needs more of an introduction. Born in 1909 in Vienna to middle-class, Jewish parents, Felix Pollak won a young writers' contest at the age of seventeen and had his first stories published in the Vienna *Neue freie Presse.* He studied jurisprudence at the University of Vienna and at the same time attended the Max Reinhardt theater seminar, directing a highly successful, open-air production of *A Midsummer Night's Dream* under Reinhardt's tutelage at the Salzburg Festival in 1933. Two days after Hitler's annexation of Austria in March 1938, Pollak had his passport confiscated, but he managed to flee to the United States. In New York, he worked as a doughnut baker, factory worker, and even door-to-door salesman before relocating in Buffalo, New York, where he began his career as a librarian. In 1943, Pollak was drafted into the United States Army and assigned to the South as an interrogator of German and Austrian prisoners of war. After the war, now as a United States citizen, Pollak took a master's degree in library science at the University of Michigan, and in 1949 he was appointed rare books librarian at Northwestern University in Evanston, Illinois, where he met Sara Allen. They were married in 1950. While at Northwestern, Pollak began his correspondence with Anaïs Nin.

In 1959, Pollak moved to Madison, Wisconsin, where he became curator of rare books at the University of Wisconsin. Here he built up the Marvin Sukov collection of so-called "little magazines," small-circulation avant-garde literary periodicals, to become the largest such collection in the English-speaking world. Pollak published his own essays and poetry in over a hundred such little magazines, and in 1963 his first volume of poetry in English, *The Castle and the Flaw,* appeared. Dropping the pen name Felix Anselm[1] that he had carried with him from his pre-war Vienna days, from this point on he published under his own name. Five more volumes followed: *Say When* (1969); *Ginkgo* (1973); *Subject to Change* (1978); *Tunnel Visions* (1984); and *Benefits of Doubt* (1988). During the Vietnam War, his protest poem "Speaking: The Hero" [see Appendix B] was widely quoted and translated into seven languages. In 1974, glaucoma forced Pollak into retirement, but he remained active till his death in 1987, translating his poetry into and out of German, and giving readings of poems he had memorized. A reading tour in Germany and Austria in his last months in summer 1987 earned Pollak substantial belated international recognition. Following this, dual language editions of his poetry, *Vom Nutzen des Zweifels* [*The Uses of Doubt*] (1989), and of his German aphorisms, *Lebenszeichen* [*Vital Signs*] (1992),[2] were published posthumously in those countries. In 1988, Sara Pollak established the Felix Pollak Prize in Poetry, administered by the creative writing program of the University of Wisconsin–Madison Department of English. The prize is awarded annually.[3]

Through their correspondence, both Anaïs Nin and Felix Pollak present nuanced portraits of themselves that shed fresh light on their complex personalities. Two recent biographies of Anaïs Nin, *Anaïs: The Erotic Life of Anaïs Nin* by Noel Riley Fitch (1993) and *Anaïs Nin: A Biography* by Deirdre Bair (1995), have both been drawn to the more sensational sides of her story: Anaïs Nin as the self-absorbed, self-deceiving erotic adventuress. This is hardly surprising, since the record is both shocking and fascinating, but as a representation of Nin's character it is incomplete and unfair. Her correspondence with Felix Pollak helps to recover a more balanced overall portrait of Anaïs Nin. Nin showed Pollak a less familiar side of herself, direct, vulnerable, and honest. She wrote Pollak: "It is because you see me as a human being as well as a writer that we became friends." In the last third of her life, Anaïs Nin's letters, such as those to Felix Pollak, complemented and often took the place of the regular diary writing she had done earlier, when she had explored her inner self and her intimate personal relationships in the privacy of her diaries. Later, in her many devoted correspondences, she expressed a more social side of her personality in the give and take of unfolding friendships.[4]

The letters likewise bring the character of Felix Pollak into considerably sharper focus. Self-effacing and ironic in his public persona, Pollak emerges in this correspondence with Nin as harboring considerable literary ambitions and inner yearnings. Of a pronouncedly Romantic temperament, Pollak was perhaps destined to be an "existential exile"[5] whatever his circumstances. Having barely escaped with his life, he understandably made a cautious career choice, which failed to satisfy the extravagant yearnings of his inner life; the needs of the survivor conflicted with the dreams of the artist. Forced to give up dreams of a life in the theater in Austria, he prospered as a librarian in the United States, but he remained spiritually attached to the vanished pre-war Vienna of his youth, his "step-

marked "approx." The place of origin of a letter, if not specified by its author, is also supplied in square brackets.

Some digressive and irrelevant passages have been omitted, but the essential content and spirit of the correspondence is here intact. This edition uses ellipsis points to indicate such omissions. A dash designates either a dash or informal ellipsis points in the original texts, used by both writers to indicate a change in the flow of thought.

Since these informal, personal letters were written, sometimes hastily, in a variety of circumstances, occasional misspellings, unintended omissions and repetitions of words, and errant punctuation inevitably occurred. For consistency and ease of reading, the spelling and punctuation of both writers have been silently emended to conform to standard usage. In no case has a silent change in the spelling of a given word or in punctuation altered the meaning or tone of the passage in question from that which it possesses in the original manuscript. Square brackets are used to indicate material not in the original letters, added by the editor to clarify a meaning or provide a reference. Footnotes at the ends of some letters provide essential information and context to assist the reader in the flow of the reading. In addition, numbered notes grouped at the end of the volume provide background information and context about persons, places, or works referred to when such information may not be commonly known or readily available elsewhere.

Felix Pollak once suggested to Anaïs Nin that Friedrich Nietzsche's phrase "Pfeile der Sehnsucht" ("Arrows of Longing") would make a good title for a collection of poems. Likewise their letters, with their long-sustained mix of comradeship in exile, idealism, and Romantic yearning, resonate to this image of "Arrows of Longing."

The Correspondence between
Anaïs Nin and Felix Pollak

1

July 1952–February 1953

A FRIENDSHIP ARISES

IN THE WINTER OF 1951–52, Anaïs Nin was a writer in despair. "Exiled, alone, cut off," she confided in her diary, "I wept at being isolated at the blockade of the publishers."[1] Fifteen publishing houses had rejected her novel *A Spy in the House of Love*, and Nin became desperate for literary acceptance and support. This came from an unexpected source: Felix Pollak, an Austrian Jewish refugee, who had migrated by way of France, England, New York City, Buffalo, New York, and Ann Arbor, Michigan, to become the rare books librarian at Northwestern University in Evanston, Illinois. Pollak had recently assisted in the library's purchase of several folders of Anaïs Nin's original manuscripts.

In this correspondence, Pollak quickly goes beyond his professional, business role to write Nin of his admiration for her work, and their friendship is born. Pollak's first letter is addressed to "Mrs. Ian Hugo," with the salutation "Dear Miss Nin," but this quickly leads to an informal and friendly tone between the two. Amid such general neglect, Nin is flattered by Pollak's avid and knowledgeable interest in her work, and she is particularly moved by his sympathy with her inability to find a publisher for *A Spy in the House of Love*. In exchange for Pollak's kind words, Nin offers Pollak gifts of her own books, and their friendship grows.

In the winter of 1953, Pollak makes the second of two trips back to Vienna to complete his examinations for a Doctor of Jurisprudence degree that he had abandoned when he fled in 1938. He is unable to arrange a meeting with Nin on his way through New York, and the correspondence then lapses for almost a year, for no clear reason.

Mrs. Ian Hugo
35 W 9th St.
New York, N.Y.

Felix Pollak
1235 Elmwood Avenue
Evanston, Ill.
July 17, 1952

Miss Anaïs Nin
Sierra Madre
General Delivery
Dear Miss Nin:

The enclosed note in *Library News* will hardly communicate much of the admiration I have for your work, but I think you ought to see it.[2] I am *very* glad that the purchase has finally come through, and I only hope you too are pleased with it. I do believe that the immaterial advantage of keeping a writer's manuscripts together in one place is the thing that counts in the long run.

Your manuscripts are kept in our Vault and will—with necessary precautions—be made available to qualified students. Although I'm not in a position to extend an official invitation to you (this is an unofficial letter altogether), let me express my private hope that you some day soon will come to visit us and your papers!

Kathryn Winslow* tells me she thinks you're still in California but she didn't know how long, so I am sending a copy of this letter to your New York address, in case this doesn't reach you.

Most sincerely,

Felix Pollak

*Chicago gallery and bookstore owner involved in negotiations with the library of Northwestern University to acquire manuscripts by Anaïs Nin.[3]

General Delivery
Sierra Madre
Cal.
[July 22, 1952; postmark]

Dear Mr. Pollak:

I do appreciate your warm letter and your notes in *Library News*. It does make me happy to have all my manuscripts in the hands of those who care about them. I have had so little general recognition that I value all the more the personal, individual, sincere one. I always wanted to visit Northwestern University—I make the trip between New York and Los Angeles several times a year but I have always been rushed. I once read at Chicago University.

Do you have all my books for your own personal use? I would like you to have them before they go out of print—

I can't find a publisher for my last manuscsript [A *Spy in the House of Love*]—so you can see why I am grateful for a letter which makes me feel I must go on writing—at least the manuscripts will be read!

I will let you know when I can visit Chicago.

Most sincerely,

Anaïs Nin

Felix Pollak
1235 Elmwood Avenue
Evanston, Ill.
July 29, 1952

Dear Miss Nin—

Thank you very much for your moving letter. That you can't find a publisher for your new book seems absolutely incredible—and very distressing, to say the least! Although I have some idea of the shameful publishing situation in this country, this attitude toward an author of your stature—now, after several of your books have been brought out by commercial publishers, is difficult for me to understand. I am certain those publishers did not make much money on your books—as they should not have expected to—but it is quite as certain that they enhanced their literary prestige by publishing you. Which apparently counts for nothing in the business which their activity has exclusively become. If any grounds for the indictment of our publishing houses of prostitution had been lacking, your case would supply the need.

I understand your bitterness, although it jarred me when you remarked that at least your manuscripts will be read; it seems rhetorical to express my conviction that also your books will be read—and more so as time goes on—and that your future works will be published, one way or another. For the same reason, I don't even want to comment about your statement about your going on writing—being one of the true and genuine writers, you couldn't do otherwise if you tried! Only why artists in every generation have to go through such agonies, hardships and discouragements! . . .

As to the small public recognition you have received—first of all, I would think—and I believe you really do too—that the private one is considerably more valuable and important, and secondly, the names of the people who spoke up for you and the contents of their evaluations should more than make up for the laudatory clichés of commercial book-reviewing (or rave-viewing) which is more and more becoming a branch of the advertising business. . . .

Your offer to give me some of your books is deeply touching. Of course, I would gladly part with my remaining eye tooth for the Paris edition of *Winter of Artifice*[4] (the scene where you stand before the long mirror dressing for an evening party, spraying yourself with perfume, in the golden light from the garden, in that setting for Pelleas and Melisande, in that light of gold "made of fine powder easily decomposed by time"—that scene on which you "labored like chiseller, with minute care" and at the end of which you break out into the eternal agonized question of the artist, "Have I got it now—or will I return to these words one day and find them faded?"—that scene, Miss Nin, is not only my favorite one from all your books, but one of the most magical and enchanting and nostalgic of which I know in English prose! . . .

Thank you once more. I am very glad you said you would visit the Library, I hope in the not too distant future.

Most sincerely,

Felix Pollak

At present: General Delivery,
Sierra Madre, Cal.
or
35 West 9th St.
New York City (after Sep 25)
[August 28, 1952; postmark]

Dear Mr. Pollak,

I liked your letter very much. I didn't want to answer you until I had found a copy of Paris edition of *Winter of Artifice*—I was in New York then—but I failed. I do have a copy of my own, an extra one, packed with the diaries in a San Francisco vault, and the next time I go there to visit my mother I will send it to you. You have a right to it, you know, with your understanding of it! At the time two motivations compelled me to deny the existence of this book. One: it was published just as the war began, immediately banned by the U.S.A. mails which endangered my returning to U.S.A. with my American husband—This was a shock. Friends who had ordered it were questioned etc. This subdued my style for a few months. But the final change in my attitude was due to my realization that when I wrote this book I was too much under the influence of Henry Miller's writing and his revisions of my work (I was just beginning to write) so when I printed the book myself (by hand, hand setting etc.) I left out the Hans part and revised *Winter of Artifice* as it is now included in *Under a Glass Bell.*[5] This hand-set hand-printed edition is now very difficult to get (only printed 500 copies) and one occasionally turns up. I'll be watching out for a copy for you. . . .

Incidentally the passage you refer to out of *W. of A.* is taken literally out of the Diary itself.

Sincerely,

Anaïs Nin

1235 Elmwood Ave
Evanston, Ill.
September 6, 1952

Dear Miss Nin—

I don't know what to say—I am overwhelmed with the prospect of owning a book I have so long been trying to find. Yet I sense that you are one of those impulsively and unalterably generous persons who would part with their own cherished possessions in order to please those they consider worthy of their presents. That you consider me so makes me sincerely happy. But I do hope you won't think me presumptuous for even suggesting that you may want to give away your own last copy. Unless you can assure me on this point, I'll never feel at ease in the possession of this book! . . .

I hope things will begin to happen soon about your new novel and I trust you will let me know as soon as the turning of bad luck occurs—as it, despite everything, must.

With many thanks for many things, very sincerely,

Felix Pollak

[California]
Sept. 20, 1952

Dear Felix Pollak,

. . . Please do not feel indebted. It is good to give the books to those who care as much as you do.

. . . About *This Hunger*. Did you know it was included in Dutton's *Ladders to Fire*?[6] Was it the original edition you wanted, the one done on my own press? I have a copy but you will be keenly disappointed. That was the last book I printed, under great stress of deepening troubles, debts, the Press's disintegration, failing strength etc. So the book is a failure. If it is just the contents, you will see it's in Dutton's copy. If it is the hand printed copy, I am sending it to you just to show you it was poor handiwork—You don't mention *Children of the Albatross*,[7] so I am sending you that—

Anaïs

Dear Anaïs Nin,

It was wonderful of you to send me the books! They came on a Saturday when I was home and everything was quiet, and I sat down with my pipe and looked at them and touched them and browsed in them, and had a magic afternoon. . . . I don't know what moved me more, your inscriptions, or the fact that you sent me the manuscript of "Realism and Reality." I like that essay very much; one sentence especially captivated me: "And nothing that we do not discover emotionally will have the power to alter our vision." That is as deep a sentence as it is simple and precise; indeed the whole piece is by far the most enlightening interpretation of your work that I have read. I'm not sure that I can equally well go along with your belief that "emotionally as well as scientifically, we are going to travel more lightly and that writing will not belong to our time if it does not learn to travel faster than sound!" I think I know what you mean, but lightness and swiftness suggest also superficiality to me (except when I think of dancing which may have something to do with your liking lightness and swiftness!) and does not quite seem to go together with the depth psychology on which you also insist and which is your great forte and which to me appears rather as a slow, penetrating, boring process. Even if it employs swift, dream-like scenes, events and symbolic patterns, they go slowly, steadily into the deeper layers of the subconscious and unconscious—like the psychoanalytic process of which your novels essentially consist. To what extent we need the symbolism of science for this, as you mention in the companion essay "On Writing"[8] (the two together, with perhaps a third one would make a superb volume, I believe!) and to what extent all this is confined to "modern" writing (did not Jakob Wassermann[9] and Hermann Hesse[10] and Dostoevsky and even Homer already use these symbolic and soul-probing devices, and actually all true poets—in the widest sense of the term—throughout the ages?) I am not certain. Am I wrong in this? It is a big theme—too big to discuss with any prospect of clarity in a letter. In any case, your essay, as all your writing, has for me a very emotion-stirring and thought-provoking effect, for which I love it and am grateful. . . .

I don't think the printing of *This Hunger* is half the failure you make it out to be! I had seen the Library copy and felt then already the great charm it has, partly through your husband's intriguing woodblocks; it is by far preferable to any slick commercial job of printing even though it does not meet with your standards of perfection, and I am very glad to own it, particularly as I wouldn't have presumed to ask you for it. . . .

Lastly, many thanks for *Children of the Albatross*. From looking into it, it is one of your best books, and I look forward to reading it quietly as it ought to be read. (Right now I am for various reasons rather harassed.) I did not want to ask for it because I intended to buy it, like all your other books that are available on the market, myself; I need not make many words to say how proud and glad I am to have it with your inscription! . . .

Most sincerely,
Felix Pollak

Felix Pollak
1235 Elmwood Avenue
Evanson, Ill.
November 14, 1952

Dear Miss Nin:

Let me, for Sara and myself, thank you very heartily for your photographs. They are exquisite. You not only are, obviously, like you write, but you also look like you write—which is even rarer. We are very pleased to have these pictures and your friendly inscription! . . .

All good wishes—
Sincerely,
Felix Pollak

[New York]
[December 29, 1952; postmark]

Your wishes for me must have been very powerful and effective for I now *have* a publisher—(just recently). Book [A *Spy in the House of Love*] will appear in the Spring, in Paris, in English, at New Story Press, 6 Boulevard Poissonière!! Thank You for wishing. And now watch for results of *my* wishes for a fulfilling new year for both of you, and peace for the world?

Anaïs

[Evanston]

[January, 1953; approx.]

Congratulations!

We didn't know we were such powerful wishers! Maybe your book had something to do with it too. In any case, we're very pleased and know how much you must be! Now I also realize that the New Story people were a logical choice—only didn't know they published books also. Yours is possibly their first, is it? We too hope that your good wishes for us may be fulfilled for we have both much to wish for—including the basic "peace for the world."

Will you offer the library the manuscript after the book comes out?

I bet you feel a new incentive now to go on writing and are full of ideas and plans and maybe even in the thick of creation already.

We hope so.

Affectionately,

Felix and Sara

Will you be going to Paris to attend the birth? It would be a wonderful excuse, wouldn't it—if any were needed! It also must be an exhilarating feeling to able to stick one's tongue out at the whole bunch of American publishers!!

[New York]

[January 21, 1953; postmark]

Dear Felix,

I can't remember when you are leaving for France and I don't have your letters here. If you and your wife are passing through New York I hope you will visit me and my husband Ian Hugo. We have a film to show you which Hugo based on *House of Incest*.[11] I will be in N.Y. at 35 West 9th—telephone Algonquin 4-9110—until Feb. 18. Do let me know.

Anaïs

[Evanston]

January 26, 1953

Dear Anaïs,

To say that I would love to meet you and your husband and to see the film is understating it greatly. Also, I know to appreciate your invitation! (In fact, it made me wish I could make the trip to New York just for the occasion!) Unfortunately, I don't see any good prospect of our being in the city in the near future. You see my trip to Europe is neither for pleasure nor for business, but is due to my wanting to take my final doctoral examination at the University of Vienna—something I had to forego when I had to flee from my native city after the Nazi invasion in 1938. Since I will use my accumulated vacation time for the trip and must be gone and back all in one month, I'll have to fly and thus will board the plane right in Chicago, with either no stop-over at all in New York, or only one between planes—I am not sure which. . . .

Still, I do hope and am confident that it will sometime be possible for us to meet you and Jan [*sic*] Hugo (whose work I have long admired), and to see the film, something that would interest me tremendously. Maybe, if I return in triumph, with the degree in my suitcase and the book accepted (!)—here we pause for knockings on wood and deep breath—then I'll be reckless and won't care whether I am back in time or get fired or anything else, and then I'll wire Sara to meet me in New York and if we're very lucky, you will be in town and answer my telephone call. (It sounds a little fairy-talish—too good to come true, but one can never tell!) . . .

Affectionately,

Felix

Many thanks for the "Preface to *Tropic of Cancer*"[12] which Mr. [Lawrence] Maxwell has just sent on your request!

[New York]

[February 4, 1953; postmark]

I am sorry your schedule is so pressed but we will be here to celebrate with you. We wish you all the fulfillment your hard work deserves. . . . Save everything for festive encounter in N.Y. I'm working hard for new book and asked New Story to mail Northwestern the last ms. Keep N.Y. telephone Alg 4-9110 — as it is not in phone book for sudden plans. Good luck and my affection to you both.

Anaïs

2

March 1954–February 1955

EXILES' LAMENT

As the letters between Anaïs Nin and Felix Pollak resume (following a gap of approximately a year), two principal themes of their ensuing correspondence emerge: publishing and exile. In early 1954, after a considerable struggle, Nin finally finds a publisher for A *Spy in the House of Love*. Pollak, with his enraptured and detailed response to the novel, helps alleviate Nin's disappointment at what she feels has been a poor reception. In their efforts to get their works published, Nin and Pollak both wrestle with the question of how a writer might attempt to adjust and survive in the commercial publishing marketplace. Eventually, as a radical alternative, Nin will conceive the notion of setting up her own printing press, bypassing all the apparatus of commercial publishing, with some success. Pollak, for his part, will find an audience in the pages of the "little magazines," small journals unbeholden to the financially motivated major presses.

Both Nin and Pollak had come to the United States just before World War II, and although it was a return for Nin, she too feels like an exile from Europe, especially from Paris, her "center." Nin finds

America sterile, while Pollak feels like a displaced person in the American Midwest. The Europe for which they both pine is not a Europe of everyday reality but an extravagantly idealized and sentimentalized construct, part memory, part fantasy, and (only) part actual experience. In their more dispassionate moments, both Nin and Pollak recognize that the ills they attribute exclusively to America are symptoms of global social change from which Europe is by no means exempt.

Nin's letter of May 1954, referring to "the good advice you gave me" and stating "I can understand so well your feelings about Europe," indicates that a preceding letter from Pollak is missing.

This section ends with reference to a correspondence between Edward Titus, a publisher and editor, and Anaïs Nin. Pollak's reflections on the way that these "battered pages" of letters from the past can reawaken a strong emotional response in the reader across a gulf of time applies uncannily well to these same Nin-Pollak letters.

35 West 9th Street
New York 11, N.Y.
[March 1954; approx.]

Dear Felix:

A little late to answer your Christmas Card—but not to say I was glad to hear from you and your wife.

At last *Spy in the House of Love* is out—after many obstacles and difficulties. Publishers here wanted me to extract from it the lie detector character and I had to find one who would publish it as I intended it to be—that was New Story Press in Paris—then came strikes, etc. Book finally published in Holland. By this time New Story had collapsed with internal dissentions—but happily British Book Centre adopted the orphan and here it is. My official publication is May 6.[1]

Today I want to write you more about Hugo's films which I have been showing with much success.[2] His way of making films is like my way of writing so I have presented the films and expanded my ideas on necessity of poetry in film or novel [*sic*]. He may get two engagements in Chicago. If these turn out well and crystallize, I wondered if you could interest Northwestern—There are many possibilities. Films only last one hour and I can "discuss" them. Or I can read from *Spy* as a form of parallelism in art—which I have done, showing principles expressed in this manner. The way of the films is always easier to grasp for students. I would like to visit you and the University—but I can only do it this way. I could be available between May 10 and 30th. . . .

I wonder how you feel in Europe. Do write me. And don't worry if this project does not interest University—as sooner or later I will visit you and film will be shown.

My best to you and your wife,

Anaïs

Evanston

April 12, 1954

Dear Miss Nin,

Please forgive the delay in answering your letter which I was very happy to get. The prospect of your coming here and showing the films is exciting and I do hope it will come about! . . .

I am eagerly awaiting the publication of *Spy in the House of Love*. That you finally could bring this publishing ordeal to a happy ending and the book to a, I sincerely hope, happy beginning, warrants the heartiest congratulations! I am very grateful that you still want to give me the original edition of *Winter of Artifice*; all the book finding services I employed could not uncover a single copy! The Library was just damn lucky to buy its copy—someday I'll tell you more about that. . . .

Very Sincerely,

Felix

Greetings, good wishes and crossed fingers (for us) also from Sara.

[New York]
[May 1954; approx.]

Dear Felix:

Our letters crossed! I'm sorry my delayed answer caused you to think I was disappointed in your answer. By now you know I knew it was good advice you gave me, but that I am aware the book came out too late for me to do anything about lectures or readings until the Fall.

I can understand so well your feelings about Europe—the ambivalence too—(Home, after all!) Whoever is not born here feels such ambivalence. I have it too. When I get discouraged with the actual trends in writing or thinking here I have a longing for my intellectual center (Paris). At other times I dread returning and discovering Europe adopting the worst of America (while I at least here, know the best). But I understand how you feel. I who was uprooted at the age of 9, and believed one could become international, and grow beyond one's immediate family, now know that for better or for worse, we remain emotionally bound to our roots—and our adopted countries or families never take the place of the original ones—

Then there is the problem of America assimilating us—which sometimes also looks like the Lion in the Puppet Show who had hiccoughs after swallowing a Christian—Every now and then America shows acute indigestion instead of enjoyment of whatever the poor Europeans have to offer!

You didn't tell me what the degree was, that you received in Europe—and what change will it make in your role at the University.

I will follow your advice later, for the Fall. Thank you for thinking out the problem and telling me how to handle it.

My best to you and Sara,
Anaïs

[Evanston]
July 30, 1954

Dear Anaïs—

Your book [A Spy in the House of Love] is marvelous! I can't say this quickly enough, for I am half ill with bad conscience and remorse about saying it so late. The delay is inexcusable and I am not going to bore you with a catalog of reasons. I feel acutely the problem of trust involved here: you have really no reason for any kind of trust in me, and as for my personal judgement of your book, this ought to be a matter of great indifference to you. And yet, you have been repeatedly hurt by unperceptive and mercenary publishers first, and have to face now, according to your letter, the ignorance of book reviewers who half the time haven't even read the book they're reviewing and who lazily and conveniently just repeat old stereotypes after each other. Thus the silence of even an unimportant reader whom you may have considered your friend (and who at the very least ought to say Thank you for the gift of the volume and the personal dedication) must have felt strange to you; I doubt that I, were I the author, could have abstained from bitter thoughts about that particular reader.

. . . I have read your book only last week. I am still reading in it and will continue to do so off and on—it is that kind of book. It is, for one thing, deeply, almost desperately serious, and the reviewers' plea of unintelligibility seems quite intelligible to me as a rationalization of their subconscious resistances to it. For being solely and exclusively concerned with the individual (and not even a typical and certainly not a conventional one); being moreover concerned solely with the most secret and disturbing aspects of life, the subterranean territory, "living as others live only in their dreams at night, confessing openly what others only confess to doctors under guarantee of professional secret," it runs head-on against all the taboos of a middle-brow mass civilization that can view man only from a sociological vantage point and find on its scanty scale of values good and evil determined merely by what is beneficial or bad for "society." The novel's whole theme must be anathema in a country that, despite its hectic attempts at overcompensation, is still laboring under the Puritan strain; for even in the "sexiest" novels produced here, sex is always treated functionally: a recurrent need, leading to recurrent acts, to concessions, whether deplored or affirmed, to nature, functions that must be fulfilled so that they can be forgotten and make room for the "higher" things. While in all your books and most clearly in *Spy*, sex is exposed as the ever-present life force, the life of the senses is all-pervading. Eros, sensuality are shown as the spark plugs that set the whole machinery in motion, as the source, the spring, the key, the Mother in the Goethe sense. Unity in manifoldedness, not tortuous and artificial emotion from reason, but reason and emotion as inseparably mated and molded together as effect and cause; instincts, drives seen as what they are: the wire-pullers of even our most rational thought processes, the tremendous hidden portion of the tiny iceberg above the waters.

Such concept brings with it the inescapable problems: the exposed, the confessed schizophrenia of the internally rich and honest and complex personality, the immorality of the ethical, the agonizing search of the possessor of a self for the selves that compose it; the lust and torment of the compulsion of living each of these selves; the fears and flights from super-egos and lie detectors; the deceits necessary for being true to one's being; the clashes of the outer and inner reality. The novel's essential theme seems to me to be a deeper variation of a sentence from Hamlet: This above all, to thine own selves be true—And the quest for the recognition of these selves, the old question, Who am I? altered with deeper insight into: Who are I? Only he who has selves and has self and only in being true to one's selves can one be true to oneself.

With all that, the resistance against your book, even the unwillingness to face it, is a testimonial *for*, not against it. You yourself in your last letter very charmingly cited the case of the Lion in the Puppet Show who gets the hiccups after swallowing a Christian. Only his indigestion in your case comes from a European heathen who refuses to be wholly assimilated into said lion, who, so to speak, throws monkey wrenches into the Melting Pot! If only the Melting Pot knew how healthy such activity is, how necessary for its own vitality! For verily, it is the Puritans who are in need of cleansing, of a purification from their poisonous purity! They won't read the book, of course, but Sabina's catharsis will be shared, I'm sure, by every understanding reader, even though catharsis is always only a by-product of drama and art, never their purpose.

I was particularly moved by an indefinable, intangible European or cosmopolitan air pervading the novel, by the nearness of a soul, a mind, a world outlook that brought back into my consciousness the smell of the streets of Paris and, unaccountably, the strong, unique, exhilarating odor of the Metro, but even more forcefully the lonely desperation and orderly dreariness of places like Superior, Wisconsin, where I worked for a spell previous to my marriage in Chicago.

God, how I longed then, how I would have cherished such breath of air from the other world, such escape from the prison into the spaciousness of a loneliness shared!

It is easy, no doubt, to find shortcomings in the novel, particularly if one dwells upon what it isn't rather than on what it is and aims to be. Even within that frame it has, like everything in life, some flaws, but they are minor since they concern things that were obviously of minor importance to you in writing the book; for instance that the continuity of the narrative does not always match the continuity of the theme, that the individual episodes remain at times somewhat separate and strung together rather than flowing into each other; or that of all the characters only the frantic, very American John, and partly Mambo, came to three-dimensional life for me. But, as I said, to create three-dimensional characters is probably of lesser importance to you and may not be your forte in general, although Djuna in *Winter of Artifice*, Johanna, Hans, and some of the women in your short stories are very visible and alive. I guess I sound like a book reviewer (which is not my aim)! Let me say, instead, how captivated I again was with what in my opinion *is* your forte: your language. Its lucidity is the more astounding as you are setting out to express the almost inexpressible and thus have to prestidigitate more in between your lines than into them. This makes for difficult and exciting reading within simple sentences. Your rhythm and music, your probing for meanings and nuances, the blood-beat and the tart sweetness of your prose cast again the old spell over me. You have the foreigner's prerogative of seeing and hearing and sensing every word as if it occurred for the first time, you know and use expressions I seldom encounter in native prose, you taste their sounds and shadings with a sensitive and sensuous passion, a nervous aliveness that is superb. The erotic fluid emanating from all your books stems not in the least from your erotic relation to words. Musical delicacies like the juxtaposition of "moulted" and "moulded" in two closely welded-together sentences, passages like "who can never reach termination as ordinary people reach peaceful terminals . . .", and many other poetic excursions into the depths of language parallel to the deep sea divings into the unconscious of the soul, leave me time and again with the one adjective that to me best characterizes your writings: *exquisite*.

I need hardly stress that I am profoundly grateful to you for giving an inscribed copy of the book to Sara and me, and for your inscription as our friend. I am glad, Anaïs, that you are! . . .

I believe that this novel (I like, incidentally, its external make-up) will in time be recognized as one of your most important ones, and will also find its readers, not many, perhaps, but the kind you alone care having. Never in the whole history of literature was there so much reason for pride at being a non-commercial writer as there is today, when such a phenomenon is not only inspiring, but actually awe-inspiring! For a voice like yours there will always be listeners, because it has the power and enchantment to *create* listeners. . . .

With all the very best wishes for you,

Felix

P.S. Re your last letter: I meant to tell you how true your observation struck me about Europe's adopting the worst of America while here at least we know the best. This says very much in a nutshell of what I also felt there. The degree I got there, which you asked me about, was that of Doctor of Jurisprudence which I had started a thousand years ago and almost completed when I had to flee the country in 1938. I can't stand incomplete things and broken bridges behind me (there were many complex motives connected with my return trip to Vienna)—the main thing is I kept my promise to myself, and did it, although the studying and the exam were every bit as forbidding as the title sounds.—I ought to apologize for not writing the whole letter by hand (I've once made a note to myself to the effect that a typewritten private letter is like a gloved hand offered in greeting) but so few people seem to be able to read my handwriting without difficulty that I feel I'm justified typing.

[California]

[August 6, 1954; postmark]

Dear Felix:

Your letter was well worth waiting for, and a most beautiful letter it was, of which I am *immensely* proud. It was not only the understanding of the book, which was valuable and nourishing, but also your understanding of what creates rejection of it, so that you not only helped the writer to continue his work but helped to diminish, attenuate the effect of the rejections to which I am, unfortunately, vulnerable. When someone can be so articulate and respond one feels spurred to continue in efforts which at other times I may look upon as hopeless. The value of any individual development research or experiment is regarded here, I know, as anti-social but I believe that until the individual is developed he is useless to society. His function in "whole" may not be immediately apparent but it is nevertheless essential. I know that I am contributing to our awareness, not to mine alone—

You need not have been alarmed about your one criticism. When there is acceptance of the basic work, a discussion of details is good. I am not sure I did right in presenting the men only at the moment they passed through the intense searchlight of Sabina's desire or vision of them. I purposely chose to intensify both the limitation of passion and its quality intensity instead of completeness in relationship. I reproach Sabina at the end for loving only one aspect, the aspect created by illusion. I don't honestly know if this would have been lost if I had done the men more fully—In this realm I am exploring I may make some errors—due to the search for *other* emphases, *other* truths—To bring out one truth one may forfeit another, gain one at the expense of another. I was being true to Sabina's inner screen and lighting. Just as when I leave out many minor characters such as are usually included in novels, I do it for the sake of concentration, not because I do not value them.

I do feel the terrible standardization of character by which America reached economic security is deeply outraged at whoever seeks an individual pattern—When doctors and scientists go off on far off beat research no one troubles them, or tampers with them because they never know when they will benefit from them. But they think they have a right to tamper with the artist, who, in the most primitive societies, was recognized as a necessity and exempted from fishing and hunting!

Of course, I could also say that what may seem left undone now in the novels, may when they are completed, no longer seem incomplete. Sabina is not finished. Nor Djuna—I'm working on completing them all—I stressed the neurosis, then the tunnel out, change and freedom from it, I hope.

Gratefully for your effort to tell me all you did—

I do hope to come sometime—with the films—Will write [Jens] Nyholm when I can do so.

My best friendship to you and Sara,

Anaïs

Sara must be wonderful because a man's wife is reflected in his attitude towards women in general.

[California]
[December 13, 1954; postmark]

Dear Friends:

This is to wish you a happy and fulfilled New Year. . . .

Your letter on the *Spy* was the most accurate and my favorite letter among all.

I wonder how you are. . . . My friendship as ever.

Anaïs

1235 Elmwood Avenue
Evanston, Ill.
December 16, 1954

Dear Anaïs—

I'm glad all went well with the manuscripts.[3] I enclose a short "write-up" in the *Library News*.

I have been reading in the manuscripts, and no matter how casually I begin to leaf through them, I find myself reading avidly and entranced a few minutes later. I'm not sure that your writing is always improved by revisions; sometimes it is considerably so, at other times I feel more of a sweep and (controlled) abandon in an earlier version, and it seems you feel this too since some passages of an earlier version appear restored again later, after intermittent charges. Fascinating, all of it, and a slight indication of all the labor involved. There may also be in-between versions, or at least pages, that go to the waste-basket; are there?

Specifically, I'm sorry that you left out the Lilith scenes, the flagellantist psychiatrist episode, etc. though I realize, and agree, that the book has more unity and consistency of theme as it is now. Only I hope you will publish these other parts sometime—they're among your most exciting and exquisite writings. Aren't they (via the diary) part of the Obelisk *Winter of Artifice?* (Lilith—Johanna, Jay—partly Hans?) At least, I'm sure I have read this before, in an even longer version, certain passages (including left-out ones) stuck in my mind —I meant to check this before writing you, but want to get this letter off, have delayed it too long already. . . .

I wish very much you could come here with your films, I haven't succeeded yet in getting any action in that respect, but will keep trying. Read a few weeks ago an announcement of your appearance at Henry Miller's water color exhibition, was chagrined again about not living in New York or having time and means to fly there for such occasions. One is so goddamned restrained and restricted, I'm straining on the bit quite a bit, last year at this time I was still in Vienna, had just passed my exam and had a few short days of ecstatic let-down, I can't even think of it—

I enclose also a reprint of a short (and shortened) article I just had in *The Humanist,* under the pen name I used already before 1938 in Vienna.[4] I suspect (and hope) that you will agree with the main idea—it applies of course not only to so-called politics, we talk on many simultaneous emotion-sparked levels about *everything.* . . .

Are you working hard on your long book?

All good wishes, Anaïs—

Felix

35 West 9th Street
New York 11, N.Y.
January 15, 1955

Dear Felix:

Thanks for the *Library News* and what you wrote about the ms. I read your article with interest. . . . I was interested in your connection with the U.N. and in your playing the violin, and the interesting phenomenon that while being aware of our social life (as I am), of the humanities—yet you never indulge in the moralizing and the rigid point of view of the American social, historical critics. Both can exist simultaneously, the awareness of humanity and of individual growth and their relationship is what you are inferring, and I so much agree.

Was also interested in your comments on my revisions. The reason you "remember" certain passages, or scenes is that I did dismantle the section Hans in original *Winter of Artifice* published in Paris—the one I promised to get out of my vault in San Francisco one day—I felt it was written under the influence of Miller's writing, it was my first attempt to transpose the Diary material, it was naively exaggerated—I recast some of this throughout—I don't believe I ever used the flagellantist episode—but whenever I do leave something out it is the judgment of the artist upon the success or non-success of the transposition. It is severe, it is the sacrifice to the perfection—But all of this in its imperfect, more human spontaneous state is in the Diary, not lost and that may be why I have the courage to leave it out of the novels. As in a musical composition I did want to take up again the Lilith scenes of earlier *Ladders to Fire,* but when I saw I did not add to its development, could say no more than I did the first time, I dropped it—Yes, a great great deal of writing is thrown into the basket. I don't work hard at revising, or re-writing, but proceed by writing a great deal and then cutting out, as if it were a film, cutting out what has not crystallized perfectly. . . .

The split between the "art" work and the natural work—the Diary —has been a cause of ambivalence. I feel my major work is the Diary —but it is impossible to give it without a transposition—Whether this added to the work, or destroyed it, I do not know. People cannot accept the naked truth. But the symbolic drama does not satisfy them either. Only a fraudulent realism (as in majority of novels) or diluted poetry—isn't it true? . . .

I am working hard on my large book but without hurrying or pressure because *Spy* failed to sell according to average standards and had been rejected by 15 publishers so that I feel the next one will not be published at all. I wonder if someday the universities will have to publish books on a small scale or else the "wholesale" will destroy all our experimental writers, the research workers, etc.

Now that you are Dr. Pollak who do you teach at Northwestern, what is your work? . . .

With my friendship to you and Sara

Anaïs

Dear Anaïs,

I just received your letter, I'm sick in bed, but I am so glad to have it that I'll squeeze a few drops of energy out of me to answer you right away. . . . Squeezing everything into the evenings and half the nights is difficult and apparently makes one susceptible to the flu, so Sara tells me, though I think that the miserable climate here helps. I was quite depressed until your letter came, aided and abetted (my depression, that is) by long newspaper stories about the effects of radiation on our health, our aging process and our genes, ruining also whatever future generations may be left. Cheerful. . . . And who can stop it? I'm sure that millions of human beings feel this way and the utter helplessness, the inability to do anything about it is the frustration of our age. And no more place to hide—nowhere.

Thank you for your kind words about my article. It isn't shortened from a book, just shortened, sounding more mechanistic, probably, than it is meant. I also have a hunch that the editors of the *Humanist* misunderstood it, thinking that I was *deploring* man's emotionality which surpasses his rationality, while I was just trying to show that the first, not the second, is the force behind our thoughts and acts and that our thoughts and acts cannot be understood until this is understood, even in fields as "rational" as politics. Not that this is a new idea, but it is, for the very reasons discussed, constantly disregarded. . . . As far as the book in progress is concerned, it consists of aphorisms, short reactions, reflections, observations (minus moralizing and plus occasional humor, I hope)—"Fame: a footprint in the quicksand of time"—that sort of thing.[5] It has been in the making over the years, an oblique kind of diary too, though of course not the *real*, monumental kind of diary for which I admire you tremendously. The mere task of it, and its continuation, is awe-inspiring, like a wish-dream, a life not lived in vain, the record of a life (and it is a *life*, not an existence kept, preserved, instead of going down the drain of time, and the recorder an artist with the courage for the truth—this, Anaïs, will make you famous, not to use a stronger word, someday, even if you may not live to see that day. Bitter, bitter, but sweet too—n'est-ce pas? I feel very sure about that, and all the pygmies that today won't even accept your books will then outbid each other to publish books *about* you. The old, old story. God knows why it must be constantly repeated.

I'm sure you are taking too gloomy a view of the prospects of your next book, but that whole commercialized situation is shameful and only one aspect of the general picture. Maybe the university presses *ought* to step in, but you know how *they* are, at least at present; novels become literature and thus worthy of professorial cognizance only after some books of criticism have been written about them by members of the English Department, and in general, the professors would rather do without the text than without footnotes. Still, there will always be a way also for the uncompromising writers like you. (How many are there??) That some of your books are now on college reading lists is encouraging in a way, though in another way it endows them with an academic respectability which doesn't fit them, it seems to me; they're not tame and safely dead enough for that. In any case, it must take more strength than most authors would have to keep on writing as you want to write and have to write in the face of that continued uncertainty of being published. . . .

I expect a great deal of trouble finding a publisher for them [the aphorisms], have had some of it already; the finished version is in German (I'm working now on the English version which consists of English originals and translations of the German aphorisms, as far as they are translatable). Artemis, a good publisher in Zürich, was interested in the German manuscript (the reason for my stop-over in Zürich, last year), but after more than a year returned the ms. with the explanation that the German market had not developed as they had hoped it would, and that they therefore couldn't take the risk after all; though as far as the quality of the book is concerned, they can only repeat blah blah blah. It *did* get me down and I didn't touch the thing for a long time, until I sent some excerpts to a German literary magazine and they published them right away in two installments. . . . To continue with me as a subject (in order to get it over with)—despite my doctorate, I don't teach anything at Northwestern, am just in charge of the Library's rare books as before; but will have to make a change soon, the salary is low and there is no chance for advancement in this set-up. The violin I've been playing for many years, since my boyhood in Vienna, then interrupted for more than ten years after arriving in this country as a penniless refugee; no cliché, this "penniless" either, Hitler permitted the equivalent of $2 to be taken out of the "Reich" and that year in New York, when I, among other things, tried to peddle silk stockings as an "agent" for a big firm, with no talent for the occupation and no success in it, viewing myself as on the screen of a ludicrous and corny movie and mumbling Rilke poems to keep the connection to my self that was split in the middle—that year seems as unreal to me now as anything I've ever read in a "fraudulently realistic" novel. (Do you see why the thought of a diary kept, to which I had not the energy and objectifying power, seems as such a wish-dream to me?) . . .

I'm prattling on and feel a little feverish, so I won't go on. I just want to say that I believe there must be a sphere between "naked truth" and "fraudulent realism" and "diluted poetry"—a sphere that is the sphere of art. For the naked truth rings as little true in a novel as the sound of a real sickle, say, sounds real on the stage. In order to produce the reality of a sickle sound, one needs a theatrical apparatus that adds the dimension of the stage; just as a face must be painted to look unpainted in the limelights. "Symbolic drama" is something else again. One voice in me (the voice of sanity, no doubt) says, "Look who's lecturing whom?", but another voice reassures me that you will agree. Do you think I could do my little part of helping *Spy* if I tried to review it? And where? As far as I know it has been reviewed in the *Saturday Review* and the *Nation*.[6] I'll be glad to try if there is a place where it may get published and do some good.

I meant to write you from the Library where I have the documents—we have just purchased a few pieces of correspondence between you and Monsieur Titus regarding your book on D. H. Lawrence.[7] That is to say, a letter by you to Titus, the swine, and letters between him and your lawyer. Your letter, Anaïs, was heartrending—why do people act that way, people who first showed sense enough to publish your book??? . . .

In friendship,

Felix

P.S. Yes, the *Winter* edition is the one you printed by hand and your husband illustrated—both beautifully done!

P.P.S. As for the individual-society relationships, I'm really interested in society only insofar as it affects the individual; the sociologist's point of view is probably the opposite. It is one of the effects society has upon us that we're made to feel it is our duty to be more interested in the "whole" than in the "part" (??) One is being intimidated to assure society of one's interest in it. One is even made to feel that this is the masculine or "mature" view, which while interest in the individual primarily, is the feminine or "immature" viewpoint. I think this is a lot of bosh. People want to be considered en masse, because they feel instinctively that they're nothing as personalities.

[New York]
[January 24, 1955; postmark]

Sunday
Dear Felix:

I didn't have your "Reflections" at hand when I wrote you (as most of my letters are written on a bus, while waiting somewhere between engagements, in flight), and I had not said all—I agree so much with your interpretation, the irrational context in political attitudes— Not enough has been written or said about this, and what you wrote was wise and accurate. As Hugo and I have been analyzed we can appreciate the truth of what you wrote. Hugo brought your article up for discussion with Louis and Bebe Barron (electronic music composers, who composed music for Hugo's films) at a little Greek restaurant last night, after a drumming class. I agree completely too with P.S. to your last letter on "pseudo sociologic point of view." You are so right when you say "people want to be considered en masse because they feel instinctively that they're nothing as personalities."

I hope you're over the flu. After the flu there is always the blues— and I hope this letter reaches you in time against the blues. The only reproach I have to make is cutting out the personal parts of the letter, calling it "prattle" and depriving me of what you must know by now is something very meaningful and important to me. What a friend thinks, feels, says informally, casually.

Thank you for suggesting a book review of *Spy*. I don't like to accept your working at that besides so many other works, and being uncertain of who would publish it. . . .

Are you restless for another or a different job—teaching? Is there anything I can do? My brother Joaquín pianist composer like my father is head of Music Department at Berkeley-UC. Should I ask him if there is anything open in other departments?

Very amused by purchase of letters regarding Titus. Ironic—to me —the uneven estimates. A letter to Titus worth purchasing—but I can't get published and even my devoted agent, a Frenchman, throws up his hands when my stories come back from *New Writing*, and even an abbreviated version of the Diary I confided to a friend in Pocket Books.* Yes I would like to know how such letters get into the library.

I have all my letters and Henry Miller's for over ten years. Do libraries ever keep such documents locked up, closed, until a specified time for exposure? I often wondered how one can protect human beings and yet preserve what may be useful later to the truth. I have to make some arrangements one day for the Diary—I travel so much. And as it is, if anything happened to me, it would hurt some people whom I spent my life protecting. . . .

Anaïs

. . .

*Pocket Books, a Simon and Schuster imprint, although Nin may well be using the term generically here.

[New York]
[January 31, 1955; approx.]

Dear Felix:

Above all let me thank you for all your activities in behalf of a film showing etc. It sounded like [Franz] Kafka's *Castle*—the labyrinthian protocols, etc. You made it humorous but I can see signs of great labor! I don't want to make it so difficult—truly. . . .

We can separate the 2 events—films take 1 hour (and discussion) and perhaps a reading to English Department. The reading can be "paid for" by sale of books, if they allow me to or help me sell them etc. You know, and I know, that I am not in the world a name like Auden or Thomas and cannot get $200 for a lecture as they do. . . .

Now if you find they will rent films ($40) without me, or my trip—don't worry—it will please Hugo—and surely sometime I'll be able to travel to Chicago and pay you a visit. I never have, on the way, because my schedule is so strenuous. When I'm in N.Y., I am overwhelmed by wifely duties (which include film showings) when in Cal. I write—and pressure on every side. The only escape and repose in Acapulco which is like the South Seas—and this because I have a brother living in Mexico City I can and must visit once a year.[8] Humorous too—Titus correspondence, an *identical* situation now with British Book Centre—no statement, no advance, no knowledge of how many copies they offset from original edition etc. I wonder why Titus kept such a record!

Anaïs

. . .

[New York]
[February 2, 1955; postmark]

Dear Felix:

The other evening we had dinner with friends—He occupies a high post in U.N. He is a very intelligent Yugoslavian lawyer—his wife a Russian writer. We quoted your article [in *The Humanist*] and he was delighted. We promised him a copy. Do you have any run-offs to spare? Otherwise I can buy this magazine. I also want to give it to a very narrow-minded Marxist Maxwell Geismar, a friend, but who uses "politics" to moralize, and literature as a cover for his political work.[9] We are fond of each other but quarrel over his limited categorizations—The U.N. is wonderful in New York—we go there to see films—have many friends there, in Haitian Section. I'm glad you are connected with it—Have you written more on the subject? Why did they *shorten* article—Could I see the entire article?

Anaïs

[Evanston]
February 6, 1955

Dear Anaïs,

Above all—good news is in the making! Yesterday, after some days of deliberation among the powers in being, I got word from the Film Society that they have decided to pay your and your husband's transportation—any transportation, plane or Pullman—to Chicago and back; that they are delighted at the prospect of having you come and present your program, which, the Film Society at long last discovers, is quite along the line it wishes to develop. The time I am to suggest to you is the week of May 23–28, and preferably Wednesday, May 25th. . . .

I am really moved by your interest in that little article of mine and am most happy to enclose a few copies; they sent me a whole bunch of them. It won't sway, I'm afraid, Maxwell Geismar, nothing sways a real Marxist, or Communist, or Fascist, or Catholic, or Puritan, for the very reasons I tried to set forth in the piece itself. But I'd be curious about his reaction; he is quite gifted as a writer, isn't he, in an intellectual fashion? The U.N. is another reason why I would like to be in New York (there are also some against living there). I gave two speeches on and for the U.N. last week, one at a dinner of the School of World Affairs, another at a U.N. meeting in one of the suburbs, despite my having resigned my chairmanship last week too. . . . I'm glad you too are interested in it! . . .

I'll be in touch with you, Anaïs. With all good feelings and wishes,
Best regards to your husband,
Sara sends greetings,
Felix

[Evanston]
Monday, Feb. 7, 1955

Dear Anaïs—

Your correspondence with Titus was bought by the Library from the Bodley Book Shop, 46 E. 57th St. in New York for $8.50. It was advertised in the shop's catalog 139 (no. 258). It consists of a page of "Sales Account to the end of October 1932," your contract with Titus (Nov. 25, 1931), a letter (undated) from you to that son of a bitch, starting, "Dr. Mr. Titus: I am writing you a human letter and I want you to answer me in a human way. A long time ago I made a request which was really a very just one, I asked you to give me either an account on the sale of my book on D. H. Lawrence, or some copies of it in exchange. You responded with a price on the remaining copies which I could not afford to pay, and never offered to give me an account. . . ." . . .

The last letter bears the head of the Obelisk Press, is dated November 25, 1935 and signed by Jack Kahane. Addressed to Mr. Titus, Cagnes s/Mer. "Dear Mr. Titus, I am now in charge of Mrs. Anaïs Nin-Guiler's literary affairs. . . . Can you now let me have these accounts? And can you also inform me how Mrs. Nin-Guiler can obtain possession at the earliest possible moment of, say, one dozen copies of her work, pending final settlement of this question?"

Here the correspondence ends. I don't know how you now feel about this and things like it, but to me it's strange, an ever renewed wonder, how the written word can preserve lived life in a magic capsule, how time, times, dates, addresses, persons, sights and smells and rooms and emotions lie capsuled up in a few pages of yellowing paper, how scenes and feelings are re-enacted in a strange place, a different country; those papers, filled with strong emotions had been composed and typed and sent through the mail and were read and discussed by the persons involved, and are now lying on this desk, a few pages of yellowing paper, an ocean away from the scene of their life, two decades away from the time of their life—and how yet they are able to re-create in the mind and soul of one who never knew at the time that any of this existed, these same emotions, how they can affect his nerves and glands. What was I doing on those dates? Growing up in Vienna, occupied with my own problems and affairs. and now, 20 years later, all this comes to life out of these battered pages. Strange.

And I notice that these very reflections of awe and wonder have given a perfectly good answer why these documents should be worth money to a Library, even if publishers in their unspeakable and mercenary greed return the creative works of that very author. Ironic— yes. Senseless—no.

Affectionately,

Felix

Please don't hesitate to let me know if you want photostats, typed copies or any other information.

3

February 1955–June 1955

THEIR ONLY MEETING

IN FEBRUARY AND MARCH 1955, Nin sends Pollak postcards from Acapulco where she is vacationing with Rupert Pole. Anaïs had discovered Acapulco in 1947 when she visited her brother Thorvald, who frequently vacationed and did business in Mexico. She returned to Mexico two or three times and the atmosphere she encountered there inspired the Golconda section of *Seduction of the Minotaur*.

On April 14, Pollak first mails Nin one of his own poems "A Living"; many more will follow (see Appendix B). Meanwhile, Pollak is busy arranging Anaïs's lecture and film screening engagement. Several letters, mostly by Pollak, that deal with the negotiations and logistical planning leading up to Nin's visit to Evanston have been omitted. Pollak orchestrates the visit completely, but remains behind the scenes, uninvited to some of the official functions. At a high nervous pitch when Anaïs finally arrives, Pollak is set off by some trifle. Sara Pollak recalls Anaïs remarking to her at the time: "Felix is without skin. How do you manage to live with it?"

Nevertheless, the whole visit is evidently a great success. On May 25, Anaïs screens Hugo's films *Ai-Ye* (Mankind), *Bells of Atlantis*, and *Jazz of Lights*, and speaks on "The Poetic Film." On the 26th, Anaïs speaks on writing and illustrates her ideas with readings from her work. Pollak's moment in the limelight comes with the impassioned introduction he gives Nin before her lecture on May 25 (see Appendix C).

Following her whirlwind visit, Anaïs resumes her peripatetic, bicoastal lifestyle, while Pollak remains, stirred and dejected, in Evanston. The poem he sends her on June 3, "A Passing Visit" (see Appendix B), captures his mood.

[Acapulco]
[February 23, 1955; postmark]

Dear Felix:

You were very clever and diplomatic and I'm delighted. Don't worry about the date. I will keep it—May 25—That should be my small adaptation to a plan in which everyone yielded and collaborated—I'm very pleased, at the whole plan. Sitting now in an open air Spanish restaurant on the square—music—guitars—carnival processions—all the delights of a country which has refused to work, to be enslaved by duty and the mentality of South Sea islanders—100 pages of the new novel [*Solar Barque*] is about them.

I wrote my brother Joaquín to expect a formal letter from you describing what you wish to do etc. Someday you and Sara must see this place. It is Gauguin's world.

My best to you both and gratitude,

Anaïs

[Evanston]
March 2, 1955

Dear Anaïs—

. . . Thanks for your letter. Acapulco sounds enchanting. I was en-
vying you intensely; unfortunately it's already over for you; I hope
you enjoyed it and had a good rest! Now, I suppose, the hard labor of
love begins again. From the shameful and tragic experiences you
have to make with publishers (I was more than appalled to hear
about the British Book Centre and its following in the dishonorable
footsteps of Titus)—judging from those experiences, the *writing*
must be the most satisfactory part of being a writer! . . .

Sincerely,
Felix

[Acapulco]
[March 7, 1955; approx.]

Dear Felix:

I should have sent you this letter sooner—I'm sorry—Acapulco is
like a drug, and one loses all sense of time and responsibility—especially time. The old beach photographer who calmly waits with his
1900 camera said, "Don't hurry—Take your time. We have more
time than life—Mas tiempo que vida."

Anaïs

[California]
[March 14, 1955; approx.]

Dear Felix:

I would have answered your long and helpful letter sooner but I
was teaching (in Spanish) at University of Mexico for 2 weeks[1]—and
only returned 2 days ago to face an autograph party, 3 radio interviews
and the usual disappointment with reviews—A strangling legend
about my unintelligibility has grown to such proportions I don't feel
I can ever dispel it. . . .

Will let you know soon what I can do,
Anaïs

35 West 9
New York City 11
[March 28, 1955; postmark]

Dear Felix:

. . . Did I ever thank you for sending me the Titus Story? It is all humorous. The necrophiliac tendencies of man are more developed that Mr. Ebing* ever gave us to know—a writer's value is all a matter of postponement. *Spy* only sold 1000 copies and now I'm the blackest of all sheep among American publishers! . . .

Amitié

Anaïs

* Richard von Krafft-Ebing (1840–1902), German neuro-psychologist, best known for his pioneering studies in sexual psychopathology.

[Evanston]
April 1st, 1955

Dear Anaïs—

. . . I am happy to hear that you are lecturing so much; each appearance, in print or in person, is another step toward the recognition you deserve and eventually will have. What you say about a writer's value being all "a matter of postponement" is so true! It is tragic that it is so, but it is comforting and reassuring too, at least to know that and to be aware of it. I think everybody has the measure of his value essentially within his soul, is at the very depth of his being quite certain about what he is and isn't worth. The world, the events of the day, people of the day, reviews of the day, can shake a true, or fortify a false belief and judgement for a while, can toss us into depression or lift us into elation—but that doesn't last. Eventually the scales return to their true position; for it is only the scales that can be affected, not the balance, not the true proportions of weight. As a matter of fact, I believe that our essential, our entirety, our being what we are, if we are something, is not even touched by the value judgements of others. Those that know of this un-value may and usually will close their eyes before themselves or won't look at and into themselves, which is all they can do to keep from becoming too aware, too conscious of the truth—for even they can't bribe this scale, no matter how much external flattery, how many mountains of empty honors and rave-reviews and best-seller lists they heap on one side of the scale. To the degree in which they know about the true state of affairs and are suppressing that knowledge into their semi-conscious, to that degree they develop neuroses. And the true artist who may be hounded to death by critics and publishers and the indolence and ignorance of the public, will nevertheless draw unlimited strength from his inner value and from the fact that he can afford to look into himself without having to flinch away and run, from the fact that he can be himself, true to himself and, as part of it, be engaged in the never ending discovery of what he really is. . . . The proof whether a human being and an artist is or is not somebody, has or has not value lies simply in the fact that the second one will always shift and change and try to please—the critics, and "friends" and publishers, and the market, and the fashion, etc. and will always be willing to prostitute himself and his art, while the first one might be despairing at times at himself, his ability, his path, the time, the world, and yet he will not waver and deviate and make compromises, he will continue to be what he is and do what he has to do—because he is he, he is somebody, and can't be and do otherwise. It is always Luther's "Here I stand, God help me, I can't do otherwise!" You can kill a leopard, but you can't make a vegetarian out of him; you can kill him, not his instincts, his essence. It is exactly the same with personalities. "People," on the other hand, are shameless with no substance, everything, and therefore essentially nothing. We both know that and agree on that, I'm sure. And by that very description we both know which category you are in, Anaïs. The criteria set forth about the first kind of artist are your portrait. Therefore you are vulnerable but inviolable—more vulnerable than the insincere and insensitive person, but absolutely, eternally inviolable! . . .

Heartily,

Felix

Can you actually read my writing?

35 West 9th Street
New York 11, N.Y.
[April 4, 1955; approx.]

Dear Felix:

The consequences of your writing me freely and spontaneously, and improvising, is that I always keep the letter to read for pleasure, whereas the others I read dutifully and conscientiously.

It was a good moment to write so eloquently on the integrity and deeper stability of the artist who believes in what he is doing because I have the integrity but also a vulnerability to rejection which for the past years has been severely tried. The humorous truth is that the reason I am so active just now is that before I went around just reading or talking and they could not raise enough money to get me there often (it would always be just the one friend in the English department) but the films always bring money and a public, and so now the films actually pay my trip and enable the English department to entertain me! The collaboration between departments (which was your idea in Northwestern and which you successfully organized) is the secret and it is both good for the films and for my work. . . .

I am saving up for you my edifying correspondence with the British Book Centre and will present the Library with a gift of it! But seriously, I believe that universities are going to have to take up the publication of all literature or the confusion between Woolworth in writing and literature will be one day incurable. I know they publish text books, psychology, philosophy etc., but they may have to publish fiction too.

Yes, I can read your writing quite well. Handwriting still has more of a facial expression than the typewriter. I rarely use the typewriter for friends, except when there is much to write, as today. . . .

The worst of living in New York is seeing friends off to Europe. First my literary agent who was French, "retired" at 37 to go and paint a year in Portugal, and his American partner thinks he is insane. Tomorrow the Yugoslavian representative of the U.N. has been promoted to some high rank and will settle in Paris.

How is your humorous book going?

Met Sam and Bela Spivak, authors of *Boy Meets Girl, Kiss Me Kate, Four (or Three) Angels*. She is better and more authentic than all her characters. Came to U.S. at age of six motherless and father-less (father unknown) with a bedspread on which some grandmother had embroidered her name "Bela" and "c'est tout." So she had to carry the bedspread around to all the immigration maze, having nothing else.

I should be working—

My very best to you both.

Anaïs

[Evanston]
April 14, 1955

Dear Anaïs,

The interesting thing is that those who can't read my handwriting react blankly to me in any other way too—experience has proven that to me pretty regularly, and that a mutual understanding is easily established between me and those who have no difficulty in that respect. That's why I was confident of your answer when I asked you, and am glad of it.

. . . I hope you won't be disappointed in general; much as I look forward to your coming, I have also trepidations. I'm sure I'll look my worst (my best is bad enough), but men aren't supposed to worry about that, I hear; quite in general, subjects, objects, and circumstances of all kinds have a way of not cooperating when an event one is very much looking forward to occurs. And one can't do much about it. I would have wished our first meeting to take place somewhat like yours with Quinones: in New York, informal, unannounced —Well, I am looking forward to meeting you, Anaïs. . . .

Before I forget—I wanted to comment on your statement that *Spy* sold only 1000 copies and that you are now the blackest of sheep among publishers. "Only" a thousand copies, Anaïs?? I think that is very good, considering the lack of fanfare and the tastes of the "general public." What do they expect of a work of art, not expressly written to entertain or compare with T.V. and *The Power of Positive Thinking*? How many copies were printed? I didn't even think they'd print more than 1000! I'm anxious to see your correspondence with the British Book Centre. . . .

I haven't written you so long, it seems—I'll probably forget half of what I want to say, time slides away faster than ever—a pity. It's our only life that's sliding away so, and with too many incidentals and too few incidents in it, too few essentials, too little living. Which reminds me—I'll enclose a poem I wrote on that subject, it will appear in a little a magazine late in the year.[2] . . .

  In friendship,
  Felix

  35 West 9th Street
  New York 11, N.Y.
  [April 18, 1955; postmark]

Dear Felix:

  So much work that I cannot take up the leisurely pen. I sent you a formal letter and several photographs to the library. I don't want to burden you with extra work. I know how much you have to do. Let me know when there is some data I should send and to whom. Do not take it all upon yourself. Yes, I too like casual meetings, but alas there are no cafés. Don't be nervous, because I feel the same way. Always afraid to disappoint people, and hiding behind the smoke screen of the work! But in this case I am not nervous. I know I will like you, and I feel at ease with you in the letters. The photos are not good but I may get better ones in a week or so. I have not yet been to Chapel Hill, going this Wednesday, one film showing and one talk with the English students. I am sending you what publicity they have already done as it may help whoever is doing it for Northwestern.

  The poem was a sad one! But there are days when one feels like that. I never did in Europe. Economics were bad but in the background. Here earning your living is in the foreground, and as you express it, meanwhile you lose your life. It's a matter of lighting. The emphasis is all wrong. That may be why Europeans never adapt themselves. Or very few of them. Because somehow, life is sacrificed here. The ideal would be to live like Darius Milhaud and his wife. He teaches for one year at Mills, in California, then goes to France for a year. We are aiming at that. Hugo, though American, has always loved Europe. I was teasing you about the book. You told me what it was. It was Quinones who described the "twinkle in your eyes." I would like to see you get the job and the life you want. I am more fortunate than most. I never could have done that writing if for years Hugo had not had a very good salary. The only time I have had to think about being practical was when Hugo gave up business to do the films, and the films were too big a drain, and then both of us had to "work." But we have a lovely home we held on to, and a camera and next year we will be able both to make films again. The films require more capital than the books.

Do have confidence in the friendship that was built up by the letters and let's enjoy the meeting as if took place in a café.

Anaïs

[New York]
[April 25, 1955; postmark]

Dear Felix:

Our formal correspondence is flourishing. It makes me schizophrenic! I mailed the 3 films [*Ai-Ye*, *Jazz of Lights*, and *Bells of Atlantis*] today to you at the Library (as I'm leaving for Cal. and Hugo has no time to attend to this as he works all day). . . .

Anaïs

[New York]
[May 18, 1955; postmark]

Dear Felix:

I am arriving *definitely* the *24th in the evening*—American Air Lines Flight 614 arriving in the evening at 6:30 Chicago time. If Evanston can be reached by limousine I can go straight to the Hotel, and can we spend the evening together, you, Sara and I? . . . Let me hear from you—[3]

Your friend

Anaïs

[New York]

[May 30, 1955; postmark]

Dear Felix:

How like you to have the delicacy to write Hugo about his films. No one but you would think of that. I was overwhelmed by your and Sara's kindness. The flowers were still lovely when I left. And at the airport an amusing incident. By mistake American Airlines handed me a "phone call." And it was the friend of yours instructing American Airlines to take good care of me because I was a famous author! The girl was embarrassed, but I thought it was marvelous and told her so. You did everything to make me feel appreciated. Hugo was very happy with his letter. And I with the entire visit which you so thoughtfully arranged—You have such a light touch. It was all done by you, but then you efface yourself, as if not to be detected. You know, that's the brand of the real magicians—of the skillful prestidigitators. I only wish we had had more time for our friendship and less pseudo-gestures in public—

I hope everyone was satisfied—and that you were not tired— One does not tire when *all* is pleasure, but I know there was strain behind the scenes. . . .

With my love to you and Sara,

Anaïs

P.S. I think the best of all results of this visit is your idea of trying to join the U.N. You belong in a bigger and more mobile world.

[New York]

[May 31, 1955; postmark]

Dear Felix—

The article on Karl Kraus* was very beautiful and inspiring. It made me want to read him and I will. Have you forgiven me for my wanting you and Sara to be there the last evening? My best to both of you.

Anaïs

Don't forget I'd like a copy of your introduction.

Austrian poet and satirist (1874–1936).

June 3 (Friday), 1955

Dear Anaïs—

There is so much to say, there would be so much to say, still, again, that I feel helpless before the task of writing you a letter. Now this medium of communication seems not enough any more. You left a week ago and left a void in me, a dull painfulness with sharp edges. This was long in coming, almost a foregone conclusion, and is in the light of reason, and of many reasons, utterly foolish and ludicrous — is supposed to be at any rate. Yet I feel pretty helpless about it. I realize full well that this sounds adolescent, one part of me is looking over my shoulder shaking its wise head, but all the rest of me is filled with that painful void. My whole behavior, I'm afraid, was somewhat adolescent, from the moment I saw you at the airport —you brought the adolescent out in me, a part which I thought was past and done with, outgrown, buried, dulled by time and America —for when I set foot on Europe it too raises its head again and comes up in me, I noticed, a kind of half-drunkenness, only much less so than now. Ludicrous, ludicrous. Yet what would happen to us if the adolescent in us would really die? Wouldn't we be empty shells, actually, zombies, like the majority that surrounds us, and wouldn't life lose really all its lure? Yearning and desire are the adolescent attributes par excellence, and if so, my mental or emotional age is 18 right now. I am afraid I was even as clumsy as an adolescent at moments, which angered me and made me laugh at myself at the same time. But enough of this clinical report. Miss you, I miss you terribly, and I wish we could have had more time, more time together. . . .

I'm very glad you liked the article on Kraus, I wish I had written that. He was a world in itself, quite incomparable, I wish you could have heard him read and act a whole Shakespeare play by himself, sitting at a desk on a dark podium, or sing a whole Offenbach operetta accompanied by a piano behind the wings. He has a marvelous voice (fortunately I could get permission to make recordings from the City Library in Vienna of some of his records still extant and it is an almost unbelievable experience to hear his voice again, after all these years, across an ocean, in an American living room which by a strange sequence of events happens to be my own); I also could collect, by several strokes of luck, all but 3 issues of *Die Fackel* and many of his books; the Library has almost everything; I'll find the missing issues yet, had many numbers in Vienna, but my father burned them all after I had gotten out—justified self-protection from the ever-imminent danger of a Gestapo house-search. Unfortunately, almost nothing has been translated (and that most likely inadequately) for his unique style is virtually untranslatable. When I think of him and all that other world, I feel so old and when I think of you, Anaïs, I feel so young—it's strange.

I too was amused by the airport incident—about the code in which you let me know about my friend's Bon Voyage message! Anaïs—if you ever want to write me something personal, just entre nous, you can do so by addressing a plain envelope to me in the Library, marked clearly and largely "Personal"; then it will reach me unopened. (Otherwise they have the charming habit here of opening letters in the Office!!)

There would be so much to say, so much that it is best to say nothing more. . . .

Write me, Anaïs—

Felix

[Evanston]
Friday, June 10, 1955

Anaïs—

. . . I'm still looking for a copy of *Steppenwolf*—out of print, suddenly. Am going to read *Nightwood*,* and Otto Rank. Did you read the article by Polgar** on Friedell† ("The Great Dilettante") in the *Antioch Review*? Would be interested to know how you liked it; I knew Friedell, by sight, he was a famous figure in Vienna; and I like Polgar very much—he comes in his short little vignettes closest to Peter Altenberg,†† only he's more sophisticated, less elementary. I've called his (Polgar's) stories "miniatures de force" which is less good than the word somebody coined about his style: "filigranite." Could you please send me the magazine back when you have finished? Thanks for the return of the Kraus article. And thank you again for that lovely copy of *Under a Glass Bell*—just beautiful! And your inscription! We're very happy to have that volume! . . . Hope the films arrived all right. It is already two weeks ago that you left—

I wrote to the U.N. Will get the aphorism ms. ready now and send it to you, if you still think I ought to.

All the best,

Felix

Greetings to Hugo

*Novel (1936) by Djuna Barnes (1892–1982).[5]

**Alfred Polgar (1875–1955), the Austrian master of the feuilleton, journalist, essayist, theater critic, and short story writer.[6]

†Egon Friedell (1878–1938), Viennese cabaret director, essayist, and cultural historian who co-authored sketches with Alfred Polgar.

††Peter Altenberg (1859–1919), Austrian feuilletonist, satirist, and short story writer, active in Viennese bohemian café circles. Known for his vivid, ironic, short pieces in his distinctive "Telegrammstil der Seele" [telegram style of the soul].

Mrs. Felix Pollak

1235 Elmwood Avenue

Evanston, Illinois

June 15, 1955

Dear Anaïs,

. . . Your visit remains a very pleasant memory—it was one of those rare occasions when the actuality exceeded the expectations and believe me, the expectations were great. Most times it is the opposite. One builds up a mental image of a person through his writings which is often at variance with the actual person himself. But your integrity and complete honesty made the image and reality the same.

We look forward to seeing you and meeting Hugo sometime in the not too distant future. I hope you conveyed to Hugo my enjoyment and praise of the films. My best to both of you.

Yours,

Sara

. . .

Box 335
Sierra Madre, California
[June 19, 1955; postmark]

Dear Felix:

Knowing me as you do you probably guessed that the only time I leave letters unanswered is when I get ill—I have dips of loss of energy, so low, that they are more like breakdowns. So I abandoned every activity and came back to my refuge. I wanted to thank you for everything, the beautiful letters, the Hesse book which was beautiful and healing, the magazines, your article, the photographs of the exhibit, the usual journalistic caricature shots quite in the journalistic tradition of making everything ugly—Slowly I will digest all these gifts here, in peace, in a small, quiet, but human life. A day at the beach, in the sun, and I can begin to thank you. I should have mailed you back the magazine—I liked the character of . . . (I can't spell his name). And I liked your article, but not having it with me I cannot comment on it until I return to N.Y. I am particularly grateful to you for your eloquence, for your generous introduction, for the fact that you are articulate and alive. My impression of university life is that it is petty—and I can see how unsuited it is to your desire for what D. H. Lawrence described as "living relationships." I do hope your application at the U.N. will give you "a richer life."

As soon as I get back my strength I will write more. . . .

I just found your article—had slipped it in with Diary for rereading so now I can tell you—it is eloquent and lyrical like a poet writing about a poet, and a good critical evaluation. I like the comparison with Woolf—differentiation—and the interpretation of the books and magic realism. But you are right, no writer with any inner richness can be liked in America. They have chosen to live as an agglutinated mass, ashamed of the self, blind deaf and dumb to individual growth as if it were a crime to grow. You are a very fine writer. And I would like you to send me the aphorisms when I return. Or if you prefer send them directly to Gunther Stuhlmann:

Stuhlmann
Criterion Books
100 Fifth Av.

from me. He is a young and brilliant German—say at my suggestion—and I will write him.

Anaïs

[Evanston]

June 22, 1955

Dear Anaïs—

Just a few lines to tell you how *happy* I was to get your letter—it was like food and drink to me, for I too have been almost sick these last weeks—for lack of mail from you. People asked me why I was looking so pale and wan, and I said it was the hot humid weather, but my heart was heavy and I was terribly depressed. You have gone deeper into my blood than I knew, it almost frightens me. I considered the possibility that you were ill, but wouldn't want to believe it and tortured myself with innumerable theories about your silence, being at times even angry at you and at myself, my letter, the poem— and just generally miserable. When finally, finally that envelope with your writing was in the mailbox, it was like a big light had been turned on in the world.

Whatever it would contain would be better than the torment of that silence. And it was a good letter, warm, full of you—except for the distressing news of your exhaustion. I should have known. I do hope, Anaïs, you are better by now and have recovered part of your strength with the aid of sun and the quiet of the sea! I wish I could be near you and hold you—Just disregard what I am saying, it's insane, only it's true—Your letter too sounded like you were scraping your last reserves of strength to write it. Please don't do that—now I can wait—write me only when you are strong enough, please. I'm glad you went back to your retreat. What you said about my writing touched me deeply and makes me very happy. I'll send the aphorisms to Mr. Stuhlmann as soon as I can. Had 5 poems accepted during the last 6 weeks, in various little magazines, will send them to you, it may be a long time till those quantities appear again. Hope you will be strong enough, soon, to work again, without exhausting and depleting yourself too much. Take care of yourself, Anaïs. Those interruptions of work on a book must be painful and hard to bridge. Do you think we'll ever meet in Paris? Do you think we'll ever meet again?? I've said too much already about my feelings toward you. So I just put my fingers to my lips and touch this paper—

Felix

4

July 1955–December 1955

LONELINESS SHARED

FELIX POLLAK'S SENSE OF HUMOR was certainly a central part of his personality and of his writing style. His mordant wit shows clearly in his aphorisms (see Appendix D), which do not spare himself as a target, as in "The artist is a person who matures earlier than the average person and stays immature longer."[1]

Nin and Pollak also discuss the merits of psychoanalysis as a way of becoming reconciled with their personal frustrations. Nin, who has for many years been involved with psychoanalysis, encourages Pollak to undergo analysis also.

Pollak offers to help Nin obtain one of the early-model [Verifax] photo-copy duplicating machines, and Nin's lack of enthusiasm for the venture illustrates the importance for her of hand-copying her own work as a stimulant to her creative processes. (Such questions concerning the role of the physical means of production upon the writer's literary imagination still remain largely unexplored.)

In November 1955 Felix and Sara Pollak make a trip to California. Nin's letter of October 7, in reply to a missing letter from Pollak, makes it clear that she is planning to welcome him, but she is forced to leave for New York to nurse Hugo. Although they do not meet in California, Pollak's impending arrival prompts Nin to share with him the secret of her double life "on the trapeze," shuttling between a husband in New York and a lover in California. Pollak behaves with exemplary discretion while visiting Rupert and Anaïs's West Coast relatives, and the subterfuge further cements the friendship between them.

While in California, the Pollaks also visit Henry Miller. Miller features as a frequent motif in the Nin-Pollak correspondence. Nin and Miller had been lovers during the 1930s, and Pollak is clearly fascinated by Miller's intrepidly unconventional lifestyle. To the end, Miller's name recurs in the letters, a reminder and a provocation.

[California]
[July 13, 1955; postmark]

Dear Felix:

I'm only now regaining strength to answer and to write, although I enjoyed the aphorisms for their *wisdom* and *wit*, but I didn't want to write negligently, and perhaps I should have for I know you hate silence as much as I do. But now you will know mine is always due to illness. I had rheumatic fever as a child and when I get a bout (after the ice cold lecture hall at Evanston—remember I was afraid) it lasts a month. As it impairs the heart all energy is at its lowest—but today all is well again after much sun and dry warmth—I am so sorry to have caused you anxiety. The aphorisms are quite sharp—I didn't quite understand if this was my copy, or one to lend to the Gunther publisher—I see it is dedicated—Did you send the carbon to Gunther Stuhlmann? Just found in your letter your reference to Aphorisms—that you will send copy yourself.

Of course we'll meet in Paris—Somehow I always feel no place in U.S. is suitable for friendship or exchange. One is always in a school, or in a functional spot, a food trough, or a transitory home, etc. I hope you'll try for the U.N. The atmosphere there is marvelous.

Every artist I have ever met here says: "I am lonely." But there is no cure for the inhumanity of space.

There is a humorous mischievousness in the aphorisms. A subtle spirit amused by the heavy literalness of words and clever at playing with them like a prestidigitator to bring out the paradox and the gentle mockery.

My warmest friendship, dear Felix

Anaïs

[Evanston]

July 22, 1955

Dear Anaïs,

I do hope you are well again; it grieved me to hear about your illness, doubly so because your visit to Evanston was the immediate cause of it. You should have warned us in advance, then we could have insisted that the halls were properly heated. I hope you'll do this in other places, you mustn't take these chances. In view of the fact that you had to suffer so long for it, your visit here was hardly worth it. Even I, who counts your visit as one of the memorable events of his life, would have sacrificed the experience for your well-being. I am very glad you could go back to the dry California heat to get your health and strength back again. . . .

I was joyed with your reaction to the aphorisms. They are a small sample—I have about 700 of them in German, which after a new critical scrutiny will probably dwindle to 500, but this would still make a slim 150 or more page volume. In English I have both more and less, since many of the German ones can't be translated into English, and vice-versa, bound, as they often are, to words and the play with words and meanings. You have, of course, immediately picked this essential gesture for your comment; the fact is that many of my most illuminating psychological insights stem not from my relations with people but from my intercourse with words. I have a lot of work to do on the English version yet, and a lot of translating (fascinating and difficult, because literal translation is seldom possible and so the thought has to be recast into another language, almost another medium, and then it happens that this not only leads to other thoughts and formulations in which I lose myself, but also that I like the translated version better than the original one, and then in turn render the new one back into the original language, and this painful —hurtful interchange often goes on for days with the inconspicuous end result of a few lines in either language). Anyway . . . I have written Mr. Stuhlmann . . . and asked him whether he may be able to help me finding a publisher. . . . I enclosed a few aphorisms as samples. . . . So far I have no answer. . . .

The form letter the United Nations sent me on my application is enclosed. It isn't so easy. In fact, without connections, it seems to be almost hopeless. I am certain they have files full of applications.

I have been thinking about your copying the volumes of your diary. If I remember right, you said you have "only" 20 volumes left to copy, and that each volume has about 200 pages. That would be approximately 4,000 pages. I wonder if you would really need the help of a library or any other institution to have those microfilmed, instead of going on with the wearisome and time-consuming labor of retyping. The University of Chicago Microfilm Service charges $.03/page, that would be $6/volume, or $120 for all 20 volumes or 4,000 pages. That wouldn't be too bad, would it? Just think of all the time and drudgery saved, and you could have even more than one copy at a minimal additional cost. . . .

Are you working well? On the translation and the book simultaneously? I'm thinking of you.

With all my heart,

Felix

P.S. To my great grief, I just got the news that Alfred Polgar, who wrote the piece in *Antioch Review* for Egon Friedell, died in Switzerland where he had gone after his exile in New York. He was past 80.

[California]

[August 1, 1955; postmark]

Dear Felix:

. . . When I return to New York August 15 I will see him [Gunther Stuhlmann] and find out what he is doing. The letter from the U.N. was colorless and functional. I wish the friends I had there had not moved to Paris—but if ever you go to Europe you will meet them—but in spite of friendships one has to go through these bureaucracies.

I'm sorry you're susceptible to the weather too—sorry you can't escape as I do. I'm all well now—You know why I can't write beforehand to universities to turn the heat on—one is always ashamed of a physical handicap and hopes to overcome it! If you are susceptible then I wish you had found work to do in more pleasant cities—California however, because it is Grecian in its physical life seems to produce its most colorless and inert population of all U.S. Universities are bourgeois and shallow—utterly without character—So you might suffer from total absence of mind while the sun does shine.

Don't feel badly at my copying diary. Your suggestions are very good—and sensible, but the truth is the diary copying feeds me when I starve for an interesting life—it becomes a means, as I copy instead of feeling it is a chore, boring, I get illuminated by fire and richness of life in Paris—and it enhances the present—Copy diary, read [Marcel] Proust as others read Bible and then I can write—However, I will study these new machines. . . . You are always so kind—

I'm taking aphorisms with me—they should be published in magazines even if a few pages at a time. If I ever buy offset machine and publish my own books again we could do yours by subscription. Someday. . . .

You have a philosophic mind, and do I detect a touch of cynicism about psychoanalysis. I know how you feel about the death of the writer you admired—It was also the loss of a fragment of yourself, of what you loved, and of your past. The sea of death carries away a little fragment of our soul's island, with each person we loved or admired.

Anaïs

. . .

[California]
[August 2, 1955; postmark]

Dear Felix:

. . . All information about copy machines—invaluable—very kind of you. I will look into all of them. They may solve publishing problem too—as I want to set up my own press again and break with indignities of commercial world—publishers, reviews, book shops and offset titles, as they disappear. Thank you! As ever

Anaïs

Love to Sara

Dear Anaïs,

. . . There are many conflicting opinions on California, some people say most of it is just an empty glitter (which sounds believable to me)—others speak highly of San Francisco, its climate, its cosmopolitanism, its "difference" or character—badly needed here and a rarity, if true—in a country where every town and city looks alike and one if placed upon a main street without knowing where one was, could never distinguish between Buffalo, St. Louis, Grand Rapids, Cleveland, or Detroit; the same landscape of drugstores, gasoline stations, First National Banks, taverns, department stores, bowling alleys, churches, office skyscrapers and slums on one side, and bourgeois porch houses on the other. Everything functional, barren and synthetic, no organic growth, no grace, no personality; cities serving the needs of those who serve the needs of the cities—objects all, none a subject. And here strangely the cult (or lip service?) to individualism. In one of the aphorisms I said that whoever is not a rigid individualist in this country, is ostracized for nonconformity—we're taking a late vacation this year or scraping pennies so that we can go to California in November for four weeks—if we can afford it. I'd like to see it (though Mexico would intrigue me more) and I want to make some inquiries at San Francisco universities about job prospects. Probably too late for this year by then, but to establish some personal contact is better than writing into the void and receiving form letters in reply. Oh—if I could fly to Europe instead! That will have to wait.

I didn't quite understand your reference to the physical life being Grecian in California and thus producing colorless and mentally inert populations. Do you mean devoted to physical culture only, body centered, without the Grecian balance and harmony of body and mind that produced so much of the "beautiful and good," the typically Greek sensuous mentality?

I can very well understand what the diary reading and copying does to and for you—I even envisaged this when I asked you if it helps you creatively. A strange, somehow sad and awesome thing—devouring one's past to derive from it nourishment and creative strength for one's future—the yesterday feeding the tomorrow. A candle burning in reverse, the wick adding tallow in burning, the flame restoring the candle it had consumed.

Was just looking over the aphorisms I sent you to see where you might have suspected a touch of cynicism about psychoanalysis. It can only be the one about the mental hospital—and fantastic as the thought sounds, I really mean it! This is not cynicism toward psychoanalysis (which I'm not cynical about) but about some psychoanalysts, followers of and frequently diluters of Freud (who I am skeptical about). Like one who, in literary criticism, asserted that Kafka's sentence "the gendarmes arrested him" symbolizes the "arrested development" of the man, pointing out the double meaning of arrested. But it so happens that Kafka wrote in German and the word he used was "verhaftet" which has not the slightest connection with the psychological symbolism. The same man also wrote that Little Red Riding Hood's red cap is a symbol of menstruation. I don't know whether this is far-fetched, or close-fetched, but it seems dragged in by the hairs, I would say! The passage expresses some doubts about psychiatrists in general and their lacking courage to practice what they refrain from preaching (for to their honor it must be said that they don't preach!) My thought might be impossible to translate into practice, but the thought nevertheless is valid, I believe. So while I'm not cynical about psychoanalysis which is probably the greatest step toward self recognition and understanding and thus hope for a better world that has ever been made, you will find a goodly portion of cynicism and skepticism distributed throughout my utterances and reactions and as part of my make-up (a skepticism, incidentally, that is skeptical also about skeptics!). And right next to these, in close proximity and good neighborliness, many great enthusiasms and stores of faith. Aren't we all that way, conglomerates of seeming or real contradictions—skeptical about enthusiasts, enthusiastic about skeptics, and our stores of faith having short and irregular store hours?

I am happy that you're interested in the duplicating machines and that they may be, even if indirectly, useful to you. The idea of using them for the self-production of books could make a dent into the power position of the dry goods salesman who dominate our book publishing—a dent that could signify a beginning of a new era. It would be a joke of high moral retribution if the same technical progress that made the publishing business monopoly possible would in its logical development serve to break it! And the prospect, however dim at present, of having my aphorisms published at your press is a beautiful and buoying-up vista indeed!

All last evening and all this morning I have been thinking about, and repeating in my mind, your marvelous sentence "The sea of death carries away a little of our fragment of our soul's island, with each person we've loved or admired." Nothing really can be added to such a sentence.

Felix

. . .

35 West 9th Street
New York 11, N.Y.
[August 18, 1955; postmark]

Dear Felix:

I didn't express myself clearly on California—I meant Los Angeles. I spent 2 years in San Francisco, and it has great beauty, charm and character. The group of artists I knew there lived with fantasy and imagination. I am sure you would like the atmosphere, more than that of Evanston! Many interesting international restaurants, and more intimacy. It is Los Angeles which is empty. I meant Greek in external achievement of physical grace, physical external graciousness in living (the homes are beautiful, for instance), *but* empty. The emphasis is all on suntan, swimming, health, beauty, but absolutely empty. I go from one house to another, beautiful, on hills, overlooking the sea, around pools, without being able to remember the people—It is physical but not even sensuous, just automatic.

I'm looking over duplicating machines thanks to your valuable information. New York is sultry limp. Everybody looks wilted. I'm rereading *Siddhartha* with pleasure.

Devotedly,
Anaïs

Chapter 4: July 1955–December 1955

I have written to my friends the Alexanders in Paris (United Nations) to ask them if there is any opening there. I'll be in L.A. in November. When you are ready I will give you introductions to friends in San Francisco. You will let me know.

Anaïs

[Evanston]
August 23, 1955

Dear Anaïs—

I think I was rash and superficial and somewhat smug in rejecting Erich Fromm's remark about the psychological background of the Little Red Riding Hood tale. Do you know him or his work? What do you think of him?[2] One puts up a resistance when the lovely fairy tales of one's childhood seem to be violated by such "ugly" interpretations, and if they lose their magic this way it would be a pity—but maybe they needn't lose it even though a deeper insight is gained. It is a typical resistance which in itself has to be explained psychoanalytically, I realize. I don't know if Fromm is right in his explanation of the red cap being menstruation symbol (it seems possible!), but that is not the point. The point is that one shouldn't judge without examining first, and shouldn't jump to rejection. I've never read what Fromm said, I've only heard a ridiculing statement about his observation, and was thoughtless enough to repeat it. In the Kafka example I still think he's all wrong (and being German he ought to know better, and surely does); but I haven't checked his statement either, will try to do so, or it would be uneasily (too easily) demonstrable intellectual dishonesty. As to the basic point—that many analysts shoot beyond the target or go off on tangents, there can be little doubt about this; but that, after all, is only human and happens in all fields and ventures.

Are you seeing your analyst in New York?[3] Thus alternating between sessions and writing? Strictly none of my business, of course, and I generally try not to ask personal or curious sounding questions, but this does interest me (you indicated something like this at our dinner conversation at the Tally Ho remember?) and you have made it so easy, by your whole being to ask and say anything one thinks (as one could have expected from your books, of course!) that I am liable to take undue advantage of it. If so, please disregard the question! . . .

The heat still unbearable, I am at the beach whenever I can, leading mainly a vegetated life, a summer variety of hibernating, all one can do in this beastly climate. I translated a few Austrian poems into English which will appear in a small California magazine in November. Received a $2 check for a poem of my own—the first money I ever got in this country for anything I ever wrote. Rather funny!

Keep well, Anaïs, all good wishes to you and Hugo,

Affectionately,

Felix

. . .

[New York]

[September 7, 1955; postmark]

Dear Felix:

I don't blame you at all for resisting psychoanalysis of fairy tales or great artists. I feel the same way. I resented the last life of Beethoven.[4] I do feel that psychoanalysis like medicine should be used only in case of illness—and not as an interpretation of Da Vinci or Beethoven or Fairy tales etc. To me it is and should remain a medicine.

Fromm always gives me ambivalence. I like his themes and his generalities seem wise (like our *fear* of freedom) but one feels he is not great.

I once asked someone (Ruth [Witt-Diamant],* whom you will meet if you go to San Francisco) what had prevented psychoanalysis from gaining the basic respect it deserves, its place, and she answered rightly, because it destroys the magic. And this is what you feel about the fairy tales—They should only tamper with illness and privately, secretly, as a professional secret.

I think for example, it was wrong of Jung to pass judgment upon Joyce—

It is this very objection you have which has maybe our age retarded in its psychological knowledge. I haven't read the book you mention. Yes, I do believe in analysis in spite of all that. I do keep in touch with it, because as an artist I am a myth maker, but I do not want distortions (the negative aspect of imagination) to affect my human life. The artist who lives *in* the unconscious is always in danger—I'm delighted you sold a poem! Did I thank you for *Steppenwolf*—ever thank you enough?

Joaquín my brother is here—so I have to rush off. We are trying to make his visit full and interesting—beach, and plays, and friends—

Will write again soon. Much love to you and Sara,

Anaïs

*Ruth Witt-Diamant, English instructor at San Francisco State College and Founder in 1954 of the Poetry Center in San Francisco.

[California]

[September 26, 1955; postmark]

Dear Felix:

I was about to write you at length about Fromm when this powerful current I call living carried me far into urgent activities consoling Hugo for the death of his mother. Taking care of my brother Joaquín, another orphan—for 10 days, entertaining Ruth Witt-Diamant—the teacher of English and Manager of Poetry Center at San Francisco I wrote you about—who is alone etc. Five weeks passed. Now I am at Sierra Madre again, my first hour of leisure. Did I express my delight that a poem of yours is being published?

The most important question now is that I remember you said you and Sara would spend your vacation traveling and would visit California—I can't find in your letters the reference to date—Anyway, I seem to remember October. So we can talk about Fromm, analysis etc. (You know I don't mind any questions. I have been analyzed for 7 years, intermittently. I believe in it completely)—when you come I want to remind you to visit Joaquín Nin Culmell, 5830 Clover Drive at Oakland, Humboldt [sic], and Ruth Witt-Diamant (hostess to all artists-writers, etc. who visit San Francisco) (1520 Willard St., San Francisco). Let me know what I can do to make your visit pleasant, if we should find you a hotel room, etc.

Now, dear Felix, there is one delicate matter which I always try to spare my friends, and it is involving them in the "pain of love divided" which is my life but as you are coming I have to tell you. Here I live as the wife of Rupert Pole, grandson of Frank Lloyd Wright, a musician and a once actor who took up the profession of forester as romantics of other periods went into monasteries. He left N.Y. 7 years ago, wounded, defeated as an actor, and I left with him in what seemed an impulsive adventure which became a crystallized existence —All I ask of you and Sara is not to mention Hugo or Hugo's film— That is all. I will not ask more. I realize it is a great deal to expect— but I do want to see you when you come and as Rupert plays viola, and has heard about you, we may have an evening of music at his stepfather's (Lloyd Wright's) house if you like this, or a visit here where we live, at the foot of a mountain which Rupert protects from fires and floods. Last year we were involved in both fires and floods! We have a car and will be able to drive you about. Los Angeles is very difficult to navigate—it is spread out and not many busses and no subways.

Tell me when you are coming, what I can do—when you would like to stay. Los Angeles proper is like New York City—crowded and active. Hollywood is like a pleasant suburb—It all depends where your friends are (we are 50 min. from Hollywood, 50 from L.A.) whether you want to visit University of L.A. or U. of Southern California, etc. We do not have week ends off like everybody else, Thursdays and Fridays are our free days. Other days we are subject to "duty" calls—fire duty if weather is hazardous etc. After the rains we are freer.

Will you visit Henry Miller at Carmel, Big Sur?

Write me about this as it is most important to plan it so it will be pleasurable for you.

Affectionately,

Anaïs

[California]
Oct. 7, 1955

Dear Felix:

Of course your visit will not cause me anything but pleasure. My hesitancy was merely due to my having to involve you in my disguises—I have no hesitation in entering any labyrinth, but some in asking others to share it. If you don't mind and your letter was what I expected—let us enjoy it. I do hope you will save enough to come because I know it is part of your effort to alter your life and your work.

Chapter 4: July 1955–December 1955

Intuitively, having lived in both places, I can suggest that you will prefer San Francisco. Not only for its beauty, but for its charm and international flavor, its little restaurants, its character—Los Angeles is flavorless, charmless, empty. I'm only here because of Rupert and his work and his family. Are you driving?

You know I always tell you the truth—

About analysis: it has saved me from the fate of all the romantics (illness, death etc.) for romantic and neurotic are synonymous and just as their lives were tragic the neurotic life is tragic. I owe it to analysis. I have even accepted cheerfully this year my final divorce from America (with blame equally shared). No publisher, no agent, total indifference, etc.

About craving to go home—I have cured myself of that (with analysis). The need of moving, voyages etc. comes out of basic unhappiness—I laugh at the things which caused me pain and rebellion.

Are you thinking of analysis for yourself? You can write me freely. Affectionately,

Anaïs

[Evanston]
October 14, 1955

Dear Anaïs—

. . . We will leave here on Wednesday, November 2nd and go first to San Francisco which I look forward to very much, from all you have told me and from what I've heard and read. We will visit your brother, if it is convenient for him, as you so kindly suggested; and yes, we want to say hello to Henry Miller, if he can see us. We plan to stay in San Francisco, Carmel and Big Sur from the 4th to the 17th, visit the universities (Berkeley, Stanford, etc.) and arrive in Los Angeles on the 17th or 18th. . . . I would like to see you and Rupert first as long as we're still masters of our time—as much as one ever is. . . . We will stay in Los Angeles from the 17th to the 27th, then back, stopping over for a day or two in Las Vegas to lose whatever may be left of our money on roulette (which fascinates me) and to see the Grand Canyon.

About analysis I would rather talk to you than write—I'll write later if we shouldn't have a chance to talk leisurely enough. Also about your (recent?) change of mind about going back to Paris. All this interests me greatly. Right now just these lines to give you what seems good news to me. Both Sara and I are looking forward to this trip and to seeing you.

Affectionately,

Felix

P.S. . . . I've always wanted to ask you whether your books aren't translated into French—and why not? I would think you would have a more sensitive, perceptive, cultivated and appreciative public there! You are French, also of course in your writing, and that's the large part of the indifference you meet with from the American public. It hurts me to read your remark about "no publisher, no agent, total indifference, etc." Divorced from America and yet "cured" from the desire to come home? Of course, so many things enter into all decisions. . . .

[California]

[October 31, 1955; postmark]

Dear Felix:

I am delighted at the news. Your trip sounds interesting and should be stimulating. I have to leave for New York Nov. 3 or 4 but I will be back in time to see you on the 18th. There are many changes—I will tell you about them.

. . . Yes—about being translated into French, it would seem logical —and I thought so too—but there is: I—difficult style to translate, II—the fact that they have many writers like me, III—the fact that they are imitating America and printing and publishing only best sellers!

A woman recently translated *Ladders to Fire*.[5] It is being read by Plon. Also: France has been under influence of [Jean-Paul] Sartre, my very opposite. After the war, they had a distrust of romantics and symbolists—The romantic, symbolist trend is very feeble.

We will have much to talk about.

Affectionately, Anaïs

P.S. But the main thing is to concentrate our energies on attaining for you a job you are happy in.

At Sierra Madre, my phone is Custer 5-3389

address 2219 N Santa Anita Ave. as Mrs. Rupert Pole

or privately, Box 335, Sierra Madre, as Anaïs Nin

[In flight, New York–California]
[December 5, 1955; postmark]

Dear Felix:

I can't tell you how disappointed I was not to be able to return in time to see you. I had looked forward to your visit. We had so much to talk about. So much I wanted you and Sara to see, and I wanted to help your stay in California. *Hugo got sick*—I had to nurse him for 5 days—I talked with Rupert over the telephone. He told me he had invited you to his family's—I hope you enjoyed it. I had told him all about you but he never remembers names. He may have sounded vague. Sometimes my "trapeze" as I call it, is diabolically frustrating. Now we are reduced to letters again!

. . . Here I am flying west while you are on your way home. I want very much to know if you like California, whether you found a job you like better, whether you enjoyed your trip—My "family" can be very charming and sometimes very difficult. Lloyd feels overshadowed by his father. . . . Do forgive me for disappointing you through no fault of my own.

Affectionately,

Anaïs

[Evanston]
December 12, 1955

Dear Anaïs—

Yes, it was a great disappointment, I had been looking forward to our meeting as to the high point of the whole trip. But life is often like that. I am sure you could not help it.

We were glad to meet Rupert, who is charming, and your "relatives." And we did have a good time sitting in that beautiful and comfortable looking house, chatting and drinking the strong martinis Rupert makes; they together with my grief of having missed you, and missing you, went to my head. . . . I hope I did not commit any indiscretions, though I did mention that I had met you at Northwestern (assuming that Rupert knew that much) though not in connection with the film, of course. I referred to our meeting in Evanston, after he told me that your travels to New York enabled you to stop over at universities; when I mentioned Northwestern, he seemed surprised for a moment (or at least it appeared so to me) but he didn't ask any questions and so I hope everything is alright. Your "trapeze" *must* be a difficult contraption to swing on, at times—I can appreciate now also the identity-preserving function of your diary. (Am I right?) And the father confessor function of a psychoanalyst. Though Ruth Witt-Diamant made the not too tactful but to her simply amusing joke that she had always suspected that your sessions of analysis invariably ended up with your seducing the analyst—"They always end up on her couch!" she cried and roared with laughter; but I don't think she meant to be malicious (and I hope you won't give my out-of-school talking away)—she just is that way; we had no sooner come into her living room than she informed us, by way of getting acquainted conversation, that Klaus Mann used to have an affair with Auden, and Thomas Mann had an affair with his daughter Erika—"What will you drink?" Those two weird looking dogs of hers snored loudly at our feet, each one using economically only one eye when he was awake, and sundry cats walked about the room while she told us how many cases of beer Dylan Thomas had consumed in her house. . . . I saw her the next evening again at the open house of Mr. Kenneth Rexroth,* and she was very quiet and self-effacing there.

It was a wonderful trip, all told—I just love San Francisco, the only American city I have so far seen (I've never been in New Orleans) that has a character and personality of its own; it is the most European-feeling city, with all those Spanish houses and street names and sundry national quarters—we had excellent weather, drove and saw quite a bit, and one sunset while we were having cocktails on top of the Mark Hopkins Hotel, looking over the bay, at Alcatraz (thinking uncomfortably of the prisoners on this castle island) and at the graceful bridge, was a memorable experience. We enjoyed very much meeting your brother, had lunch with him on the campus; he laughed when I told him what you had said about his being "hopelessly European." He is one of the few people I met in that part of the country who would rather be in New York, but I can understand it in his place; for a musician nothing in this country can compare with New York or take its place. . . .

We both liked Carmel; (Sara's trying to figure out what she could do to support both of us there so that I would have time to write and in a way it sounds beautiful)—and among the various little magazine poets we met, several seem to have made just such an arrangement, some "helping" their wives in making pottery or running an employment agency—I don't think these schemes work out too well in the end, psychologically. I rented a car in Carmel and we drove up to Big Sur to see Henry Miller (after having made an appointment, of course). The drive was breathtakingly beautiful—only when we came to the Big Sur Inn, Sara begged off, she can't take heights very well and was a little dizzy driving so close to the edge high above the ocean. So she stayed at the Inn with the poor monstrously fat, immobile, grotesque, but very intelligent Mrs. Dutgin and her bizarre and quite drunk husband, while I went on alone, exhilarated by the air, the sights, the driving, and the prospect of meeting H. M. We had a very interesting afternoon, he was somewhat reserved and suspicious at first, being pestered unfortunately by a lot of curious tourists who wanted to see the man who writes so many "dirty words."—But we established contact after a little while and then things went along fine. I liked him very much, he was close to what I had expected, and also his new wife seems very nice. He was particularly interested when I—touched off by a coincidental remark of his wife [Eve] about three "lost" manuscripts—told him that they were not lost, that I had seen them a few weeks previously in Ben Abramson's shop, and that I could probably recover them for him, at least in photostat. (I'm working on it now.) He would not let me go down alone—it had gotten dark before we knew it—but drove ahead of me to the Inn so that I could follow his car at those hairpin turns, and thus Sara too met him, after all, and was very pleased about it. . . .

Los Angeles I didn't like at all, as you prophesied, an anticlimax to the whole trip. Ugly, sprawling, a village in search of a city, as someone remarked, and unless *los angeles* like what is worst and most standardized and dirty in America, they must have long since left that town—except for the fallen angels who became film stars. Even the moon looked phony among those palm trees along Sunset Boulevard which in turn, looked like giant toilet brushes to me, pardon the metaphor. And Las Vegas too—brassy and stupid, as expected. Even the gambling halls lacked the erotic flavor and air of elegance and excitement of the European counterparts—croupiers looking like gardeners in shirt-sleeves and green aprons instead of tuxedos; instead of the demimonde (with few exceptions) bleached little dolls and molls with their sugardaddies from Grand Rapids; and assorted

Babbitts, who found oil in their backyards, playing "craps." Well—! We played a little roulette, I won two $8 jackpots (beginner's luck) and ended up with a loss of $17—which is good, considering what we saw other people lose (who had more to lose to begin with)! Still it was interesting. . . .

And now, sad, sad to say, we're back in our grooves. And I have to rely again on pen and ink in talking with you. Some subjects need the give and take of conversation, are difficult to correspond about. But we have to make the best of it. Work piled up in the office, work and correspondence piled up on my desk, tiredness in the evening, and slim chances, probably, that I can sneak in a letter during working hours for quite awhile—as I before sometimes succeeded in doing. So I am glad that I could write you at least at length. . . . . . I just got the good news that a Vienna magazine has accepted a batch of aphorisms—the first I sent out in two years; will send Stuhlmann a copy. Write me about yourself Anaïs, and the changes you mentioned.

Affectionately,

Felix

. . .

*Kenneth Rexroth (1905–1982), San Francisco–based poet, translator, and critic.

[California]
[December 19, 1955; postmark]

Dear Felix:

Your letter about your trip was so interesting, and I enjoyed it— Felt slightly consoled for missing you—You both made a lovely impression on the "family"—Our letters must have crossed, and by now you know it could only be Hugo's illness which would cause me to disappoint you and myself.

Your description of Ruth amused me. It is true she is not a symbol of delicacy or subtlety, their very opposite—but under her rough wings she shelters the artists. It is true she is not malicious. She spoke the truth, even if out of context! I did reverse the roles with Otto Rank —but the analysis which succeeded was done by a woman and no personal complications ensued there.

There are things I would rather talk to you about than write—But since the talk is so far away—for the last 8 years I have been happier here—but I felt I should give my marriage every chance of "repair" and the "passion" time to prove it was an illusion. If it is, "illusion" is winning out—That is all I can say for the moment. . . .

You were of course, perfectly tactful and sensitive. Nothing went wrong. Rupert's haziness about places, facts, names, is part of his personality. . . .

Spy is appearing in England, so they want a new novel to follow, so I have gone back to finish the one I was working on—I'm deeply concerned about time—I need time to work on Diaries but I spend ½ day on housework—and now on Xmas gifts etc.—and if I stay here I could also have to get a "job."

I hope too, you will pursue the United Nations project—I feel you'll be happier there—Somehow, university life is always cramping —Intelligent friends of mine everywhere in education, say the same thing. The personal life is cramped.

Remember someday to see Marcel Marceau. That was the highest emotional experience these last few months. Supreme eloquence of the body—He is a mime, a pupil of [Jean-Louis] Barrault. . . .

Your friend
Anaïs

[New York]
December 30, 1955

Dear Sara and Felix:

This year was kind to us in allowing us to meet and become friends, but not kind enough in interfering with our meeting in California.

My wishes for a happy Christmas and a New Year which will fulfill all your desires,

Anaïs

5

January 1956–October 1956

THE NECESSITY OF
A RICHER LIFE

IN LATE 1955 POLLAK gives Nin a gift of Hermann Hesse's novel *Steppenwolf*. Living on a level of sublimation far greater than Nin's, Pollak saw himself as a would-be Harry Haller, the hero of Hesse's *Steppenwolf*, an outwardly conventional, inwardly multi-faceted personality who breaks savagely out of his bourgeois straitjacket.

Now at the emotional heart of this correspondence, Anaïs Nin, having shared her secret with Felix Pollak, encourages him to unburden himself also. Pollak replies with a seven-thousand-word handwritten confession on the travails of his inner life and of his marriage. In a scarcely believable later addendum, Pollak even confesses to a perverse longing for the adrenaline-filled days of Nazi persecution. Nin is moved by his confidence in her and offers more details on her own, often surprisingly banal, domestic life and its frustrations. She berates herself for a lack of courage. Rupert is also disillusioned with his work in the forestry service, which he gives up to become a junior high school mathematics teacher. Struggling financially, Rupert and Anaïs move to a two-room apartment. The extent to which both Nin and Pollak reveal their inner selves in this section is remarkable, even as they each proclaim, in Nin's words, "the necessity of a richer life."

Felix Pollak's poem, "What It Always Comes Down To" (Appendix B), which he sends to Anaïs Nin on February 18, 1956, captures a sense of their mutual romantic longing.

[California]
[January 9, 1956; postmark]

Dear Felix:

Just reread *Steppenwolf*—and feel I didn't thank you enough for it. The first time I read it was in the maelstrom of life in New York and I did not get all of its essence. It is a beautiful book and so subtle and so full of the knowledge of elusiveness of character and reality—That is of course why you gave it to me.

What I most regret about missing you besides the personal exchange and sharing is that I feel I could have helped you with this matter of finding a better work—since it may be a long time before we can talk why don't you write me about the things which trouble you which I feel in overtones in your letters, references to psychoanalysis etc. My intuition may be wrong but I do feel you are troubled. You know I believe in sharing. I have always answered your questions.

Curious thing, that I know a *Steppenwolf*—in life—Rupert's father [Reginald Pole] (not his stepfather Lloyd) who is an English ex-Shakespearean actor, very ill and very tragic and completely isolated. He haunts us like a ghost—but cannot commune with any human being. I was reminded of a deeper Pirandello—who played with facets and paradoxes so well.

How is your work?

Did you know an English publisher is bringing out a biography of Henry Miller?[1] I had a big struggle to be left out of it and only succeeded in part. It is a very cheap and journalistic one by a character I always considered a caricature double of Henry, a kind of valet to

Don Juan, a Sancho Panza with Don Quixote—not that Miller is either, but the relationship had that quality. It is unfortunate for Henry. America does enough cheapening of its writers without Europeans adding to it.

The best novel I have read recently is Romain Gary's *Colors of the Day**—translated from the French—alive.

Anaïs

Les Couleurs du jour (1952; translation by Stephen Becker, 1953). French novelist Romain Gary (born Romain Kacew in Vilnius, Lithuania; 1914–1980) won the Prix Goncourt for *Les Racines du ciel* (1956; *The Roots of Heaven*, 1958).

[Evanston]
Jan. 12, 1956

Dear Anaïs—

I am sure your intuition is seldom wrong, and it isn't in my case. But these things are awfully hard to discuss in letters. It is not a matter of candidness—I feel I could be utterly truthful and open with you, without reservations and inhibitions, but it is almost impossible to analyze one's inner life, and the way it is connected to external circumstances and to other persons and their lives and backgrounds, short of writing a book—and you're the last one I have to tell that to. You have written—you are writing—books (maybe one book, altogether) on just that theme. Only, to make it literature, it has to be taken out of the realm of the private (which still remains personal)—and what you're asking me to talk about is private, involved, requiring a psychoanalyst's couch rather than letter paper. Notwithstanding the fact that you, I realize, could be an ideal analyst for me—except for the acute danger of personal involvement (as far as I am concerned) and added complications rather than their dissolvement; though sometimes added complications are solutions, are may be just "what the doctor ordered." And so one faces two dangers: trying to tell too much—which, in a letter, would still be too little, even though it might become a monstrously long one—or to be glib and surface-skimming, which is really to evade the issues. Added to this is the matter of clarity (difficult to attain), of balance, fairness to others involved (sketchy remarks or complaints can sound very treacherous, disloyal, vicious, without being meant to)—and to avoid, in general, a tone of complaint, which I don't like; for I believe that people can—to some extent—direct their lives, and if they are not satisfied with their state of affairs, either ought to change them, or be quiet about them; if one is too weak, too timid, or otherwise incapable of doing something about one's troubles (or if one really doesn't want to do anything about them) one should realize this and not blame the world, others, circumstances, etc. for it. If one persists in talking about all this, the chances are that one wants only to talk, that one really doesn't wish to change anything. Don't you agree? (I admire you for doing something about your problems, e.g. Hugo!) Yes, Anaïs, you have always answered all my questions (and I appreciate this, just as I appreciate very deeply your concern and your wish to help me)— but you too knew in your answers always just how much to say and how much to leave unsaid, what to reveal and where to stop. So I will try to say briefly as much as can briefly be said.

As for my references to psychoanalysis—my main concern here is whether it would help me creatively. For one of the things that troubles me very much is that I have achieved so little, that I have to show so little for my age—and the feeling that I have more in me than I have even begun to bring out. I suspect analysis may help my creativity, but at the same time I fear it—for two reasons: for what it would do to my life (for psychoanalysis is not one of those patent medicines to philosophies of Adjustment and Peace of Mind and Peace of Soul, and Peace of Glands, so contemptibly in American vogue)—and I feel latent urges of rebellion which could easily become acute; (maybe they should, but that is easy to say, easier than to do, though I have taken risks at various stages in my life—but all those things are so much more easily coped with by characters in novels' wish fulfillments, wish dreams, projections often of the authors who live vicariously in their own creations). But there is also the opposite fear in me, I suspect and this is really blasphemy, but our ambiguities seem quite capable of housing prayer and blasphemy very close together—the fear that analysis may prove too successful in releasing my latent creativity, that the need to write would become urgent to the point where I could no longer hold a job—a job which (though better in that respect than many others) leaves me basically only a few precious marginal tired hours a night for doing what is most essential to me. This is very painful, fundamentally wrong, a sin against sense and the spirit and the body too (I hardly ever get enough sleep that way and I am tired all day and still tired when—after chores and Sara's requirements of companionship—I can sit down to work in the evening). But what is the alternative—if one is not either a slick, facile prostitute who writes what the public or the publishers or the critics want and pay for—and then what is the point of writing at all, any other job is equally noncreative, some are more creative even—or if one is not a genius, either talented enough to be successful on one's own terms or young and unencumbered and reckless enough, and a genius, like Henry Miller, not to give a damn what happened. I don't fall into either of those categories, I am happy and profoundly sorry to say—so what is my alternative than to go on living on the margins of my existence and writing in the remnants of dull days? Why do you think even this letter to you, on my conscience for so long, is so late in coming? Even at this moment, I'll have to interrupt again and go home for dinner— I am writing this in today's last hour in the Library—the only worthwhile thing I've done all day. And that is the reason why I am not too interested in another job, even though it may in respects of interest, money, location, etc. be a better job. For, when it comes right down to it—a job is still a job, the same necessary evil, the obstacle in the way of what I really want to do. A job is a means to an end which eliminates the end. I know that hundreds of artists and writers are in the same predicament—and produce. So, again it is only partly the circumstances, and largely myself who is to blame.

One more word on analysis before I close for today—I'll say one other thing about my present job tomorrow (I hope!). In the course of our references to analysis I had a few arguments with Sara. . . . What the argument was about was Sara's contention that it would be very hard for me to be analyzed. (She was—but I sometimes wonder how successfully.) Why hard? I asked. Because, she said, I have built up very strong defenses, have developed a very rigid pattern of outlook and behavior, have made a very definite adjustment (how I hate that word!!)—and it would not only be extremely difficult to pierce the shell, but it would also be terribly painful for me, maybe more than I could take. (I hope I am relating her words and meanings correctly.) I answered I didn't agree with her. I had all my life been prob-

Chapter 5: January 1956–October 1956

ing into myself, attempting with great and very often painful honesty to analyze my motives, not the sham and surface and easily digestible motives into which our true desires are commonly rationalized, but my real urges and intentions and beliefs. I've all my life been working on this and myself, trying to get to know myself without blinking or shrinking. Which, I added is more than most people do, or attempt to do, or even partially succeed in doing, because it is the hardest thing in the world.

Therefore I believe I would be relatively easy to analyze, having a certain amount of insight in myself, having done, in fact, to a large degree what an analyst is supposed to help one doing. And being not inarticulate and being in the right atmosphere—rather uninhibited, I think it would be fairly easy, though of course still painful. How necessary, how beneficial, I could not tell. I am beset by conscious, and semi-conscious, and no doubt unconscious memories that bother me, and often talk aloud to myself, shooing them away when they come up. But I am not to any troublesome degree neurotic, I have despite my sensitivity, a rather robust core of health (I believe and hope) and apart from the (important) question of creativity, I don't see any acute need for analysis. . . .

January 20th

. . . This is again stolen time and Mr. N. [Nyholm] can appear, or call for me, any moment. Which fits in with what I want to say about my position here. Considering any job a necessary evil, this one has the great advantage that I am my own boss—except for Nyholm. He does pay much more attention to me than I cherish, but at least I am alone in the room (except for a part time student assistant) and having during my first years here thoroughly organized the collection and procedures, I can now let it run fairly easily by itself; there is no great run on my books by professors and students, and thus I do have a little time for myself, work on the aphorisms, correspondence, etc., on a desk sufficiently covered with papers to make it hard to determine what exactly I am doing. This, to me, is worth a lot of money; and even a medium-size raise in salary with, most likely, no free minute to myself, is a dubious prospect. Not that the time that I devote to my own work ever amounts to much on any one day, and it is always a tense, uncomfortable kind of working; but even that is precious. . . . And as for limitations on one's private life—the University as such, or the colleagues, do not interfere, snoop or bother; my limiting factors lie elsewhere. When I frequently feel fenced in, cornered, confined, it is largely not Sara's fault but my own—if "fault" is the word at all. I probably should have never married in the first place —I don't think I am cut out for it, and I waited long enough, as it were. When I finally and with some trepidation took the step, it was to a large extent due to the cold, cold atmosphere in this country, where it is so incredibly difficult to have a satisfying affair with a woman, to find some measure of human warmth, depth, passion, where my past, my standards, my whole being seemed to make for an increasing isolation, and erotic encounters tended to accentuate my loneliness rather than alleviate it. But that is only half the story—the other half, or three quarters, was of course Sara's warm, generous, devoted personality, her maturity, all the good qualities which I have never ceased to appreciate. But everything is complicated, complex, hard to put clearly in its place. In contrast to the just mentioned feelings of coldness and isolation which made me want a companion, I also need a great deal of privacy, of being alone with myself—more so, I believe, than most people. This militates against marriage per se. I remember how happy I always was when I, after an evening with a woman—with Sara before marriage—or after a weekend night, went back to, or was left alone in my little apartment, where I could close the doors on the outside world, where nobody could enter, where I was alone with my thoughts and dreams, my books, my work, my letters, where not even anybody's noticeable attempts not to be noticed or not to disturb me, disturbed me. There was never enough of that, there was my violin and chess (partners or postal)—and the hours of plain easy lounging even, of which I can do a great deal, always were cut short by having to go to work on whatever obligation. But I enjoyed my solitariness, that's what I'm trying to say, I've never in my life been bored when I was alone, but frequently so in company. All this is probably not so unusual but it doesn't describe an ideal marriage partner, I think, unless his mate is of a very similar nature. Sara's temperament is very opposite to all this—partly the attraction for me, I suppose—she is more extra- than introverted, outgoing. . . .

I remember when the question of marriage came up between us, that I voiced great apprehension about my ability of making not only the considerable adjustment necessary for marriage (for someone like me, and relatively late in life to boot) but about the additional adjustment of becoming suddenly the "father," the guardian, the companion, the "older friend" of a 13-year-old boy. Here I was swayed by assurances and promises. In this respect I am still shaking my head about myself. Not that Sara did not try to keep the promises — they were simply not possible to keep. Mark is a good, intelligent boy, but I have a [too] vivid recollection of my own youth (childhood, puberty) to be interested in young people (I even have the urge to make up to them some of the things that were done to me) — and I like children, to the extent to which a person like me can like them: for a while, for, even more than marriage, I would want to turn them on and off like a light bulb, like an electric switch. Which of course cannot be done. . . .

I may have actually been jealous, when I had arguments and quarrels with Sara and felt the two of them forming an alliance against me, the foreigner in more than one respect. I had hours of great loneliness and bitterness then, and again impulses of flight and the frustration of imprisonment. Sara said on some occasions that I would act quite differently if she had a daughter instead of a son, and I could of course neither consent to nor deny the possibility. Although with me it has always been the personality that was the decisive factor in my reaction, even in animals! But how can one prove that? But it all affected our relationship, though Sara never kept up that alliance against me, is, in fact, much more conciliatory than I am, much more ready to admit being wrong and to try to "make up." She is a very good person really, trying hard to do the right thing by everybody, being (overly) concerned about everybody, anxious to see and make everybody happy and her one complaint against me is that I try to make her over, to change her, that I correct her too much, etc. That is a hateful thing to do, trying to make people different from what they are, particularly if one, like I, believes so strongly that everybody should be what he is, and I am disgusted with myself, for I know there is truth to that assertion. I am a tyrant, I suppose, without wanting to be one, more: while hating to be one. So many things bother and disturb me, my aesthetic sense, my taste, my ear for false tones, my impatience with conventionalities, frills, commonplaces, artificialities — all those things being such of course only on my personal scale of values, things as they appear to me. It's all quite subjective, of course, and I feel the same towards my own actions. I am, in one word, hyper-sensitive (as you yourself observed and said) and difficult to live with. I know that, and I warned Sara about it before we got married. . . .

. . . The belated shock of a sudden and belated fatherhood and at-tendant complications made also a stroke through my libido, so to speak, and apparently to Sara's, and the times of our affair seem long ago. Indelicate, I suppose, to mention this, but it is an essential part of the answer to your question, what was troubling me. And in turn this affects one's hunger and appetite for life itself. It is not one thing, of course, not one big thing that could be dealt with and changed, it is a maze, a filigree net of many small, evasive things, the formida-bleness of trifles. Besides, everything is so difficult in this country— apart from the difficulty in my particular set-up of even going out alone without going to great lengths of concocting stories and lies, and sneaking around. I hate to sneak, I hate to hurt Sara, who is loy-alty and (a bit clinging) devotion itself (and she would be hurt to the quick by my having an affair, by my "deceiving lies" with another woman), I haven't even got time, money, a car (so necessary here) (suburb!), and with frustration and desire begin to mingle resigna-tion, lack of energy, tiredness. I dream of Europe—it's becoming a *The Secret Life of Walter Mitty*[2] state of affairs. It frightens me. I am obviously not "well adjusted." To become so is an acute danger which makes me feel chained and confined. For the emphasis, in all cases almost, seems to be on adjusted, not on well. So far this has not much to do with America—as far as the diagnosis is considered. The condition can occur anywhere, and no doubt does. But the cure, its possibility, has to do with Europe. . . . I often have a corny but beau-tiful vision of the ideal life for me: a garret *sous les toits de Paris*, or Vienna (which I once had) near a good bordello, with just enough money to live without going to work and thus able to do my own work, meet people to talk and play chess with, and free to prowl the streets and pick up strange women for wonderfully fulfilled life-filled, mystery-filled encounters without inhibitions, without entanglements, without responsibilities, duties, and all the clay that begins to creep like a fungus over all beauty when you come too close. Not without masks this vision, of course, corny, adolescent, immoral, irresponsi-ble, a Walter Mitty dream—I know. I just wonder about the rightness of the standards by which all this is so wrong and so impossible. I have had times at least close to that—and they probably spoiled me for my present life, and for this cold, commercial country where ugly brassy business women disguised as whores can be contacted in "saloons," after rounds of drink-buying, to give strictly functional performances at outrageous prices. . . .

I could write on—and yet, what could I add, what good would it do? This is so sketchy that less, not more, would be indicated. Unless one can give really a whole picture, with foreground and background, and fairness to all concerned, anything in between too much but not enough will distort rather than present an external and internal reality. Everything is inconclusive, must be so, in most situations. Do you have any suggestions? Can you help me? Do I even need help? And can anybody, except myself, give it to myself? Certainly, things are troubling me, but is that not the case with most people? I don't know any cure-all answers for any of my problems, and I doubt that there are any, or that anybody else knows them. But I do hope, Anaïs, that you will comment on what I wrote, as frankly as I wrote it. I am glad, in a way, that it is on paper, fragmentary, superficial as it is, but I would feel almost naked and betrayed if you wouldn't tell me what you really think of it all. . . .

I was very happy to hear the good news of the English edition of *Spy* and that you, on the strength of it, have a publisher again—hearty congratulations, Anaïs! It is easy to say I told you so, and it is easy to tell one that things will work out at the right time—but I have infinite faith in you as a writer and in your eventual recognition—not by the mass, but by more of the few. I hope you will be inspired by the fortunate turn to work well on your new book, despite the new (?) developments with Hugo. Will you reciprocate in kind and consider me worthy of your confidence in that connection? . . . Am so glad that you like *Steppenwolf* so much—after my spotty fragmentary confessions which leave always room also for contrary moods, thoughts, desires (even motherhood and fatherhood can be wonderful, I'm sure, even the attachment, the love to one woman—provided she has many within her—can be "a consummation devoutly to be wished for" as Shakespeare puts it)—after my confessions you will know too why I love this book and what it means to me.

"The knowledge of elusiveness of character and reality"—Yes, of course, that is why I gave it to you, who knows so much about this herself, whose very theme this is. . . . I believe that even famous artists can be much lonelier than we think and one individual letter can mean more to them than ten laudatory reviews. Have you considered writing Hesse a few lines? I know he reads both English and French, and he may well know your name and your books—if not, I am certain he would appreciate them and recognize in your writing blood of his blood, spirit of his spirit. . . .

When I mentioned the glory of fatherhood, incidentally, I remembered Miller's new discovery along that line and his almost comical, though touching, but actually close to maudlin description of his belated father role in the book he's writing about his life on Big Sur. The passage that made me rub my eyes and laugh out loud is quoted in Emil White's "Big Sur Guide 1955" and reads as follows: "My eyes are moist with tears as I watch them moving tenderly and reverently amid a swarm of golden memories . . . days drenched with sun and nights spangled with stars and 'Oh, daddy, come quick, see the moon, it's lying in the pool!' And besides the adoration of the neighbors, a dolt of a father who preferred wasting his time playing with them to cultivating his mind or making himself a good neighbor. Lucky the father who is merely a writer, who can stop his work and return to his childhood at will! Lucky the father who is pestered from morn till sundown by two healthy insatiable youngsters. Lucky the father who yearns to see again through the eyes of his children, even though he became the biggest fool that ever was!" And that from the man who was forever spitting the world in the eye, who wanted to blow the whole world to bits, who remarked of his pregnant first wife in *Black Spring:* "She was crying for sympathy and not a drop of sympathy in the house" (I'm quoting this from memory)! Both touching and funny and incongruous. But then, there were always many incongruous traits in Miller. He is a synthesis of incongruities. About the biography of his by Perlès, Miller's clown, and your only partly successful struggle to be at least not named by name, you've told me when you were here—at our taxi ride from the airport (which for me was the best part of your visit here—I'm egotistical enough to prize it even above your public performances!) Yes, too bad that Miller's life—which of all people's lives needs no re-telling

by anybody else—should be presented in a cheaply journalistic manner, and by a European to boot! . . . With great affection and friendship,

    Felix

    . . .

                           35 West 9th Street
                           New York 11, N.Y.
                    [February 2, 1956; postmark]

Dear Felix:

    I was very much touched by your supreme act of friendship, that
of sharing with me a painful and deep revelation of your personal
life, and I want to say first of all, please do not feel badly after being
so truthful because I know that sometimes when one utters one's
most secret thoughts, the truth, they seem treacherous to other human
beings. But the truth is *never* treacherous, and it is so much beyond
the personal, that the story you have to tell, and Sara, are like two dis-
tinct truths, neither one damaging to the other. We are concerned at
this moment with *your* truth. There were so many little evidences of
distress that I felt, perhaps because I am always driven to this kind of
facing of truth, that I felt it would be healing merely to confront it.
My impression of all you tell me is not of a neurosis at all, truly, but
of the universal human drama of conflicts between desires, and the
restlessness every thoughtful creative human being feels to fulfill his
potencies. What I had guessed was the necessity of a richer life. Freer
too. At the same time you recognize the value of what you do have,
and the needs which made you enter this situation. Analysis would
not deprive you of one or the other but merely help you to reach for
the major ones and cease the inner strife between the needs. You presented such a well-balanced picture, the negative elements, as well
as the positive, in the marriage, in the job, in the problems, and then
completed it all by expressing the fantasy, the wish: life in Europe
with its greater personal freedom. What can I say to help you? That
we are all caught between life (in Europe) and earning a living which
is all America has to offer.

    There are two solutions, I feel. It lies mainly in choosing the place where life has more to give you in the realms which nourish you. Analysis is working at this expansion and liberation from the inside, but it can be worked at from the outside. There are places where "jobs" are less demanding and the life more nourishing. I am sending you a booklet on jobs in other parts of the world for both of you. What I feel is that given the elements you have, some of the fatigue is due to the lack of expansion within the life itself, similar interests, friendships etc. What you describe as ideal is a kind of bohemian life which exists in San Francisco and in New York. Perhaps, if you don't want to revolutionize your whole life, you might tend all your efforts at getting a job that is not just a job. It is the bourgeois structure of life which makes full living impossible in American University life. Small towns. The atmosphere itself is constrictive. In Paris, for example, I could live all my lives out, both home, husband, and the other—In New York too—Perhaps you should strive for that.

About Sara. Dear Felix, every relationship has its negative and its positive side, destructive and life-giving. I feel that you see this, and make a balance in your heart, as you did live out your artificial fatherhood to the best of your abilities and I can see it was difficult. The kind of life in which the writer can exist *is* attainable. I think most of the evils of American life come from the fact that we let the job dictate the form of life, rather than aim at the kind of life first. If I were a man I would choose the place and life first, and then the job. What you seem to need most of all is a kind of life in which you can live fully.

In return for your sincerity, I will tell you what I can. It is very simple. All my life I have been married to Hugo. And all my life I have had romantic outside attachments. But to none of them I wanted to be married. But eight years ago I met Rupert, and for the first time my passion was also a human, happy relationship. But I could not make the break, because Hugo is, as it were, my whole family, mother father brother son, and lifelong friend. The conflict grew so acute I went to analysis, and fought for a wholeness I could not achieve. And there I am. On a trapeze. I know what I want. But I cannot act upon it. Hugo has been analyzed all this time and seemed to be freed of me, but won't relinquish me. I have very little time left, both to live and finish my work . . . because I have a bad heart. What I wanted, I never reached, because it is harder for a woman. Her life is shaped by the man. I should have been married to an artist, and lived an artist's life. I would have made a marvelous wife to a great artist—but—"on épouse ses propres faiblesses" [one marries one's own weaknesses]. The only two men I chose to live with are not adventurous, obsessed with security and a shelter, a refuge, a nest.

I may not make it—

To return to analysis and you. You should not *fear* it. If you find the right analyst, this acute rebellion you worry about (that it might explode) is the very one analysis dissolves. As for the changes it might bring about, they might not be the ones you fear, but completely different changes you did not imagine. Do not dismiss the idea. When you say you cannot afford it remember: it usually helps to improve the professional status, income etc. and every analyst knows this and that just as the creative potential is increased, the earning one also, and you may start with difficulty but find ways to pay it, in increased energy, output, work, confidence etc. Even I who never earned a penny, finally earned a little last year! In other words, the *fears themselves which you mention, are the ones which stand in the way of your fulfillment and not the outer situation.* The fears should be examined —for example the idea that if your writing impulse were liberated you would do nothing but write etc. These fears demand great energy, at the *controls*—and removing them releases all this wasted energy. As a friend I would ask you *first* of all to try analysis, to obtain the life, the relationship the creativity you want.

If you decide against this—and I feel you would not need very much [analysis]—then the next one is to change the life outwardly, job and place etc.

To help Sara I will write you *both* a letter. I know what to say.

As one writer to another, let me say that you described and stated your position, your feelings, beautifully and lucidly. You write extremely well.

Your friend,
Anaïs

Dear Anaïs—

I am very happy with your answer to my letter; it is as perceptive and human as I expected it and makes me appreciate our friendship more than ever. You were certainly right in your intuitive diagnosis of the need for a richer and freer life—more life and less existence—and were probably right also in the therapies you suggest. Whenever I am stimulated and animated, encounter my kind of people, find a free and alive and creative atmosphere (as on some occasions during the California trip), I emerge like out of a dungeon—and the sinking back into it, the dungeon of stuffiness, dullness, mediocrity, routine, is accompanied by dread and exasperation. This is very, very true. As to the direction into which I should try to move, your letter has thus given me added clarity and impulse. The difficulties of doing so in actuality may be greater than you think, though. Even your brother spoke with almost nostalgia of New York, adding, "but what can one do—here is my job and to find an equally good or better one in New York is not easy." Still—I read the sentence a few days ago, I forget where, "fulfillment depends on the quality of wanting." Some truth in that. External circumstances, surroundings, etc. are not the whole solution, but are no doubt an important factor. As for the things that are surrounded by the surroundings—the inner situation—yes, I will think about analysis. Whether I will go into it, whether it can be done, I don't know yet. . . . How beneficial it would be, I could feel already by the effect my confidential letter to you has had: I felt much relieved after having written it (without any doubt or anxiety as to your reception of it!) And your assumption that it would be healing merely to confront the problems in a coherent and truthful way, was quite correct. (To thank you in a meager sentence would be utterly inadequate.) Still, I am, alternately, even more aware of the need for changes; to talk things out helps, but is by no means enough. Let me think about it further.

I wish I could offer you any help in your own problem! It has been weighing on me ever since. And let me say, Anaïs, first of all, that you will never have reason to regret your confidence in me! I am deeply aware of the fact that you have so much more at stake than I by being so frank and disclosing so much; I am grateful for your trust and will not fail you! What can one say—what can one suggest—one cannot even blame psychoanalysis for having provided no solution, for as you say, "I know what I want. But I cannot act upon it." That is it, that's exactly it. Certainly it is much to know what one wants, most people have no idea although they may think they know, and analysis and self-analysis can bring about at least that important realization. But then? Then to act upon it is another matter. For it involves not only ourselves but others, and what they want. And analysis can hardly bring about—or be required to accomplish—the dissolution of someone's love, or need, for another being. Thus your saying that Hugo had been under analysis all this time and seemed to be freed of you and won't relinquish you, made me feel sorry for him too. There are no magic drugs to bring about, or eliminate love from one person to another. And you indicate that you yourself need him too, particularly his father role is easily discernible in *Spy*, doubly so when seen in the perspective of *Winter of Artifice*. For your books, while they certainly transcend your own single, individual life and experience, are sufficiently and consciously autobiographical in their raw material to allow one certain insights, don't you think? Thus when I read *Spy* and pondered the various episodes, I made a note to myself about Sabina: "A daughter and a mother in search of a lover." Do you think this is wrong?

While Hugo, painful as it may be to him, seems capable of facing the reality of Rupert (even though he may try to call it "illusion"), Rupert (and his family) apparently could not face the reality, the continued reality of Hugo. And the strain this must put you under— even technically, mechanically, in external arrangements, apart from the eternal split and need of being ceaselessly on guard—this I grieve to contemplate. Of course there are two kinds of tension, the unproductive, and the productive. And yours may well be the second. I would feel extremely bad if I were sure that you had to create your work despite all this, rather than because of it. An artist's nature is cunning too: sometimes he, subconsciously, strives for the generation of tensions the release of which is his work; in that sense the artist is like a self-winding watch. This may not be so at all in your case, of course—as I said, I'd hate to think that it weren't. In thinking about it all, several specific questions came to my mind—questions which again would be easier to ask and answer in direct conversation, but until then it may be a long time. Thus, while you have the tact to ask me only in general, I shall put the specific questions to you; but I hope you won't feel in any way obligated to answer them or some of them! When you referred to your romantic attachments while you were married to Hugo, I couldn't help wondering whether he was, or wasn't at all jealous (he must have known about some)— and whether you were ever jealous about his relations with other women which I assume existed (though I don't know, of course)? And how would this compare with Rupert's reaction (if you would, however superficially or temporarily) get involved with another man and he would find out about it? And you, in his case? Does his mother know that you're not married to him? She impressed me as rather bourgeois and on the conventional side, as a woman who would rather pretend she didn't know what she doesn't approve of, than admit she knows. (But I saw her only very fleetingly.) (You made a remark once that your "in-laws" could be rather trying at times, as well as charming at other times, and I couldn't help wondering about difficulties from that quarter.) And Rupert himself? Does he think you and Hugo are divorced? (I cannot help, while my mind keeps asking logical questions, to hear a whole chorus of inner voices chanting at me, "Felix, stop that, that is strictly none of your business!")

I'll stop asking questions. But there was one remark you made in your letter, Anaïs, which gave me a sensation of dull pain—I would not want you to answer me this in reference to your future, or its problems and solutions. You know as well as I do that people with bad hearts can live a long time, if they take care of themselves on the one hand and refuse to consider themselves invalids on the other. I know you don't the second, I hope you do the first. Are you under a doctor's supervision? Of course your particular trapeze does not make for serenity and calm. I very much wish I could help you. Hugo's refusal to "relinquish" you—does that mean he absolutely refuses a divorce, or more than that? (Questions, questions again!)

I think I understand one thing about you better than before: you live in and for the day but you are very much concerned about time and its passing, aren't you? (As I am, too.) And your refusal, for instance, to date your letters, is not symbolic of your unawareness of time and its relentless departure, of your disinterest in the dimension and quality of time, but on the contrary, an indicator of so much awareness and interest that it manifests itself in an unwillingness to face it. Strange in a way, since you believe in facing and confronting the basic things — but understandable too — as an irrational and futile (so terribly futile) gesture. . . .

If I can help at all — in any way, please let me know. With friendship and affection,

Felix

. . .

[New York]
[February 18, 1956; postmark]

Dear Felix:

I am so sorry I never wrote you about the poems — always did not want to write hastily — waiting for a calm moment to say more, but eyes tired from trying to finish new novel for English publisher to follow *Spy*. I like "On Listening to a Dead Poet's Recording," the lyrical last lines, "o were once more flesh, this shell impelled . . . under a pin's caress . . . to rehearse death." And "Zoo," very eloquent plea for freedom. I like "What It Always Comes Down To." "Toned by the hours" is a Debussy phrase. It is also like a miniature painting. "Trees through a Window"[3] is graceful way of expressing the mysteries of being and seeing. Very delicate. "Are we two separate identities?" You have a fine touch, like Paul Klee. They express your sensitivity well. We should send them somewhere, but I wonder how you will react to the impersonal and brutal way they have of saying no — or even presume to tell you what you should write. It makes me hesitate.

I wonder if you could not apply for a fellowship and make a literary project of some kind. Some friends of mine professors in Claremont are very cynical about fellowships. They say anyone with a title, and some far fetched pedantic project can get it, and then you can write what you want. Some study or research into some Viennese Library on some century or subject they don't know — You might write about Hesse — And then you would have time to write for yourself too. I am sure you could write a sympathetic study of a writer, for the sake of writing —

Forgive me but I have not written Hesse. I would have wanted to write a wonderful letter and at this time I am over burdened. A friend who lives next door has just returned from the Hospital, a woman composer [Peggy Glanville-Hicks], who needs attention and care. I also wanted to write you and Sara a joint letter—but I'm off to cook dinner!

Anaïs

[California]
[March 7, 1956; postmark]

Dear Felix:

I'm returning the photograph you lent me. Hesse looks solitary and tragic, doesn't he?

I left many of your questions unanswered for lack of time, and now your letters are within the last diary, under lock and key outside of the home—because I am leaving for Mexico Saturday (R's vacation which he plans for a whole year) and I want to write you now because in Acapulco it is impossible. Life there is so completely physical. As I am writing about the place in the new novel, it will be wonderful to renew my impressions. It is utterly beautiful—the tropics. When you get up, awakened by natives who sing while they work as the Spaniards do, you get into a bathing suit, and drive to the beach. There we stay all morning, swimming. We return for lunch, cook a light lunch and sleep—for it is hot and everyone sleeps, even the bankers, lawyers, doctors, etc. All the shops are closed. At four when it becomes again fresh, we either go for another swim, or to visit friends—or to a dancing lesson. Return home for a cocktail. Dinner at Spanish restaurant open on the square, from where you see all that happens in the little park. Musicians come and play for you. Natives offer things for sale, baskets, or puppets, or combs, or flowers. Watching people, cars, tourists etc. is endlessly interesting and amusing. Sometimes somebody sits down with us, to tell us their troubles. We advise them on travel problems and love problems, being experienced! Then we go to a movie, with all the villagers—fishermen, store keepers etc. The tourists don't go there. The movies are bad, and mostly in Spanish. After the movies we go dancing. The nightclubs are all on the beach —beautiful. The music is Cuban, or jazz. It is a life unknown in America, and it is dedicated to pleasure.

The Mexicans have a high respect for life. None for work or

achievement. We always return renewed, and happy just to know that such a life does exist somewhere, without thought. Just sweet and human and physical.

You'll read about it in *Solar Barque!* But better still I hope someday you'll see it for yourself. So this is my letter from Acapulco. . . .

Your friend

Anaïs

Box 335 Sierra Madre,
California
[April 9, 1956; postmark]

Dear Felix:

When I wrote you a long description of what Acapulco would be, I angered the Gods and they decided otherwise! Rupert was ill all of the two weeks with severe bronchitis, and we were very blue not to be able to enjoy the place. He only swam 3 times at the end and most of the time we read pocket books and sat on our terrace. But it is still a place you must see where the child-like people are as happy as the Polynesians, and deliver one of all guilt. They are completely irresponsible. They laugh when things go wrong. But life is heightened. Even Rupert admitted how dull and tame America seemed by comparison, how unexpressive and gray. The musicians stalked us as usual, guitars, or drums from Veracruz —

I did receive your post card, and I know you were being your usual thoughtful tactful self by not writing a letter so I would not feel I should write one too.

For Easter we stopped at Taliesin West at Scottsdale, Arizona. Frank Lloyd Wright's wife is Russian so we had a Russian Easter in a fabulously beautiful setting. It is a fellowship architecture school based on the old pattern of Master and Disciples—a Feudal life really, with music, dance etc. going on by the students, collective cooking etc. It is interesting to see the types of young Americans willing to submit to such autocracy by a great artist. They do. They live there as in a monastery and cannot leave it even after they marry or have their degrees—I often think of the problems of your life, and wish I could help you solve them. I know your imagination demands a more interesting life. But life sets the romantics such traps. Will it console you to think I am in such a trap—trapped in family life, bourgeois life, duties, very small, and can hardly manage one hour of writing a day? I hope now you'll write me how you are. Mr. Lesley was so kind, sent me a tape of the talk (I always feared I had not given enough, not talked well—I always do) and his broadcast has caused people to write me and order books.

I'll be here until end of April working on *Solar Barque*—having replenished my supply of sun and beauty. I still regret missing you on your trip west.

With affection, Anaïs

[California]
[April 19, 1956; postmark]

Dear Felix:

I was teasing when I wrote, "Will it console you that I too am trapped in a life that is mostly duties—human life?" But I meant also that it is a human problem one shares with others and is therefore more bearable when shared. And so is the fantasy of robbing banks and running away to South America. Then you hear about an artist Yanko Varda[4] in Sausalito who seemed to have escaped all human traps who lives on a barge, teaches painting only two days a week, built his own sail boat, lives free and according to his fantasy—and suddenly we are all asked to contribute $10 to save him from the consequences of back unpaid taxes. I'm less deserving of sympathy than anyone else because I have been given time to write—and have written enough even if I didn't write another word. I still think it's not irresponsibility we want but freedom and nourishing expanded heightened life. Have you written to the United Nations? I have such a feeling that you belong there. None of us can return to Europe but we *can* find a more international universal form of life. . . .

It is because you see me as a human being as well as a writer that we became friends.

I bear in mind the long sincere autobiography you wrote for me as a gift of friendship and I hope it illumined your way.

Anaïs

[New York]
[May 24, 1956; postmark]

Dear Felix:

You must never worry when you can't write. I understand better than anyone how difficult it is to sustain a correspondence in our lives—sometimes I stop too—my eyes get tired, or as in N.Y. I'm under terrific pressures, so never worry. . . . Every time I'm in N.Y. I keep my ears and eyes alert for jobs of greater interest for you. We entertained recently some friends from Zürich who are in touch with publishers, reviewers, etc. in German. I thought of giving them your aphorisms but they are in my Diary in Sierra Madre—and in any case they would want them in German. Do you have another copy? . . .

Of course I realized (when you wrote me about your "other" needs) the ones which were fulfilled by Sara, a home, a deeper love, it is just that in America it is more difficult to live in all directions. The pattern is rigid. Everybody works to maintain it, not to liberate, to help others to be free.

Hugo and I have at last reached a freedom—which he now has—and you can only *give* it to the others when you yourself have it. I do feel that if you could get a job in N.Y., you would have the possibility of finding ideal work—every day one meets someone in contact with bigger lives—from everywhere. For example, this week friends from Zürich, then [J. M.] Tambimuttu who runs a poetry magazine [*Poetry London–New York*], French friends connected with *La Table Ronde,** etc. Friends from the U.N.—a man who represents U.N. in Haiti, and in Cuba. Some of it is mirages, lives you touch, and cannot reach yourself, but the opportunities are there. I will write to Hesse. This letter I'm writing on the bus! . . .

Affectionately

Anaïs

*Parisian monthly (1944–46; resumed publication 1948) featuring contributions by leading writers such as T. S. Eliot and William Faulkner.

[California]
[June 23, 1956; postmark]

Dear Felix:

Rupert's quest for a new profession has made me wonder if teaching would not give you more freedom—to write. About the pay I don't know—but it seems California pays the highest salaries, and that there is a severe shortage of mathematics teachers. Three months free in the summer and holidays and the possibility of transfer to cities you might like. Have you thought of this?

R. is tired of the exigencies of Forest Service—It's like being a doctor, always on call, so little pay (less than a postman), no hope of promotion unless you accept living in the sticks, in trailers in isolation —and he wants a home—The transition may be very good—College teaching is even better, less hours etc. I always regretted not having trained for that—I wonder how you are getting on in your restricted apartment—Felt so sorry, as there are enough obstacles without cramping inhibiting neighbors. I don't know if I wrote you from New York—to read *Waiting for Godot* by [Samuel] Beckett—and to send your poetry to Tambimuttu, once editor of *Poetry London* now editor of *Poetry London–New York*. His address is

Tambimuttu
338 East 87
N.Y.C.

I saw him in N.Y. It is strange to see a neurotic Hindu—I don't know why. Dressed like one, with long black hair, but alcoholic and with ulcers etc. without any mystical poise! It shows how contagious neurosis is—that even a mystical Hindu can catch it—How is work at the library? You did not tell me what you thought of Perlès book on Miller—I think it is a tabloid, reads like a cheap confession magazine—Critics have been harsh. It has not done Miller any good, has it? Copying volume 68—and struggling with *Solar Barque*. . . .

Anaïs

[Evanston]
June 30, 1956

Dear Anaïs:

I couldn't teach mathematics to save my poor soul—or even my dear life! I always barely passed that subject by the skin of my teeth, and sometimes a little skin went with it. Literature, psychology, philosophy, logic, sociology, anthropology, economics, languages, music, art, stage directing—all the humanities, yes. But science, mathematics, chemistry, physics, history, even geography, anything connected with machines, with mechanics, with engineering or business—no. Neither interest, nor talent, and when I had to pass exams on those things it was always a traumatic experience, a matter of fear and trembling and utter, paralyzed, impotent confusion and dumbfoundedness. Partly probably the result of poor teaching and terrorizing teachers and of an inferiority complex along those lines that was more the result of conditioning than of inadequacy. For I remember that for a short year we had a marvelous, human young math teacher and there was one kind of algebraic equation in which I excelled, being on top of the class. But as soon as he was transferred and my positive fixation became a negative one on his successor, I was back at my old "minus satisfactory," one precarious step or half step removed from flunking. On the other hand, I love chess, as you know, which some people say is related to mathematics and which, no doubt, can be played mathematically too. But I don't play it that way, I detest that kind of playing, I live dangerously, at least on the chess board. —I like to gamble, take risks, figure out brilliant (and frequently failing) combinations and always pit imagination against calculation. When I bring it off against a good player, I have a feeling of triumph and almost artistic achievement. When I am defeated by sober, grinding technique and science, I *feel* defeated, not only on the board. That game is such a symbol. Anyhow, God preserve us from the even, well balanced minds that can do everything equally well (with equal mediocrity, as a rule), excel in nothing and fail in nothing. Long live the poorly adjusted! And so I pat myself smugly on the back, highly pleased with all my shortcomings—for they prove that I'm nearly a genius, don't you see? Rationalizations are a wonderful invention, aren't they? . . .

Felix

[California]

[August 20, 1956; approx.]

Dear Felix:

I've had the little magazines you sent me by my bedside and read all the poems slowly. They have both a philosophical and a romantic wistfulness—and I like their simplicity. Thank you, and thank you for the clippings. Did you send some poems to Tambimuttu?

In full business of moving—Here we did have space—and in the other place none. So it is a problem of shrinkage to which as an old traveler I am used to but not Rupert. Yes—of course Forestry was not appropriate, but then nothing in my life with Rupert is appropriate. When I met him in N.Y. he was on his way home, defeated as an actor, wounded by a bad marriage. In following my physical passions I have always ended in worlds in which I did not belong—It is only in my marriage to Hugo that I came closer—but even then that too was a bourgeois life—I inwardly rebel against all of Rupert's family life domesticity, his reading only *Time* magazine, completely bourgeois habits—monotony—duties—family—and nature—and California— and his friends. After 8 years the conflict has grown complete— between a passion and a way of life completely unsuited to me—but isn't that woman's destiny?

Soon I'll give you an address—

Devotedly,

Anaïs

[Evanston]

August 23, 1956

Dear Anaïs—

Just received your letter and I feel closer to you than ever. Such familiar chords. . . . I too want to thank you for your confidence and openness. There are such ironical aspects to your story, such ultimate tragic ironies! For one thing, physical passion has led many men and women into worlds into which they didn't belong, but it was almost always a departure from a bourgeois world into a Bohemian or Proletarian world where at least the passion could thrive. But to be led by one's passion into a bourgeois cage—that is diabolical! To do the unconventional, to do exactly what the Philistines frowned upon and condemned—and by that very action to land again in a conventional bourgeois set up is a fantastic trap. I hope I'm not using the wrong words, too strong ones, I'm just thinking out loud in a general way. (Although I feel more specifically than generally about it!) Specifically, too, I had that very very proper bourgeois impression also when I met Rupert's mother and was wondering about it. During the light conversation Rupert mentioned that he had met you at a New York party to which neither one of you had wanted to go. He said something to the effect that both of you disliked the hostess, and his mother overheard that remark and whispered reproachfully, "Rupert! One doesn't say such things!" I don't think I showed it in my face, but something in me stood on its head at that moment, and I tried hard to picture you in that environment but couldn't. Incongruous, utterly incongruous. And I thought, if it hadn't happened that you had to be absent, you may have preferred not to be present right then.

Passion has to be strong to overcome domesticity—not to become domesticated itself. For me—when (you know what) becomes "sexual intercourse" which is only one step removed from "marital duty," passion and lust and joy and excitement all wilt and wither together and I prefer fasting to eating surrogates. But that is personal, referring only to myself. What I meant to say is, passion can overcome so many, so many things, it may even overcome a proper, domestic, "wholesome" bourgeois atmosphere—and there can be no greater triumph for passion than that. The poets have always celebrated the wrong feats of passion—the overcoming of distances, time, obstacles of nature and intrigue—things on which passion actually thrives, which increase it. Those are not passion's real feats. When it can survive the lack of obstacles, tranquillity and monotony and security, the domestic nest and Philistine harem, then passion has won a victory, then it is an occasion to shout "Hooray for love!" Don't you agree? . . .

I am somewhat eager to meet Hugo. No, Anaïs—I don't agree at all that the conflict between a passion and a way of life is "woman's destiny." It may be her—and sometimes man's—deplorable lot in this civilization (and in many preceding ones, it's true) but it is far from her destiny.

They are very different things, warring-with-each-other things usually. Sometimes I think that our whole autobiography can be reduced to the formula: the struggle of our fate with our destiny.

Warmly,

Felix

Box 335 Sierra Madre,
California
[August 26, 1956; approx.]

Dear Felix:

Just a hurried note while moving—I enjoyed reading "Utopia or Anachronistic Reflections on H. B. Yearbook"⁵—It was clever and humorous and very true— . . .

I agree with all you wrote about the power of love to conquer certain situations—Perhaps outside of Forest Service (which is like the Army) I may succeed—but forces of conservatism etc. are stronger so far—Yes I hope you will meet Hugo—He is a curious mixture: what he shows in his engravings and films he does not act out or live out. In life his primary concern is security and money! This half is what drives me away—But what brings me back always is his infinite goodness to me—his sincerity.

I am to blame you know for all the fantastic ironies and traps . . . because I did not have the *courage* to live with insensitive men (such as Miller) and the only 2 sensitive ones I lived with were timid and bourgeois and not bohemians.

Didn't you find *Devil in Paradise*⁶ a truly cruel book—and you never told me what you thought of Perlès' book—half of it untrue.

A bientôt—

Anaïs

. . .

[California]
[September 1, 1956; approx.]

Dear Felix:

I meant to write you as soon as I received the magazine which I enjoyed so much. To see the poems printed makes them seem like paintings in a gallery, and then you notice how much they gain by comparison with others, and you can see them with objective appreciation—but we were in such a transitional state, spending all our free time looking for a place to live in the Silver Lake district, and all our evenings with family, music, relatives.

We found a place—2 modern rooms with a patio—the wall hides the boulevard—and it has beauty which is rare here—and next time you come will be there—Sept. 1—1732 Silver Lake Boulevard (but I will give you another address to write to).

Thank you also for the aphorisms. I want to try my friends in Zürich whose brother is a publisher—but it has been an upside down period—Rupert hates change, is fearful, and very strained.

His disillusion with Forest Service hurt him—I've hated it from the beginning so I have no difficulty giving up a petty, bureaucratic, and most un-romantic profession which endangered R's life (he almost burnt his hands once). Meanwhile I have typed and copied and written—and today got good news that Avon will reprint *Spy*—very amazing, since the book did not sell—but I'm happy—It sold out in England, I think I told you.

Rupert will teach mathematics in a junior high school—We will be more independent and he will work less hard and be able to build his house by the sea.

How was your summer? The summer must be lovely by the lake . . . I hope you've had more peace and time to write. I'll be here until Sept. 15—then New York.

Hugo has been travelling—He loves that.

Toute mon amitié

Anaïs

35 West 9th
New York City 11, N.Y.
[September 20, 1956; postmark]

Dear Felix:

You can write me at above address. Came back to rain and autumn but also to a pleasant interview with Avon pocketbook editor [Thomas Payne], to my surprise a cultivated well read man—not as I expected a roughneck—(he did Nathaniel West* and [Francis] Carco,** etc.) who reads French, etc.

Then again trying to finish *Solar Barque* handicapped by duties and activities as I am in L.A.

I wish your next trip were New York as we could make it so interesting for you and Sara.

One couple I have to see is a beautiful tall Jewish girl who married a negro dancer and has two children, one named for me because of "Child Born Out of the Fog" and so I am, as it were, the mystical godmother!

Tell all my friends to save their $.25 for *Spy* because Thomas Payne tells me pocket books are only allowed in the stands 2 to 4 weeks (more are printed than there is room to display) and then are all sent back like old magazines! What a system.

How is your month? What phase, cycle, low or high?

My brother is on his sabbatical from Berkeley—his letters make me homesick. Paris—Madrid—London.

This is just to give you an address—in a rush.

Anaïs

*Nathaniel West (b. 1906, d. 1940 in an automobile accident), New York–born screenplay writer and novelist based in Hollywood.

**Francis Carco (1886–1958), New Caledonia–born novelist, lived in Paris, moved in bohemian circles, and was attracted by the exotic and criminal elements of the Parisian underworld.

[Evanston]
September 29, 1956

Dear Anaïs,

. . . . A few poems have come out since I've sent you the magazines. But the real great news is the news in the making—toward a wonderful climax or a terrible anti-climax. I received a letter from Tambimuttu, returning the poems I had sent him, except one. He wrote he was holding this one for further consideration. I was quite excited because his is a first rate magazine and would be by far the best in which my poetry has appeared up to now; and I have been on tenterhooks for the last four weeks—his letter was dated August 28— and every day I bicycle home on my lunch hour to look at the mail and my blood pressure rises. I don't think it can be much longer, and I am very particularly pleased with the would-be choice of this poem for it has a close connection with you; it is, in fact, for you. If it ever comes out (in *Poetry London–New York*) you will understand what I mean.

You see—even children are named after you—this is surely a wonderful tribute to a writer, particularly when such people are involved and their choice based on such a beautiful, tender story as "Child Born Out of the Fog." I was moved and pleased.

Also, am very glad your association with Avon is so beyond expectations pleasant and prospective. I will watch out for copies on the newsstand—and have (and am continuing to) spread the news, needless to say. I am sincerely glad for you, Anaïs—also needless to say. May this be a success that is only the beginning of further and increasing successes. I have told you before, that all my money—the little material and the larger spiritual currency I have—is on you as an eventual winner! If only someone would buy the diary and make you financially independent. . . .

I hope I wasn't tactless or crude in some of my remarks in my last letter to you. I sometimes say more than I mean as my pen glides over the paper. A pen on a paper seems to have a life and compulsive sequence of its own—is it led by subconscious forces or by artistic impulses—which don't falsify but sometimes distort just a little—magnify or minimize and in any case project oneself into the addressee? I hope nothing I said sounded like a request for intervention and hence your announced letter to Sara. If that was not what prompted your card to her, it would be very good of you to write her, she was immensely pleased with the card! She wanted to write you right away but decided to wait for either your California address or your arrival in New York. When your letter came she again said she would send you a card and if she does not get around to it, it is not for any lack of impulse of doing so. There are many things to be said for her and against me. What relation is perfect anyway? . . .

. . . We have seen apartments and even houses (which Sara's brother would help us buy)—however, not only are the prices here outrageous but I am internally resisting the idea of buying a house and being even more chained to this locale and all it entails. (I remember your saying somewhere that you all your life had tried not to find a house to live in—except that you said it better and more charmingly pungent; I can't recall, at the moment, your exact expression.) Well, I feel the same way—in a way—though in another I cry out for peace and privacy and for being my own master and at least not at a landlord's or other tenants' mercy and subject to their noises and disturbances, so that I finally can sit down, in the little time around the day's edges left for it, and work. I don't know what will happen.

In a way I envy Miller his wooden castle overlooking the Pacific— Yes, about the Perlès book. Next time, I'll write about this in some detail. Too much for now. Of course, *Devil in Paradise* is a *cruel* book. But most books of Miller's are somewhere cruel—and tender at the same time. And I too, I must confess, developed a great dislike of Mr. Moricand as I went along: what should, what could Henry have done? What would I have done? What would you have done? Let your whole life be messed up more and more by a quirkish parasite? Maybe he should never have let him come to America. False kindnesses usually result in real cruelty. Yet, Miller is a passionate man, an element, and this explosive violence and reciprocating hatred runs all through the *Tropic of Cancer* and makes it the cathartic book it is, as you yourself acknowledged in your memorable preface. If it is not too bold of me to say so, I feel that you are still very much attracted and attached to him, even if those feelings express themselves today in an ambiguity with a negative prefix. Although I don't know the real circumstances of your breaking up—and would give much to know! I sense that Henry acted badly toward you and hurt you deeply. And you say yourself that you "did not have the courage to live with insensitive men (such as Miller)" although it must have been more than a matter of courage. Not that courage, whatever that is, is not involved in all our decisions. Almost everybody has fears and is afraid of many things—and with good reason. (I mean, good cause.) And although we feel a little contempt for people who are so concerned with "security"—somewhere we may crave it too. I don't believe in coincidental choices, basically—especially if the pattern is repeated. Anaïs —you know I love and admire you—you must not mind my saying things to you which I, strictly speaking, have no right to say—and (I assure you) wouldn't say if I didn't love and adore and respect and admire you. Or, if you prefer my putting it this way, if I weren't your friend. Besides I'm sure you know all this, and more yourself. (And, still more besides, there is always the possibility, that I am quite wrong and know too little. For actually I know little about you, though I sense some.) I, anyway, am in the same boat: scorning the craving for security and yet having not enough courage to give up the security I have achieved.

I understand today the attraction wars, revolutions, invasions (like the one of Hitler), prospective uprooting and exile have on many people. I had a beautiful, vivacious, brilliant woman cousin, who wrote me from Prague where she and her husband and two small children had to flee from Hitler when he invaded the Sudetenland. I remember, and still have somewhere, the last letter before she was caught and gassed (together with her husband and one of her sons); her last letter full of exhilaration, saying, "At long last, something, even if it is the devil itself, has broken our prison and set me free (what irony!)—not stagnating—that is the main thing. Felix, you know I'm crazy, but I am happier at this edge of the abyss than I've been for many many years!"

I've made (am making) another attempt at having my cake and eating it too by combining security with my longing to go to Europe —I've applied for a university grant from Northwestern to go to Vienna to write about Karl Kraus. No librarian has ever before applied for those grants usually given to faculty members but with a Ph.D. and a subject to work upon which—in some way—may also be helpful for the university and the library—I was told by the chairman of the grant committee that I may well be considered eligible—and there always has to be a first time. In any case, I should apply and the committee would consider it. So I will—tomorrow. . . . Since the Kraus archives are located in Vienna and the purpose (at least the approved one) of Fulbright grants is to contribute to the mutual acquaintance and understanding of Americans and other nationals, it is doubtful that I would get a Fulbright to Vienna. But I think I'll apply anyway because a cynical (but informed) professor told me that the chances of getting a Fulbright award are exactly as great as drawing a certain number out of a hat; and candidates, he avers, are in effect chosen by the same procedure. So we'll see. As the irony of fate will have it, we'll have a house just before we go away. Life is strange. Where are the snows of tomorrow?

Affectionately,

Felix

. . .

17129 North Occidental Blvd.
Los Angeles 26
[October, 1956; approx.]

Dear Felix:

I was so disappointed with Tambimuttu's letter—and the poem not being printed. It was a witty poem, skillful and it should have been done. So many disappointments.

As you can see I started a letter in N.Y. which I couldn't finish! Life flowed by so fast that I cannot remember if I answered your long letter—What of the project to write about Kraus—and going to Vienna? I know how much this means to you—I pray it comes through.

In New York I did many interesting things, as always—Saw Caresse Crosby who is now the head of Citizens of the World—a woman who visited Paul Bowles and told us about his life in Tangiers, his house, and his plans to go into the desert to record Berber music before it is forbidden by the new regime. I also had a second talk with my publisher who is cultured and frank—Returned to find R. very unhappy about his teaching, more work than in Forest Service, hours of correcting papers at home etc.—Became interested in *The Mandarins* [1954] of [Simone] de Beauvoir—did you read it? Never liked her before but this book is meaningful and problem touches not only the French—but all of us—Now I'm reading her *L'Invitée* [1943]—It's curious—She is a bad artist, documentary—no style—but it is sincere and strangely feminine—whereas her book on woman [*Le deuxième sexe*, 1949] was so old-fashioned suffragette style.

If you go to Vienna you'll be passing through N.Y.? When? I'm eager for news—I get sad when you tell me about your eagerness to hear from Tambimuttu—One should not care so much (but one does!) Or else have a life so full one has no time to care to stop and be hurt.

Completely reconciled with Hugo—Analysis has transformed him—It only makes trapeze more difficult.

Hard at work on last typing of *Solar Barque*—to send to England.

Why doesn't Evanston put out all your poems? Do they not have a University Press? Good luck with project for Vienna.

Anaïs

6

October 1956–April 1958

LA VIE TRIVIALE —
A LIFE OF TRIVIA

IN THIS EIGHTEEN-MONTH PERIOD of relatively infrequent letters (Pollak writes only four times) the former energy of the correspondence begins to flag. In January 1957 Pollak again fails to meet up with Nin as he is passing through New York City, and he is despondent. Nin complains of "low energy," and Pollak of his exasperation with "domestic trifles." Pollak abhors the commercialized "mess they call Christmas," and Nin too feels the stress of "holiday neurosis," catering to her relatives' expectations of "forced joyousness" at the festive seasons. They are both embroiled in "la vie triviale," "a life of trivia." Pollak despairs in particular for his physician brother Hans, a conventionally successful family practitioner.

Pollak also feels especially trapped since both his application for a university fellowship to pursue a critical study of Karl Kraus and his overtures to the United Nations prove fruitless. Nevertheless, his steady publishing success continues and he is particularly gratified to receive an admiring note from William Carlos Williams.

Nin is leading an active social life in Malibu Beach during this time but her writing and publishing are stalled. Meanwhile Rupert's dream house designed by his stepfather Lloyd Wright (the son of Frank Lloyd Wright), a project about which Anaïs has mixed emotions, is finally coming closer to being built.

1729 North Occidental Boulevard
Los Angeles 26
[October 9, 1956; postmark]

Dear Felix:

I am deeply sorry, and share with you your disappointment regarding the fellowship. Such a foolish reason too — to save myself at such moments I always think that the world is irrational and makes no sense at all — it helps. It is when one tries to think intelligently and humanly that the acts of others (particularly fellowships and critics) seem absolutely pathologic, above all petty, limited. I hope you will go on trying. I was so busy in New York I did not try to see Stuhlmann; if I had known you had no news of him I would have made an effort. I am writing the Weisses a note — and Stuhlmann too. (Mrs. Ruth Witt-Diamant got funds for Poetry Center in San Francisco from Ford Foundation engagement possibilities — paid —) It is one o'clock, the sun is shining on the little patio I have which I can see through a large wall-to-wall window. There is a hill across the way, and Silver Lake not too far (I walk to it) and many pines so it gives a small illusion of Switzerland — Everything in America is *like* something else. It has no beauty of its own, only imitations. I have typed all morning, *Solar Barque.* Last night a party at Malibu, the best sculptress out West [Cornelia Runyon], seventy years old, a house by the sea, her sculptures made of semi precious stones, her son cooking meat on a large brasero stove in the studio. The old but magnificent and impressive Austrian actor who took the role of the Indian in the film *Moby Dick* [Frederick Ledebur], his son, a writer. Dudley Murphy who once made *Emperor Jones, Ballet Mécanique,* and then settled down to run a glamorous Motel on the Beach, a meeting place for

movie people, lovers, and travelers between San Francisco and Los
Angeles. It so happens we live in what is called the Viennese section
of Los Angeles.

Anaïs

[California?]
[December, 1956; approx.]

Holiday Greetings

This is a photograph of Lippold's* Gold Sun mobile, a good symbol for the artist, who continues to create such beauty in a troubled,
destructive world, a great symbol for us

Anaïs

*Richard Lippold, American sculptor (b. 1915), specializing in intricate
suspended structures of wire and sheet metal.

Box 26075 Sunset Boulevard
Los Angeles 26.
January 4, 1957

Dear Felix:

I hope your holidays were pleasant. I hope you and Sara do not
suffer from the holiday neurosis, which is due to the simple fact that
it is one time of the year when your memory is forced by associations
to return to the past, with both sadness, regrets, or revulsion. In either
case, a forced joyousness is expected of one which sometimes one
does not feel in the mood to give. I came the 17th because R. had his
vacation. We had a few days of beach weather, then came the fire
and so many of our friends' homes were involved, that we shared
their anxiety. One professor of art lost the studio he built himself and
all his life's work. My Viennese friend Renate [Druks],¹ the painter,
had her young man sit on the roof wrapped in a wet blanket, all
night, watering the roof. So many tragedies—not all the houses were
rich people's, many artists, and many workers had little shanty homes
in the hills.

My life is too full and too exhausting and I am not doing much
writing. In New York the whole apartment needed redoing. And
Christmas shopping for H. Here Christmas shopping for the posses-

sive and impossible double family. They always leave the Xmas tree for me to decorate and I filled it with Japanese branches of colorful token of happiness they carry on feast days. Tonight quartets. And thank you for your thoughtfulness in sending cards to both lives, you are the only one who thought of doing that!

Devotedly,

Anaïs

[New York City]

Tuesday, January 8, 1957

Dear Anaïs—

This is my last night in New York after a short stay of six days. . . . I hoped very much to find you here and was deeply sorry that I missed you again. It had been one of my main reasons for coming here, though I knew it was a gamble. I talked to Hugo on the phone the first evening, but unfortunately could not see him since he was involved with family passing through here. I was sorry, needless to say. He told me you're working with [Christopher] Isherwood* in Hollywood on a film script of *Jean-Christophe.*** I was interested to learn this.² He said you may be back here in a week or so. Bad luck for me.

I had an interesting time, saw several plays, met Tambimuttu (rather pathetic, poor, toothless) (he says an accident) in his gloomy bare apartment, liked his wife. Also saw Djuna Barnes (allegedly quite a feat), found her a sick, sarcastically bitter old woman who made slighting remarks about a lot of writers, except Dylan Thomas whose voice she admired. When I finally asked her, in some exasperation, "Whom do you like?" She answered evenly, "I like nobody." I refrained from asking whether she liked herself, for she had given me the answer to that question already. Also poverty and bareness. Yet she rejected the offer she had seen from a pocket book publisher to let *Nightwood* appear as a paperback because they didn't offer her enough money, she said. She just finished her first play which will appear shortly. When I said, upon leaving, "I hope you will feel better soon" (she has asthma and some back trouble) she replied, "Thanks. I probably won't"—and closed the door.

I'm leaving tomorrow noon, will see the U.N. building in the morning and maybe ask once more about a job possibility. Passed by your house several times, had cocktails at the Pelican Bar. . . .

I feel we have drifted apart somehow lately, Anaïs. Largely due no doubt, to my dull letters full of domestic trifles. Your life is interesting and dynamic and to hear of my routine and static one must bore you—as it does me many times. Yet it is the inner life that counts, after all—and at least there some activity takes place with me.

I had sent Tambimuttu three poems again, weeks and weeks ago, but he is utterly disorganized, does ghost writing for money (lying in bed to keep warm) goes only occasionally to his office, owes the printer over a thousand dollars for the first issue and $3700 for the new second one which just came out, eight months after the first. (It is a very good issue though!) He hadn't even looked at my poems yet—and there one waits for an answer in such a turmoil of hopes and fears. Disillusioning.

Maybe we'll meet yet again, some day.

All the best,

Felix

. . .

*Christopher William Bradshaw-Isherwood (1904–1986), English-American author, playwright, and collaborator of W. H. Auden.

**Novel in ten volumes (1904–10) by Romain Rolland (1866–1944), French novelist, dramatist, and essayist.

[California]

[January 11, 1957; approx.]

Dear Felix:

About our losing contact—please remember when I wrote you once that if ever the correspondence became intermittent rather than continuous it would always be due to low energy! Your life does interest me because it is yours, and on the contrary I have a keener sympathy for whoever is trapped in a life which does not correspond to his temperament because I have never achieved this except by "stealing." I understand your life—I'm sorrier than I can say to have missed you in New York. Again! I would have liked to entertain you, etc. and Hugo would have liked to know you and Sara—By now our letters crossed each other! I was so interested in your description of Djuna Barnes. Yes, I had heard similar stories—As far as I can surmise her life "broke" in the drama described in *Nightwood*—I believe this ending—the woman metamorphosed into a dog, a beast—was a fantasy possibly based on a partial truth. She was hurt, wounded, and became the bitter growling character she is now. I saw her in Paris in 1935 when she was a beautiful, elegant, Amazonian red haired arresting person. But even then—no love. I wrote her my first fan letter and she never answered—I have never left a letter unanswered from that day on. And Tambimuttu—a wreckage. I could have introduced you to other people—Let's hope one day it will coincide. I would give anything to have the courage to break with this life—and stay with Hugo.

I'll be in N.Y. January 15. Please write me there—

Affectionately,

Anaïs

> 35 West 9th Street
> New York 11, N.Y.
> [June 3, 1957; approx.]

Dear Felix:

I'm so glad you sent me the magazines. My eyes are tired and I am writing so few letters, and so I feel I get an undeserved present when I get one! I like "Primeval Sin." It's a truth which needs to be told again and again in many forms. And I liked the humor of "Just Asking." You are being published so frequently, one day you'll be able to persuade them to put them all in one book. The "Dream" I had read; it is wistful, and it is the best poem in the magazine. But "They Are the Pitchmen of the Lord" was new to me, and a good poem it is, an expression of pure values.

Never hesitate to write because you don't know where I am. My mail is forwarded on both ends. And don't be disappointed if I write less. My energy is dwindling.

Just noticed I had not read "White Lines on Blue."[3] This is the subtlest of all, with very fluid images and original tones. Your most impressionistic one. . . .

In the "Bomb" I feel you were growing bolder with words, with individual use of them, composition of them for your own meaning, more innovation and freedom of language (contents were always good). I hope you are having a happy summer. I will keep the magazines until you ask me or need them.

Anaïs

[California]
July 12, 1957

Dear Felix:

. . . Your poems *are* written with intelligence and consciousness but that is not a lack of freedom. If you want to write from a dream level or unconsciously try working from the night dreams as surrealists did—collect them—keep them—nurture them (By wishing a dream before going to sleep, one does dream!) And by that entrance you can reach the darker realms.

Rupert kept summer for the sea house but his stepfather Lloyd has been too busy to make the plans (he has a sketch planned which he calls the Carousel for Troubadours. Evidently we inspired a flight of fantasy on his part.) So we are sad. We go to the beach every day and Rupert takes courses at night. Nothing definite about *Solar Barque*.

Yes I am in [Kenneth] Anger's new film.[4] . . .

I am reading Erich Fromm's book on *Art of Love* [*The Art of Loving*, 1956] and [his] *Escape from Freedom* [1941][5] and Byron's life by Maurois and [his] *Lélia*.[6] I suppose you have read all this—they are not new.

Affectionately,
Anaïs

[California]
[September 10, 1957; postmark]

Dear Felix:

Such a long summer without letter writing. As Rupert was free from teaching we began June 20 a schedule which forbids all work. Getting up late, rushing to the beach, then too late doing errands or duties (such as nursing Rupert's father) and out in the evening again, as this summer I made many friends. Gore Vidal took a house by the sea with Joanne Woodward and Paul Newman (actors), and we went to typical beach parties of Malibu Colony, which means people straying in and out with drinks, in bathing suits and talking films. There we saw Christopher Isherwood, Carl van Druten* etc. Then I made friends with Romain Gary of *Colors of the Day* and *Racines du Ciel* (Prix Goncourt) and Lesley Blanch** of *Wilder Shores of Love* [1954], and so we were invited to all their consulate parties, truly international. Then Renate my Viennese friend (the one who gave the imaginative costume parties) was separated from Paul and began a Sabina existence, with dramatic love affairs and always a crisis—such as entanglement with the son of Edward G. Robinson, etc. So the summer passed, strange for me, little reading, no inner life, no writing. I met Hugo on his vacation in Acapulco for two weeks and that was the same. I believe I sent you a card from there but I am not sure. We had kept the summers free to build Rupert's house but Lloyd Wright was too busy and only last night showed us exquisite design he calls Carousel for Troubadours which looks like a Mississippi River boat and a Carousel simultaneously—utterly beautiful so that Rupert's life if it is a trap not good for a creative artist (Renate was saying everyone is watching this marriage of nature and art) is a beautiful trap at least. No writing but I am healthy and brown and cured of rheumatic fever. Now I have told you all, and I hope as a reward will hear how you and Sara fared this summer. . . .

Affectionately,

Anaïs

*Possibly Nin means John van Druten (1901–1957), the English-born playwright and collaborator of Isherwood; see note on Isherwood in Pollak's letter of January 28, 1957.

**English writer, married to French author Romain Gary (see note to Nin's letter of January 9, 1956), who served from 1956–60 as French consul in Los Angeles.

[New York]

[October 2, 1957; postmark]

Dear Felix:

It always gives me pleasure to read the poems in magazines, like seeing them dressed up for a party. I'm returning them today because the 9th I leave for Los Angeles Box 26049 Sunset Boulevard 2005.

Would suggest you send all these magazines with your poems cut out with title of magazine to a poetry publisher. They would now make a book of which you could be proud. I suppose you read *Justine* by Lawrence Durrell. You do not have the *Black Book* to lend me—I lost mine—Are you in touch with anyone in Paris buying books for you?[7] *Justine* is truly beautiful—Sara will love it too—tell her to read it. . . .

    Anaïs

[California]

[November 7, 1957; postmark]

    Coincidence: Read at a poetry group—met Boyer May who is making me read over radio. He casually mentions "my friend the poet Felix Anselm." So! I ordered magazine with your poem in it. May tells me aphorisms will appear in book form. Wonderful! Are you offended with me? It seems like a long time without a letter or are you proof reading and your eyes tired too? I'm so happy about aphorisms being published—where? In New York Nov 12 at 35 West 9th N.Y.C. 11. Love to you both,

    A

[Evanston]

November 14, 1957

Dear Anaïs,

    . . . Your summer sounded most interesting—not exactly productive, artistically, but sensuously enjoyable and luxurious. I have a secret (sometimes not so secret) hankering for that kind of life, temporarily at least. We're all ambiguous, or multi-guous about these things, I suppose. Art is pain and thus opposed to the pleasure principle which drives us. Then, as with all creation, the pain mingles with an even greater pleasure and alternates with it, while the purely vegetative and hedonistic life pales and becomes pallid. But both are intricately related, each the cause and effect of the other. Even to say, that your summer with Malibu Beach parties and movie people was not artistically creative is probably a great fallacy: out of it may come a profound artistic creation; while too much work might produce staleness and the desire for the sensual and sensuous life. But whom am I telling this? You know all this far better than I. I am just the contrary: I sometimes think of lovemaking while I am working and of some marvelous sentences while making love. Oh well. . . .

Your friend and my *Landsmann* Renate sounds interesting. And to meet one's husband in Acapulco and another round of parties: isn't that the way, somehow, to keep romance alive, as the "normal" and "moral" marriage can't do? I know you must have had much grief from your trapeze act, but the compensations must be even greater—or you wouldn't try to retain that precarious balance—despite occasional wishes, I'm sure, for resolutions. One of the wonderful things about you is that one can think out loud about you to you and know it won't be taken amiss, or considered impudent. This is so, isn't it? I envied you even more when I read the other names you mention of the people you met. . . .

I'm slowly progressing from your summer letter to your fall cards. . . .

. . . Boyer, incidentally . . . got his wires crossed about my aphorisms. *New World Writing* is considering a selection of them.[8] . . . [I] finished also the draft of an article on pornography, in connection with Miller's work; interesting and not bad, I think, but I can never tell until I let it rest for a while and then work it over. . . .[9]

. . . All the very best, Anaïs.

Affectionately,

Felix

[New York]

[November 19, 1957; postmark]

Enjoyed your long letter and will answer it when I return to Los Angeles Dec. 10 at leisure—Swamped in work now as I am working for a new woman's magazine—*Eve*—pub. Feb. 1—and distribution of *Under a Glass Bell*. I have to sell 50-cent copies to cover cost—Please help me by posting announcement in students' magazine that students can buy books at .50 (intent of project is to make books at cost for students)—or in the English Department. I intend to go on to publish *Solar Barque* too if I succeed with *Bell*, and other writers' reprints— noncommercial. When I sell directly for $1, I can give the writer .50—It might work—for a non-profit scheme.[10] Letter soon,

    A.

[California]

[December 9, 1957; postmark]

Dear Felix:

Your letter under influence of martinis was charming!* I never answered your long ones well—so I will try tonight, while I listen to Rupert playing with a quartet. The dog is snoring. One wife is knitting, one husband is correcting mathematics papers. . . .

Gemor Press: word was composed of Gonzalo Moré, the designer of the books and the partner of this press (also the hero of *Four-Chambered Heart*). When you quote remarks made by people I shiver at the way people interpret one's life—Everyone should write a diary if one loves the truth. I was in Acapulco alone when Gore [Vidal] came for a visit and got jaundice and nearly died in Mexico City. We didn't elope—I went to Guatemala to nurse him and as soon as he was well, I left. We were very close friends, *c'est tout,* a mother and son. He was 18 years old then.

Yes, the prologue was an error—a denial of all I believe made under the influence of guilt—People around me made me feel guilty because they seemed to feel if one gave up the dream, fantasy, art, beauty the world would be saved, and people no longer hungry or unhappy. And I believed this—I almost destroyed the stories then, but thank god this artist was too strong and even though I apologized for them I published them, I was influenced by a romantic unreal socialism but it didn't last long.[11] Yes, I know where reality lies now— You are right. Soon I hope to publish a little book on writing which is a more stable affirmation of my beliefs.

Yes I have faith in my publishing venture—I now have a distributor.[12] If you have patience the aphorisms will get done. The distributors will not take any book not by a well-known writer, which means we will have to distribute it by mail ourselves. . . .

Eve—Assistant editor Lawrence Lipton. They need stories (not poetry because he is surrounded by poets and is a poet). I don't know if I will be part of the staff. Meanwhile I did a letter from N.Y. and they will print a part of *Solar Barque*—Why don't you try your aphorisms on Lipton? I would. Send them to

Lawrence Lipton

P.O. Box 129 Venice,

California

. . . In one of your letters your said you could think aloud with me—and that pleased me.

I wish you would write me about Perlès book—I hated it. It was such a false, cheap picture of everything and so shabby of H. and me—It was a shock and I never forgave Henry allowing it. . . .

I understand how much you have to do—We should not indulge in long letters—I wonder how you *ever* read.

I'd like to see your article on pornography when you have done it! . . .

Sorry I won't be in N.Y. when you go near there at X-mas! Affectionate wishes for the holidays, may the New Year bring you much publishing.

Anaïs

*This letter is missing from the record.

[California]

[December 27, 1957; postmark]

Dear Felix—

. . . So many letters, so many activities, so many people—I hope you had a beautiful Christmas East—Sorry I was not in New York—Here we are preparing for a family dinner, preparing to visit Frank Lloyd Wright's first wife in a Hospital—Lloyd's mother. She is catatonic and recognizes no one—It is a visit to the dead. She does get moved when Rupert sings to his guitar—serenading the dead.

Can't wait for holidays to be over—Hate them, force you back into the past, the real labyrinth—After New Year's life will begin again.

I sit in the eternal automobile of California, waiting for Rupert and everywhere I go carry writing pad.

May the New Year bring you and Sara all your wishes.

Anaïs

Chapter 6: October 1956–April 1958

Evanston,
January 7, 1958

Dear Anaïs—

This is a preliminary note only. . . . The selection for *New World Writing* has come back. It was a blow. A rather curt letter accompanying them, from the assistant editor saying they had been seriously considered but finally the decision was negative. I don't want to alibi, but a printed line at the bottom of the letter paper may have contained part of the answer. It read: "Good reading for the millions." These observations of mine which are largely satirical and critical of our uncultured civilization in general and of American society and morality in particular just can't qualify as good reading for the millions. God forbid. The *Saturday Evening Post* and *Reader's Digest* fill that bill quite well, thank you. *New World Writing* is better than they and often brings good things; it is a desirable place to be in; but there are increasing evidences of caution and catering to the "general public." If that impulse continues unchecked, another brave attempt will have ended in the failure of success. The mass market will have another victim. I may try *Botteghe Oscure* or other good places that don't cater to the millions.

On the positive side: when I returned from that family vacation (more family than vacation!) I found a fan letter waiting for me, forwarded by the editor of *Arizona Quarterly* where a poem ["Think of the Planes Flying"] has recently appeared. (I'll send you a copy.) It was really a postcard and who do you think it was from? William Carlos Williams. I was non-plussed, non-minussed, utterly incredulous. No stranger had ever before commented on anything I ever wrote— and then this! After I recuperated, I wrote him a short note of thanks. I'll have the card photostated and show it to you. The editor of *Arizona Quarterly* enclosed a line, saying "Something for your scrapbook." Indeed! Thanks about the information about Tambi. I'll send him something again soon; have a few things out.

I was interested to hear about your connections with Lawrence Lipton. I met him when I was in L.A. and found him an interesting character—very knowledgeable, well read, an extreme ego-maniac, given to blowing his own horn, given to riding hobby horses ("disaffiliation" "dedicated poverty") a typical California cultist (jazz poetry, together with Rexroth)—very shrewd, more of a journalist than a poet and basically interested in one topic: Larry Lipton. . . .

I too hate the mess they call Christmas—really only a pretext for merchants to do business. The whole season gives me Santaclaustrophobia, as I've noted down. And the past, yes, your last letter, Anaïs, sounded depressed. You can put a lot in a description in a scene: the dog snoring, one wife knitting, one husband correcting mathematics papers. In the midst of this a wild bird caged: Anaïs Nin. The woman of the Paris of 1938! Oh God, and this macabre scene, out of the book: Rupert serenading his living dead step-grandmother in the hospital. Terrible—but the scene has at least dimension its very starkness of quiet tragedy. It exists in the sphere of the *vie tragique* in contrast to the sphere of the *vie triviale* to use the terminology of Arthur Koestler.*

I am most depressed by the trivial—as I have just experienced it again at my family visit. (No snow, therefore no skiing and only visiting relatives and their friends.) I love my brother dearly, he is a wonderful, devoted doctor who works much too hard so that nothing of his life remains for himself, his own growth, his own privacy. He has practically none. Too good for his own good, almost a saint, bottling everything up within himself, he has become provincialized, belongs to the local rotary club, has no self, no zest—or at least all of it held down by duty and routine. Taller and much better looking than I with an engaging smile, he yet makes an older impression, though he is the younger, and all is in a minor key, and even gray and I have a hard time communicating with him, breaking through a hundred barriers of small talk. Basically there is nothing to say and my heart is heavy with pity and bitterness: he had much more in him, but he carried all the burdens, asking for more and more; he supported (and supports) our mother, has four children, two houses, is doing financially well but at what cost! And he hasn't, with all this, a room of his own, where he could retreat. Everyone is pulling on him, patients, mother, wife, children, and he asks for more, let an uncle and aunt come from England and live and practice upstairs above his office— my uncle, too is a doctor, a dermatologist, 69 years old and an egotist, who looks well and takes life easy (as he should). Well—I can't get into all this but it is harassing for me, I feel sad and guilty and rebellious and as nervous as a cat there and my style is cramped to the point of becoming a different, sorry kind of person, whose very voice sounds strange and stifled there. And yet I can't tear myself away from there, have a futile but fervent desire to protect Hans and help him and cheer him up and liberate him—all in vain of course, and bringing only startled dismay upon myself, from all sides. Mark met us there too, on his vacation from college. On top of it all, I picked up an intestinal virus and was pretty sick for 24 hours.

As I said—this is only a preliminary note. That it grew . . . is not my fault—only yours: you are a listener that makes a talker out of me. . . .

With much affection,

Felix

*Hungarian-born English novelist, journalist, and critic (1905–1983), best known for his anti-Communist novel *Darkness at Noon* (1940).

1607 1/2 Silverlake Blvd.
Los Angeles 26
[February 26, 1958; postmark]

Dear Felix:

. . . About publishers and editors. Recently my experience with magazines would make a horror story. Above all, if you deal with them *don't care*. Send your aphorisms to Jane Morrison's *Eve* Magazine.

But think that you are playing roulette with a dumb deaf and blind machine—that is publishing. The sensitive and intelligent ones hate themselves, sell out every second for their wives and children and drink themselves to death on the "expense" account. They can't bear to look a writer in the eye!

They are, I found, on the lowest echelon of gangsterism. They steal spring binders, never read manuscripts until they are prodded with Neptune's trident or harpoon and judge them according to hangovers, indigestions or their failed love affairs. Deal with them as little as possible. *Do it all yourself.* It is one of the most corrupt worlds of all. This year, thanks to my friendship with one of them, what I have discovered is hair-raising. All of it is "fixed," like baseball and prize fights: reviews, best sellers lists, etc. *All* of it.

You see they are terribly wrong. The millions don't want what they are given—I had a report from a 15-year-old in a high school—

professor gave them "The Mouse" to read. They responded and understood *perfectly*—The story was never published in a magazine—I had to do it myself!

I'm so glad William Carlos Williams wrote you. His praise is genuine and valuable—Lawrence Lipton is a pathetic failure, a pseudo, fraudulent person, lost in the deserts of California. Your judgement was right in every word—"more of a journalist."

I just gave up [on] *Eve*, after seeing the first number. But in their blind accidental way they are publishing my friends, so I still send them material. I can't write for it anymore because the rich woman who runs it thinks I'm too sophisticated for them (as editor)—No, please don't call it to the attention of the library. It is terribly common in appearance and contents except for the writers I sent them, very poor. Your description of your brother the doctor very touching and sad.

I do understand why you wondered why I didn't answer a letter in which you put so much of yourself, and your life. Remember if ever I don't answer it is exhaustion, of eyes particularly. I know how you feel, loving the family and yet rebellious.

Thank you for all your help on *Under a Glass Bell*. Send aphorisms to *Eve*—even if it is not *our* magazine it will go to 75,000 people and *New Writing* is no better. None of them have any true vision or integrity.

Write to 35 W. 9 as I don't know how long I will be here. They will forward.

Affectionately,

Anaïs

[California]

[March 3, 1958; postmark]

Dear Felix:

I am getting response from your announcements on *Under a Glass Bell*—4 so far. It's wonderful.

Did read your article in *Trace*[13]—very amused by the wit and the truth—Have been quoting your remark on longevity! Good effective work for writers. Wish it were in a better magazine. That is why I now believe in "Do It Yourself!" You must find a way to publish poems and aphorisms.

Anaïs

Dear Felix:

I did not make myself clear.* It did sound like a contradiction to say: *Eve* is not good, and then: send your aphorisms. I wrote impulsively, because of my disappointment in its appearance. The art editor is no art editor. But nevertheless the magazine (while not a literary one) is half filled with my friends' work, good stories, good photos, etc. The reason is this: there is a split between the editor and the publisher (backer). The Editor is employed by the backer. She likes all I do, say or send her. But backer only allows certain things to slip through: one is humor, she responds to that very much and you have a gift for saying truths humorously, the other is a good story in the sense of story telling (not mine). Jane [Morrison] is struggling to establish her values. She may fail. But I have continued however to supply them with material because I get such pleasure when a friend of mine gets a check. I told them the truth about the art editorships. Jane may win, if the first number succeeds. But I understand that if you have a chance of being printed in a really literary magazine, then forget about *Eve*. I just wanted you to understand the seeming contradiction. I am out on two counts: no humor and no story telling. Even the material I send, for fear it may be "Intellectual," Jane does not tell the Editor who sent it! It may not last. And forget about it. But don't feel that I suggested your contributing to a bad magazine! It was a magazine we were all trying to make good. *Tant pis* [So much the worse]. If aphorisms come out in *Partisan* or *Botteghe Oscure* that would be marvelous and no comparison possible. In fact I am glad now you did not send them and jeopardize so much better an appearance.

Anaïs

No, I never saw magazine anthology—little magazines. I never saw, either, and would love to, an article by Rebecca West** on my

work, and one by Stanley Kunitz.†[14] I don't know how to research in
libraries. I get confused and lost in the Public Library. Did you ever
see the Rebecca West article? It was quoted. In fact I have been asked
so many times for a proper bibliography and am absolutely unable to
do it.

*Nin is evidently responding here to a letter that Pollak sent her in reply to
her letter of February 26, 1958. Pollak's letter is unfortunately missing.

**Dame Rebecca West, pseudonym of Cicily Isabel Andrews, née
Fairfield (1892–1938), British journalist, critic, and novelist.

†Stanley Kunitz (b. 1905), American poet, teacher, and editor.

[Evanston]
March 10, 1958

Dear Anaïs —

Now you are angry with me, and I am very angry about myself too.
I knew as soon as I sent that letter off* that I shouldn't have sent it. I
am terribly sorry. I knew how well you meant and I sounded stuck-up
and bombastic and overdramatic, excited without reason and generally like what I am: crazy. . . . Maybe I drank too much wine that
evening although I don't want an alibi. Please do write me a line of
forgiveness, and forget that whole nutty letter of mine. That comes
from obeying impulse without check and saying everything, on the
spur of the moment that goes through my stupid head. I'm old
enough to know better—I should be, I mean. . . . My Fulbright application was refused—no reason given, just a form letter. . .

More soon. Best, Remorsefully,

Felix

*Another reference to Pollak's missing letter in reply to Nin's letter of Feb-
ruary 26, 1958.

[California]
[March 17, 1958; approx.]

Dear Felix:

I was not at all angry—I felt I had not made myself clear. I do understand. Irritation at magazines and publishers is well justified. It

was I who expressed myself clumsily—Forget about it—You know I understand emotional reactions and have plenty of them myself. We have always been spontaneous and I don't want to watch my words any more than you do—One's pride is so offended in U.S.A. that one gets touchy. I understand and there's nothing to forgive. Thanks for the advice on magazines to write to for *Under a Glass Bell.* I will as soon as I find energy—Friendship with [Aldous] Huxley* now: he is better than his books.

    Amitié

    Anaïs

*Aldous Huxley (1894–1963), English-American novelist and essayist, most famous for his dystopian novel *Brave New World* (1932), moved to California in 1932 and became interested in parapsychology and in LSD- and mescaline-induced mysticism, which he wrote about in *Doors of Perception* (1954) and *Heaven and Hell* (1962).

                             [New York]

                     [April 12, 1958; approx.]

On April 18, I fly to Brussels where Hugo will show his new film [*Melodic Inversion*][15]—On May 1, I will be at the Hotel Crillon, Place Vendôme, until May 15 or so—then California—the library can order *Eve* from Editor, Jane Morrison, 8250 Vista del Mar, California. Swamped in work, preparations for trip, bronchitis, and yet want to acknowledge letter and thanks for the Little Magazines not yet arrived. If not, send them to New York address. . . . Will write— My best to you and Sara.

    Anaïs

7

May 1958–April 1959

ILLNESS AND REALITY

ON APRIL 22, 1958, FELIX POLLAK suffers a myocardial infarction which hospitalizes him and necessitates several months of convalescence. His reflections on his own near-death are especially poignant. During this time, Anaïs Nin spends the summer traveling with Rupert in France and Italy. Her richly evocative letters back from Europe ("the flavor of Europe is enclosed in this letter") help revive Pollak's spirits ("I need your letters, Anaïs. I am living vicariously reading them") but at the same time his close pass with death, and the staunch devotion of Sara, make him, to use Anaïs's term, "revaluate" his life and appreciate his concrete situation more.

Anaïs Nin had experimented briefly with the drug LSD. She did so in order to confirm her intuition that such heightened consciousness is already available to the creative artist. Pollak, the skeptic, does not experiment and is predictably not tempted to do so.

Nin's health is also quite frail. In March 1959 she is hospitalized with bronchial pneumonia. This, combined with her efforts to have her work privately printed and to distribute it herself, as well as her responsibilities as the New York editor of the new bilingual journal *Two Cities*,[1] draws much of her energy away from her own writing. In summer 1959, Nin self-published a short fiction, *Solar Barque*, which later became the opening section of *Seduction of the Minotaur*. As in the past, Pollak praises Nin's new work, but now in more measured tones. News of Jean Fanchette's acceptance of two of Pollak's poems for publication in *Two Cities* revives the sense of intimacy between them (*"Enfin une famille!"* [a family at last]) but the former close bonds seem now weaker.

[California]
[May 30, 1958; postmark]

Dear Felix:

Not hearing from you must mean you are still resting. Wonder what you would like to hear? Can I send you California sun without the emptiness of their life? Read a book on Aliterature ([Henry] Miller, Beckett, Kafka, [Henri] Michaux, [Antonin] Artaud)[2] in French. You do read French I remember. Read Artaud's works Volume 1—If you are still lying down reading and it would give you pleasure I would send you a few Diaries. Do you want that? I wrote to Eve Miller about trip to Paris. She responded beautifully—Tried to take them to [Lawrence] Durrell's life near Nimes—

At the typewriter every day at 7:30, copying Volume 54—Lawrence Durrell's first appearance in Paris.

Did I tell you about experiment with LSD lysergic acid? A more refined drug discovered by a Swiss chemist similar to Mexican Mushroom—They hope it will cure the world of neurosis. It not only opens up the unconscious (short cut) but you understand and are aware at the same time. I only took it once to prove to myself and others that it is the unconscious and the world of the artist, not a *new* world. It was like the *House of Incest*. Huxley's book on *Doors of*

Perception is by no means the best. He is a scientist, not a poet. He is an intellectual and admits having no visual sense at all—no visual memory.

Do you have *Booster*³ in your collection? Lawrence Durrell wants me to include his *Womb* story—I believe in the *Womb* number of *Booster*—in publication of *Asylum in the Snow*. If you do, is there anyone in the library who would photostat it for me that I can write to, some student? . . .

What I tried to tell you in my incoherently happy letter* about Paris is that we are right in what we feel and think and that our criticisms of America are justified—I was beginning to think in my desperate aloneness that I *was* alone—but as soon as I stepped on the soil of Europe I realized with marvelous lucidity that a whole continent is like us. As Giraudoux** expressed it: *"L'Amérique c'est tout simplement le contraire de la France"* [America is quite simply the opposite of France].

I think some of your physical troubles come from this absence of ambiance, the atmosphere which is necessary to us. Mental atrophy, indifference, silence are three American attributes which kill life.

Did you try for your fellowship to write on Hesse?

Get well

Anaïs

*This letter is missing from the record. It appears to have been sent to Pollak about the time that he was hospitalized.

**Jean Giraudoux (1882–1944), French dramatist and novelist, whose works combining the worlds of fairy tale and classical myth influenced Anaïs Nin.

[California]
[June 10, 1958; postmark]

Dear Sara:

Since you were so kind as to write to me about Felix' illness, I have written to him several times and have not had one word from him. I am worried and wonder if he is still resting in hospital. Do write me if you have time. I sent him a record. I was not sure about sending books. We are preparing to leave for Europe June 20—so I would like to hear from him before that. After that, write to 35 West 9—it will be forwarded. I think of you both and pray for good health.

Affectionately,

Anaïs

Dear Sara:

Please do me a favor. After *Solar Barque* is printed, I wanted to instruct printer to send manuscript to Head Librarian, but I have forgotten his name (always see Felix as Head of Library!) Could you send me his complete name? I want to attend to this while I am here as they can't hold ms. and can't mail it to me in Europe.

I do hope Felix is gaining strength. This must have been very hard on you too, I know, for you give him life and warmth, and I hope he is successfully recovering from shock.

Affectionately,

Anaïs

Dear Anaïs:

This is the first letter I'm writing by hand instead of dictation since I came home from the hospital last week. I am deeply touched about your concern and should have written you sooner. Partly I wasn't up to it, partly I wanted it to be more than a note (though this was foolish and caused you to worry which I am sorry about), partly the visitors whom I didn't let come to the hospital, are coming to see me at home now, and so the days have gone by. I am getting better, I'm glad to say, my strength is gradually returning, I'm walking around in the house, reading, scribbling notes to myself. I can't tell you what your letter from Paris meant to me—it did more for me than my pills and I received every ounce of spiritual oxygen you enclosed. Anaïs—I know so well what you mean, what you felt breathing the air of Europe, and my heart was so full of longing and nostalgia, it was almost unbearable. Everything within me rallied to the desire, the wish, the will, the prayer—unaddressed, except to the élan vitale in the universe and in myself—not to go down without *living* some more. I was re-reading *Siddhartha* in German, and then *The Fall* by [Albert] Camus (a monstrous book, well done) and I covered the inside cover with the names of the cities in the world I want to see before I die: a long list and I'll not do it, I'd have to be almost a millionaire to see that much of the world and to live and experience it, but I vowed—if I am able—to see a part, a small part of it yet. I thought over my life and the view of so much unlived time, time gone to waste, time stolen, time squandered, life-time gone down the drain haunted me as I was lying on that hospital bed and made my mouth bitter. And who to blame? Myself most of all, but in re-building, re-working my life in my phantasy, it still was difficult not to fly off into pure wish and dream, but to cope with the circumstances beyond one's control. At least, it was no new activity for me. I smiled only inside of me when the doctor told me, "now there's one good thing about this—at least you have time now to think about basic things which one doesn't do when one is up and occupied with one's daily work routine." I'll never know the answers as to the sense of things—but at least I am not a total stranger to some of the questions. Even the few answers I know—I don't know whether I'll be able to act according to my knowledge. But I'll try—God, I'll try! I'll never forget the sky in the window of that hospital room, when night came and Sara had left; and a big silent plane flew directly toward me with one big bright headlight shining ominously—the image of the angel of death—and my fear and utter solitariness and utter helplessness, the aloneness of one with one's arteries and one's pulse and breath, and the one thought: *I haven't lived enough to die!* One will probably always cry this, when the hour comes, but *I* must add to the scale of living—

Enough of that. One can't convey much of it anyhow, but to some very few human beings—with whom one is together in one's alone-ness—one doesn't have to. You have helped me more and shown more concern than any other friend I have. Except Sara, of course, whose many qualities include friendship. We didn't tell my brother and mother—they would have been terribly upset and my brother would have flown here immediately, the emotional strain of which would have been bad for any of us. We called my mother on the phone on her birthday, four days after the attack, muffling the hospital noises as well as we could, and I dictated to Sara letters to the family which she typed at home and brought back for me to sign. Sara has been wonderful, visiting me every day, though it was a very long trip for her on the subway to the other end of Chicago—the only hospital where our doctor works. I was deeply moved by her devotion which was born not of duty but love. I'll never forget her this standing by me in many big and little ways and her instinctive understanding. She will write you separately. . . .

I am doubly glad to be here again, as I wasn't too lucky in the matter of room-mates in the hospital. Had a private room for the first 2 weeks, then moved in with an extrovert furniture salesman who talked incessantly, was triviality personified, flirted in an obnoxious manner with all the nurses and had innumerable phone calls and inconsiderately noisy visitors. When he finally went home, an old crooked politician moved in, a real con-man from Chicago's prohibition and gangster era, who was visited by shady characters and made shady deals right there on the hospital bed. He had—and it might be true— more money than he knew what to do with, and he loudly (and undisputedly by me) proclaimed that Europe (where he had been during World War I) had nothing in the way of landscape or in *any* way that could compare to what America has, and when he read in his paper about the French upheavals, his profound comment was, "oh well, those damn Frenchmen never were any damn good anyway!" I wouldn't have argued with him even if I had been able to afford it. Poor bigger 'n better—fool!

But those things interfered of course with my reading and thinking —and reading had become such a hunger with me and part of the living to be re-couped and made up. The resident-doctor interfered in his way—maybe justly so—when he saw me reading the "Meridian Books" paperback *Existentialism from Dostoevsky to Sartre*, which is very interesting; he told me I shouldn't do any "heavy" reading but read Agatha Christie instead, so I suffered through a supposedly "funny" book from the rental library truck and became sadder by the page. And there were other incidents to lift one's spirits, like a woman's hysterical cries "murderers! murderers!" at the nurses one night at 3 A.M. when her father—as I found out the next day—had died a few rooms away. A hospital, it turns out, is not a very suitable place for sick people. Not if they want to get well. . . .

. . . Almost all of Henry [Miller]'s communications to me concern business, various editions of his books, records, etc. for the Library (or me) to buy. Of course, he writes (or paints) so much, that he has to economize in his correspondence. But I could never write to him as I write you. There would be no response, no real show of interest, no sym-pathy. Yet he was generous and spontaneous when I was there, saying *"you* I'd like as a neighbor" and urging me to throw everything overboard and move to Big Sur. To live on what? He smiled. "One always finds a way. Nobody starves." Maybe. Maybe he is right and I'm just a conventional coward. His own life proves that he was right—at least for himself. But he is something of a genius—with the ruthlessness of a genius—

I know (from a few articles) of the drug you mention. Fascinating. I'll write more about it next time. Even my pen is giving out. This is a long letter again, written over two days with many intervals. I still tire easily and suddenly. I must come to a close. (It seems hard to write anything now that doesn't sound ominous.) While reading Nietzsche the other day I was struck by a phrase "Pfeile der Sehnsucht" which means "Arrows of Longing." Wouldn't that be a good title for a book of poems? I must get my aphorism and poem mss. into book shape, that is the next order of business.

Before I close this letter I want to tell you what I scribbled the other day about you, on reading *House of Incest:* "A.N.: She is not avant-garde, because there is no rear-garde to follow her. She is garde-less, unguarded, she's not even on her own guard, bent only on lifting the seven veils of her being, to discover and express the reality underneath "reality," the subterranean reality, the sub-reality, the surreality, the super-reality of the gold buried in the soul." I hope you approve.

And now your brief statement that you're going back to Europe in a few days. It shook me. Is this just a trip or does it presage or prepare a major change in your life? Are you going for good: Two voices within me contradicted each other. One cried "Go! By all means, go at least you who may be able to!" and the other voice said "Stay here!"

Though externally the distance wouldn't be greater than it is now, and internally physical distances don't count. You'll let me know, won't you—also whether you can be reached in Europe directly. *Thanks for everything.*

Affectionately,

Felix

[June 22, 1958; postmark]

Dear Felix:

Your letter was very moving and how well I understand the wishes you made and the dreams which sustained your life—the pure love of being alive. And I do hope the strength of these desires (expressed in naming the places you had not yet seen) will now carry you into the form of life you wish. It is very strange: they say it is neurotic to oppose one wish to another and create a conflict by stating them as black or white. But I never saw as sharply before the choice one has to make between Europe and America: the means by which America chose to liberate itself: economic and political obsession became the means of creating an automaton, an inferior type of human being, a brave new world. Europe is suffering and paying a high price for disregarding both—but it *is* still a higher form of human animal—and I see no signs of Americans becoming rich inwardly, rather the contrary, Europe is imitating American exteriorization and emptiness (I won't mention proofs of this, you probably know them). At a certain point of one's life one has to choose to pay the price for what one values most. At this point I will pay any price to live with people who have something inside, I cannot take these robots anymore—As soon as the choice is made one can work towards it—The magic lies in the inner decision which ultimately coordinates the outer events. When I returned I knew forever that this was a one dimensional continent and would never be more. Russia and America—the future—

Now to answer your questions. I really think the diary would be too violent an upheaval just now, but I promise someday to send it to you—There are problems—such as having a locked place for them for your peace of mind and mine—the fact that as I am leaving for

Illness and Reality   127

Paris I can't attend to mailing or shipping or the details of selection etc. The Diary is a disturbance—I know that—Will you wait till September when I return?

I appreciated all you wrote about *House of Incest*. *Solar Barque* was delayed. I am correcting the last set of proofs—don't know publication date but if I am away it will be mailed to you. . . .

Yes, I know about Henry. His lack of sympathy, of *feeling* for others, empathy, is his greatest flaw. He does not have it even for those close to him—Eve—her problems, her tiredness (too many visitors, too much lavished on his children, too many meals to cook for worthless strangers etc). But perhaps such egotism is necessary to creation —the capacity to use others—I wish I had that. How much of my energy has been wasted on sympathy—on fulfilling others' wishes, on my desire to give each man his dream—Rupert's dream the most crushing of them all and to which he is quite willing to sacrifice me (he knows now it is *his* dream, not mine) a house in Malibu. I am sitting in our car now while he visits Real Estates to sell the lot we have now and start anew as this one is too expensive to stabilize. It is in a slide area! Such an *external* dream when there is a whole world to see! . . .

I can't answer about Europe yet—H has a fine job there—I don't know if I can transplant R.—This summer is a test—a trial, an experiment—I *do* want to return. I'm dying here. I have nausea and loneliness.

Take care of yourself. Get well—Yes this may have been a blessing to revaluate your life—

Affectionately,

Anaïs

[Paris]

July 18, 1958

Dear Felix:

Was so glad to hear from you and that you are feeling better.* Didn't want to write for fear it would incite you to tire yourself writing—The flavor of Europe is enclosed in this letter, it is the flavor of meaning and the flavor of life itself—It is strange how one feels that in the smallest or darkest rooms human beings lived—they did not float in unreality and lack of contract as in U.S. *La vie vous prend à la gorge* [Life takes you by the throat]. Americans don't *feel* this—they are dead you know. I feel myself vibrating as I stand in the middle of Rue Huchette medieval, all in charcoal, somber and gay, I feel the life currents—resplendent in the middle of shabbiness. Last night we had dinner in the Place des Tertres, in Montmartre. It was filled with tourists, but the character and atmosphere of old Montmartre so powerful *they* seemed not to be there. What was there was the Paris of Picasso et Ses Amis, of the middle ages—of every artist—and as we looked down upon Paris its charm made me feel tender and ready to weep as I never feel in U.S.—At the right there was an old House—the window was open. We could see a table with a greenish oil cloth, on it a long bread, a bottle of wine, heavy white plates. We could only see the old hands of the people who were eating. A hand passed a basket with 2 peaches on it. It was all the paintings of the world, quiet, resisting time, everlasting. It is the only image of duration and eternity I have seen in a long time. . . .

I am lying down in a not beautiful room at the Crillon but it is in Paris. As I step out I smell the honeysuckle from the American Embassy gardens. Not far away was the houseboat. I try to live in the present. Every now and then the past submerges me, but memory is a magician and only the good is remembered, the best of Henry, the best, the distillation of high moments.

Hugo is pursuing only Dame Fortune—day and evenings, but in August Rupert comes and we will rent a car and travel about—Now and then, rarely, I run to the Left Bank. Talked with [Maurice] Girodias** —*Lolita* by [Vladimir] Nabokov will be done in U.S.A.! Isn't that amazing? It is very well written but the most erotic book I have read in a long time. It is allowed to be mailed—Girodias has a "permit." The inconsistencies of censorship![4] No, we are not permanently in Paris. His work will keep him traveling back and forth—What do you mean by smaller setbacks? Do you feel weak? Physical or a matter of mood and feeling? I'm so glad Sara added little note about saving to come to Europe. Do not let people scare you about prices. Already I have found many inexpensive restaurants—ways of living etc.—

Affectionately,

Anaïs

*This and other references in this letter—to "smaller setbacks" and Sara's "added little note about saving to come to Europe"—indicate that another letter from Pollak is here missing from the record.

**Maurice Girodias (originally Kahane; 1919–1990), French publisher of banned books, including Nabokov's *Lolita* and many other classics of modern literature, founded Olympia Press in Paris in 1953 as a successor to his father Jack Kahane's Obelisk Press.

[Evanston]

July 31, 1958

Dear Anaïs,

So happy to get your letter! How can one be homesick for a city that isn't even one's home? Worldsick would be a good word: sick for one's world of which Paris is so much a part. I saw last night the film *[Under] The Roofs of Paris*, beautifully done, but what I fell most in love with, again as in *Red Balloon*,⁵ were the cobblestones and houses and lanterns and streets and windows and bistros and long breads— particularly the cobblestones. Yes, we're saving.

I'm much better and stronger, happy to say, no more setbacks, it was mostly nerves before. Your description of those hands behind the window was beautiful. Perfect enough, as it is, for use in a book or story, so I copy it for you: you may want to use it sometime. I know so well what you felt. Tried to put it into a poem once, but failed. (Also because—it's possible—the flavor is missing behind the same idea in American windows, American houses.) What a country for you and me to have gotten into. South America even would have been better —any romantic country!

I'm particularly glad that you find the Parisian Paris beneath the increasingly American one—a friend of mine in Trieste writes horrible things about the Americanization of that city: and I saw it in Paris and Vienna, but also the resistance to it; so far it was only a thin superficial coating with enough places untouched by either tourists or U.S. commerce. Particularly Vienna is extremely conservative both in good and bad things and underneath the façades nothing really changes. . . .

Together with [*Under the*] *Roofs of Paris* we saw a fascinating film in which Picasso painted; exciting throughout, if sometimes a little arbitrary, or so it seemed. Did you see it? But what poetry in René Clair's direction of the *Roofs*, what atmosphere, and what wonderful restrained acting, what photography, what reality and superreality, what humanity! Only the snow, when it fell, didn't look real. That's the difference to Hollywood. In Hollywood only the snow looks real! I loved it. Before I close, I am copying your beautiful description:

> What was there was the Paris of Picasso et Les Amis, of the Middle Ages—of every artist—And as we looked down upon Paris, its charm made me feel tender and ready to weep as I never feel in the U.S. At the right there was an old house—the window was open. We could see a table with a greenish oil cloth, on it a long bread, a bottle of wine, heavy white plates. We could only see the old hands of the people who were eating. A hand passed a basket with two peaches on it. It was all the paintings of the world, quiet, resisting time, everlasting. It is the only image of duration and eternity I have seen in a long time—

And you have captured and preserved it. Those are live moments, I love them, they haunt me. "It is strange how one feels that in the smallest or darkest rooms, human beings lived—" I need your letters, Anaïs, I am living vicariously reading them. Live, taste all of it, stay as long as you can—it never comes back.

Affectionately,
Felix

. . .

[Avignon, France]
[August 5, 1958; postmark]

Dear Felix:

I've had no mail in a week so I don't know how you are doing, but R. and I are on the road, in a small French car, seeing all the Riviera, and driving to Italy—The charm, the beauty are continuous and incredible—Everything has flavor, savor and sap and pollen! Magic. We swim, eat, walk, drive, drenched in beauty. R. is swept off his feet—I do hope you are feeling better.

Affectionately,
Anaïs

[Southern France]
[August 18, 1958; postmark]

Dear Felix:

Your letter was so thoughtful and interesting—To send me back my words to you on a postcard, only a writer would think of this— And I'm so glad you feel better.

We drove into Italy, to Rapallo (Ezra Pound's place) and Portofino where Maupassant sailed his Bel Ami sailboat into the port. Portofino is unbelievable. A medieval town, with houses of a later period in ochre and coral—small—intimate. The cars cannot enter it. The cafes line the port. And Germans, Italians, French, etc. schooners, sailboats, yachts etc. Such a flutter of flags, dresses. The Italian women wear white high-heeled wooden shoes so you hear the clatter as in Holland, wooden shoes and shawls—The shops are filled with lace made by the Italian women, flowers of lace dentelle au fuseau—It was Golconda again—(I hope you didn't try to read the ms. It was so full of corrections—the new book is ready—wait for it). On the way back we stopped at Este—a medieval town high above the sea—built for eternity—of such beauty—and then Vence where we could not visit Matisse's Chapel.

Rupert's curiosity and American go-go made me see more than I would have alone—I tend to choose a place I love and have a deeper relationship to it—but it is also good, as by the time I return I will know where I want to come back. Portofino in Italy—St. Tropez in France—We are on our way there for a day, on our way to Nimes to visit Durrell, then Barcelona to visit my brother Joaquín—

I tried to get your *Winter of Artifice* in Paris—I will mail you *Lolita* —It can be mailed by a freak of the law.

I got your letter at Monte Carlo—where we arrived tired, took my mail to the beach and read it in the sun. Truly, I don't believe we ever capture the living moments though one tries. I think I may have at times in the diary because it was written at the moment—at white heat—I cannot capture the essence of Europe—but it is something so precious that I don't see how I can ever go back to USA—Yes, American influence is strong—The young dance to imitation Jazz— Some Italians sit looking at television in cafés instead of talking to-gether.

Chapter 7: May 1958–April 1959

But it is only on the surface—The American emptiness of spirit they do not have. Françoise Sagan* gives a good imitation of American boredom with life but it does not become genuine boredom. And boredom and emptiness and the violence of the contactless schizophrenia is deeply American—When you can't *feel* you resort to violence—The Europe I see is almost as Mexico was, deeply *alive* in the only way which matters—You only have to see how they can sit together at a cafe in Portofino having a dinner which lasts all evening, all sparkling with interest in each other, in others, in enjoying the night, the spectacle, the air—

To write letters I get up at 8 and sit at cafe until 9 when R. wakes— The coffee is not good, there is skin in the milk, but the sea is violet and gold, the table yellow, the waitress smiles genuinely (in Golconda, *Solar Barque*, I described the American couple who did not see each other), and people *look* at each other with keen interest— Now you will get in with us in a small French car and ride for a few hours only to St. Tropez—

Write always to [Marguerite] Rebois. Affectionately,
Anaïs

*Pseudonym of French author Françoise Quoirez, who published *Bonjour tristesse* (1955), a novel of adolescent love that created a literary sensation, when she was only nineteen.

[New York]
November 9, 1958

Dear Felix:

A maelstrom of activity. Up at 7 with Hugo—breakfast and talk— and after that a jet plane ride from person to person, occupation to occupation. I would have written you much more from Europe—energy alone is lacking. The truth is I have created too rich a life and now I cannot stop the impetus. I love it and it is too much for me— When I get down all of Europe experience I'll send it to you—Meanwhile I am terribly sorry one of your letters was lost—you put so much into them—The 5 weeks of travel with R. on the road were too hard for the P. Office—yet I hated to be without it too—so it followed me about and strayed. But I wrote you when I came back.

Re-printing the books has been a wonderful experience.[6] People write me, and I no longer feel I write in a vacuum. How I wish every writer could do this. Perhaps my Press will grow and grow.

How is your health? Your work? . . .

Visits from Montgomery Clift's brother—telling me how good his brother was in *Miss Lonelyhearts* film—from a boy who stole *Under a Glass Bell* once from Gotham (original) when I needed one and she was keeping them for more important people! A girl I never knew before who called me long distance after reading books, Jim Herlihy *(Blue Denim)* and I visiting a place near the Ferry downtown where artists live, a loft where they once made *sails*—It still says: sail making and has a wheel which used to bring sail up and down—Guy Daniels who writes for *The Nation* and translates from the Russian— (if ever library needs a freelance job on this done). A girl from Germany—[Ines] Kaiser—who translates Henry James and Durrell—A girl who weaves fabulously, lace-like hangings but of wool—from Chicago, [Lenore] Tawney—an Indian film you should see *Pather Panchali*—can't spell name—will get it from *Cue*—

And on the 15th I return to peace, work and a little uneventful life —to help Rupert grade his papers and wash his glasses of all shapes for chemical experiments.

More poems?

Was your heart troubled at the time? Was it emotional? What were you thinking of? Everyone I know who got back to Europe feels the same way—They adore it—but they fear the problem of work and earning a living there—what a conflict!

Affectionately,

Anaïs

After Nov. 16

1607½ Silver Lake Blvd

Los Angeles

[Evanston]
November 30, 1958

Dear Anaïs—

It took really till this long Thanksgiving weekend for me to write you this overdue letter. Forgive me. With my new schedule (2 hours for lunch so I can rest) and therefore one hour longer work in the evening, I hardly come home before 7 (although we have now a car which I enjoy). After dinner, rest again and so the evening is gone, allowing me only to read a bit but hardly any work on week-days. It all has "to wait till the week-ends," and they pass too too swiftly. But I am grateful and give thanks on this Thanksgiving weekend that I feel well and am up and about and alive. People say I look better than before, getting much more rest than ever.

But above all—your book [*Solar Barque*]. I've read it first in the ms., then in the beautifully printed and illustrated version. I like it very much.[7] It has wonderful passages, full of music, wisdom, style, insight, some reading like poetry, some being poetry. And yet the parts seem to me somehow bigger than the whole. I feel that your unceasing journey into the interior took you farther and deeper in your earlier books—*Winter of Artifice, House of Incest*, and *This Hunger* above all. There seemed to be more urgency there, more drive, more passion, more daring, a hotter flame. Here are all your themes but somehow (Michael, Diane) they're only touched upon, they're not developed and the various episodes don't quite seem to jell into one inter-acting unit, a "story," as it were. Do you know what I mean? . . .

The sensuousness of the atmosphere of "Golconda" made me nostalgic; this is beautifully and fully realized; and if the "passive passion" as I named it in my thoughts, was intentional, then it too permeates the book and comes off; but sometimes I felt it was too passive a passion; and I wondered whether some of the purely descriptive passages (beautifully lyrical as they are) could come out more strongly by being absorbed by a tenser, tighter story-line, by becoming more intrinsic than extrinsic. (When I say "story," I don't mean any kind of conventional plot, needless to say, just a greater inter-dependence, inter-action, mutual necessity of the various episodes, chapters, parts. As in *Spy*.) The part of the book I liked best is the long chapter that begins with the bus ride on p. 88 and ends on p. 116. The description of the people on the bus is quite excellent and Hatcher and his American-made crutches, and the "scream through the eyes of a statue" are magnificent. And as I said, many individual sentences, words, paragraphs, metaphors are superb. Perhaps—and this is quite possible—the whole book will gain as only a part of the larger canvas. (Do you think that *Solar Barque* might come as an earlier part in the sequence, as pt. 2 or 3, and that *House of Incest*, as part 5, closing the cycle? "All I know is in this book"!) I have your photograph at the end of the book, the same which you gave me and which looks at me from the wall above my book-case as I'm writing this. I hope that the reservations I mentioned are not hurting your feelings. There is no doubt that even if I am correct in my criticism, even if the book has some of these shortcomings, that it—despite them and with all of them—is a beautiful and meaningful performance. . . .

As always,
Felix

[California]
December 9, 1958

Dear Felix:

I am alone in the small apartment with tropical patio. Rupert is singing and playing guitar to his old companions of the Forest Service. I wanted to answer your long letter, as I feel both grateful for it and yet feel you should save your strength for your own writing. I appreciated your careful and thoughtful analysis of *Solar Barque*.

All you say is true, right, *if* the book stood alone. But I took you *inside* of Lillian, who, if you remember, tried to enter life first by violence (and failed) then by escape from her husband and children into artist world (and failed) then by uprooting into nature—It is Lillian (not me!) who is drugged by nature, but finds she cannot have relationships (thus they are all sketched in), enter life deeply through nature. She must first liquidate the "shadows," the subterranean life. Thus the characters as she *sees* them. (Just as Sabina also saw partially, only the lover). Lillian sees only the surface—

It is quite different from earlier books. *House of Incest* was neurosis, not nature—*Winter* an effort to understand—Here nature is beautiful, but Lillian cannot become One with it—And now we are ready for the next development—You see, the books are interdependent. Here Michael (*Children of the Albatross* in love erroneously painfully) has now withdrawn also into Nature—exotic places. There is no passion because Lillian is not ready for it—It is a different atmosphere. Those who encounter *Solar Barque* for the first time only find relationship to nature, exile—

It is indeed not presumptuous, but generous of you to be concerned with editing of total volume. I am a very bad editor and proof reader. *Solar Barque* was edited by a professional and thus better—But neither you nor I have the time or energy to do such a job—I will have it done, though, I promise you. *Spy* was the worst, complicated by it being printed in Holland—

No—I don't think you have favorites—although everyone has—and has a right to. *Solar Barque* though the simplest to me was the least understood. The simple attempt to take you *into* Djuna, into Sabina, into Lillian, so that you see the world as they do—was a dangerous experiment. For then everyone thinks I am the one who is seeing the world thus! Yes, the "passive passion" is an experience too, necessary to Lillian who was *too* aggressive—

I give the key when I refer to "drugs"—Golconda as a drug—Lillian is learning passionately—(remember her violence in *Ladders to Fire?*) or becoming feminine—

All you say was very interesting and very right in its own way—It is I who have not made clear that *House of I* came first because I reversed the Journey—proceed from the dream outward. *House of I* was the dream—and all the characters move in and out of it. Lillian enters dream of tropics, dream of voyage, and comes out too—*changed*—

I can't be hurt when someone makes such a tender and severe effort to tell what he loved and what he found missing. All my efforts in writing were to say what had not been said and to do this I sometimes have to pursue a more oblique and circuitous route—In fact if any review had shown half the care and thought and balance you did I would have been glad—

I by-passed reviews—No copies sent to reviewers. I consider that they distorted my work and find that without them I get a much truer vision from my friends—Your letter more valuable to me than any review—Something to ponder—This way I have arrived at a direct connection with those who read me.

It was so kind of you to take so much time and energy over *Solar Barque*—Save yourself for the poems—for life—

Life here—you ask? is peaceful, regular. I work all day from 8 am to 4—Only 1 hour of housework—Evenings Rupert plays quartets and I go on working or we go to a movie—Very rarely a party—I have one disciple, a daughter (?) Greek girl who is writing a good novel—

Thank you again for your effort to understand and clarify and help—

Anaïs

[Evanston]
January 6, 1959

Dear Anaïs—

I returned from a visit to my family in Gloversville, hoping to find a Christmas or New Year's card from you. This is the first year that I haven't received one and it makes me sad. The reason for your silence I must assume to be my letter about your book, despite your saying that you appreciated it. I most certainly did not want hurt you. . . . I admire your books vastly, as you ought to know, but I would hate to become an insincere or undiscriminating rubber stamp with the word "Bravo!" written on it, no matter what the occasion. I don't think you would appreciate and respect such an attitude. I don't think blanket endorsements and uncritical unperceptive adulation is what you can want. . . . And let me stress—unnecessarily I feel—that I don't care about Christmas cards and such conventions *per se*; only in this instance I felt it indicated annoyance and disappointment on your part and this saddened, annoyed and disappointed me in turn. . . .

Felix

[California]
[January 11, 1959; postmark]

Dear Felix:

My long letter regarding *Solar Barque* should have reassured you completely about my reaction to *your* letter—didn't you receive it? I wrote you a long letter in which there was not the slightest hurt—friends can't hurt each other by honesty—The only reason you didn't get a Xmas card was that I had the flu at Xmas week, nursing Rupert, and the task of writing hundreds of cards when I write to my friends all year (Xmas cards should be only for people one only communicates with once a year) seemed overwhelming and I gave it up—I write so much, professionally, for friendship and now with the Press that sometimes I'm overwhelmed—Please reread my long letter—in

answer to yours—Holidays are a strain—were they for you?—I'm
sorry you worried—you should know me better!

Anaïs

. . .

Mount Sinai Hospital
[New York]
March 5, 1959

Dear Felix:

I'm here with bronchial pneumonia—I won't write much as I feel
weak—Received your letter yesterday. Glad you sent poems to *Two
Cities*—Appreciate your response and help in all matters—This "gen-
erosity" of the self (which has nothing to do with money) is rare—
Your activity in behalf of the books has born fruit. I got several letters
from Evanston and orders from friends or students of yours—My
cards are at home or I would give you their names. The Press has
made me a poor correspondent for my mail is heavy and I try to answer all the letters.

I am more convinced than ever that we should attend to our own
publishing. Less waste of energy and where there is no frustration
there is also more energy—If you added up money, time, and psychological damage through all the years you sent out poetry you
could have had long ago a little book to enjoy, to give, to be reviewed
and even sold in certain places. How many people do you think
would buy a book of your poems? When you send them all I will get
you an estimate. I can lend you the cost of offset. From the library
you can probably do a mailing of an announcement.

Is your photo machine in the library able to offset printing upon
any paper or only photo special paper? I have had an idea for a dis-
tinguished design—But here cost would be lower on paper and we
might have to resort to offset at home. You know the Japanese accor-
dion books? I thought it would be ideal for poems—But if you want
something simpler you can find an engraving or a line drawing to offset on cover. Remember *Under a Glass Bell* cost only $.30 offset.
What is costly is printing—*Solar Barque* cost $1.00. But you are not
in this for profit and all you need is to cover your expenses.

And now I'm tired—

Editor of *Two Cities* is Jean Fanchette, 23-year-old poet, novelist, critic, friend of Lawrence Durrell, and mine since last summer. His name was on the announcement.

Two books are being sent to you by my faithful cleaning woman —I would have sent you a copy of *Two Cities* anyway as one of the friends—but this may help next number. As you see I'm trying to consolidate our little world—organize our work to dispense with frustrations. If you do your poems I will send you a copy of my mailing list.

A bientôt. Affectionately to both you and Sara

Anaïs

[New York]
[March 9, 1959; postmark]

Jean writes me he will publish your poem (or poems) in [*Two Cities*] No. 2— We have hopes of backing—all of us are working hard—As soon as I get announcements in English will you post one in French Department and English Department? Would College paper accept a notice? I'm so glad you're "in," with us all. *Enfin une famille!*

Anaïs

[Evanston]
March 9, 1959

Dear Anaïs—

Can't write you a real letter, but want to tell you how sorry and disturbed Sara and I are to hear about your illness. I do hope you're getting better by the time this reaches you, perhaps out of the hospital already; that's why I addressed this to your home address. I too was in a Mount Sinai hospital, the New York one is supposed to be one of the best—though one should avoid all of them. I was doubly touched that you wrote such a long letter to me from your bed. Also about the letters contents. More about that very soon. I'd very much like to publish a book of poems under the imprint of your press and with the offset process you suggest and we might be able swing it financially, but I'm not at all sure in my mind that I have enough poems I care to collect between book covers. I am getting slowly better, perhaps, though I feel depressed about my writing at times, but the progress is marked by increasing difficulty in writing. . . .

I hope, and Sara joins me, that you will soon be completely recovered and that you will take good care of yourself! I hope Hugo does so too.

Amitié and affection,

Felix

[Evanston]

[March 11, 1959; postmark]

Anaïs—

Your card and news has been a tonic for me, thank you so much for writing me this! I am very curious to learn what Jean took and am proud to be a member, *enfin, de cette famille* [at last, of this family]! Glad to hear from Mr. Olson* that you seem to be out of the hospital!

Amitié,

Felix

*Richard Olson, colleague of Pollak's in the Rare Book Department of Northwestern University Library.

[New York]

[March 19, 1959; approx.]

Dear Felix:

Talisman and *Morningstar* must have come when I was ill. I do not remember reading them—or else I thought you were building a collection for future reference—I do like the pointed humor of "Seeing Double" and the deep tone of "Manichean."[8] How you manage to infer and convey so much with such simplicity! I'm mailing them back. Thank you for sending them to me. I will write Jean. He has allowed himself to be swamped and was near breakdown when Hugo saw him in Paris. He did not realize what it meant to run a magazine! He has a job, a child, a wife, etc. Please be patient. He did say he was going to print one or 2.

Anaïs

[California]

[March 31, 1959; approx.]

Dear Felix:

Thoughtless of me to write you when ill and again, but as soon as I left hospital after 11 days, burdens came too heavy—others' problems, stresses, Varda in trouble, a couple came to have their violent scene before me, etc. I had to run away—to Los Angeles. Your poems came just before I left. Can I hold them until I return? *Two Cities* not out yet. R. had Easter vacation so took care of me. Still feel as if lungs were deflated. 8:20 P.M. and in bed already. Send poems to *Folder*, Daisy Aldan, 57 East 82. Just published anthology and may do another—preface by Wallace Fowlie—will write soon. 1607 ½ Silver Lake Blvd, Los Angeles 26.

Affectionately,

Anaïs

[California]

[April 2, 1959; postmark]

From Jean Fanchette's letter. "Poetry by Anselm is good—3 poems have been selected for *Two Cities*."[9]

Anaïs

Would library accept gift of books of poetry? I have an overflow—

8

April 1959–September 1961

SUCCESS AND RECOGNITION

IN APRIL 1959 FELIX POLLAK is appointed curator of rare books at the University of Wisconsin in Madison. This new position boosts his self-esteem and lessens his dependence on Nin for outside support. With newfound assertiveness, he scolds *Two Cities* editor Jean Fanchette for not answering his mail. A prickly exchange ensues with Nin, who excuses the inexperienced Fanchette and declares herself "keenly disappointed" in Pollak's petulant behavior.

Now too, Nin begins to enjoy some sporadic recognition and success: a story published in *Vogue*, an enthusiastic reception for a reading at Harvard, a contract with Alan Swallow to publish all her novels, and the offer of a visiting professorship at Los Angeles State College. To Rupert's incomprehension and dismay, Anaïs refuses to accept the latter, perhaps because this would confine her to Los Angeles and prevent her from conducting her bi-coastal life. On the positive side for Rupert, his dream house is completed in summer 1961, and he and Anaïs move in.

The friendship between Anaïs Nin and Felix Pollak is still alive, but Nin talks increasingly of abandoning letter writing under the press of other work. Teasing her for her postcards, Pollak agrees that "penny cards are better than silence," and this section ends with a new resolution that each should write shorter letters. Signs of a break can be seen.

Evanston,
April 16, 1959

Dear Anaïs,

I was most happy with the message of your card. Only wish Jean F. [Fanchette] would write me too and tell me *which* three poems he is taking and send the others back so I can mail them out again. Maybe it's in the mail. Ordered a subscription for Northwestern. Hope the first issue will be out soon and there will be enough money and support to keep the venture up. How are things going?

I have a good bit of news to tell you—at least I hope it will prove to be *good* news: we're leaving Evanston and will move to Madison, Wisc., where I have accepted a job with the University of Wisconsin. Also as Curator of Rare Books, but on a much larger scale, with the rank of Assistant Professor and chances of further advancement, with a whole floor and plenty of expansion space for the rare books, in a new, air-conditioned, and functionally beautiful building, with a substantial raise in salary and two staff members as assistants. I didn't even know of the job, was approached about it by the head librarian, Mr. Kaplan. He had been looking for a year; my predecessor, unfortunately, died—of a heart attack while swimming. I hope this is not a bad omen. Every change of course gives one a lift, unless it is a real change for the worse, and I feel rather exhilarated. Sara, too, is happy about the developments. Of course we dread the moving—all those books!—and the problem of finding a new place to live won't be easy for we have become very spoiled by our beautiful little coach house

Chapter 8: April 1959–September 1961

which I had hoped you would one day see; it is truly charming and we won't be able to duplicate it and its privacy. And we'll miss our friends and the Library, too, which has become in many respects a part of me. Quite especially the collections I have helped building up, like the collection of your manuscripts and books, the Karl Kraus collection, etc. From those I part with a sense of real loss and feel like a deserter leaving the care for them to some unknown successor. But there never is a gain without a loss and there shouldn't be a standstill. I am particularly happy thinking back to almost exactly one year ago when I had the coronary (April 22) and thought I was ready for the ash can. To be well again (and hoping to stay so for a slice of time) and to move on to a new job is a wonderful and exciting feeling. Someone said to me the other day I looked as if a burden had been taken off me, and I said I felt that way, except that I knew there was another burden already waiting. Sometimes the interim period between two burdens is the best, the period of floating. And I am also aware that what I really want is NO job at all but the merest fraction of what my salary will be as a regular income so that I could just write and read and travel; but if one *has* to work, one might as well make the most of it. I'll leave the Library on May 31st and begin work in Madison on June 15th. Sara, under contract to teach till the end of June, will follow me in July. . . . Is not Frank Lloyd Wright's famous farm-colony just outside Madison? Was sorry to learn he died. He was a controversial character but led a rich life and a long one; one of the rare and lucky ones. We will correspond still before I leave, I trust, and later I'll write you our new address, of course, or better a box office no., since we may be settled only temporarily for some time.

I do hope you are better, Anaïs! Forgive the typewriter, but I have so many letters to write and so much work to do that I try to save my strength. I won't write more for today, therefore. Sent you a magazine. Keep well—

Affectionately,

Felix

. . .

[California]
April 23, 1959

Dear Felix:

So *pleased* with your change! I feel sure it's wonderful. More salary will enable you to travel—and a change is good anyway. I always feel Nyholm did not appreciate you sufficiently. *Congratulations!*

Do forgive Jean Fanchette for not writing—He is 23, inexperienced, he works as a medical student during the day, just had a child, and bronchial pneumonia! But I'm sure he will now. I know what you feel is a cumulative impatience with all editors! I don't blame you—

Things are going well—200 subscriptions and first number paid for. It will be properly distributed by Fanchette.

Yes I understand how you feel about leaving your collections, but think of the new ones you will create with more power to expand!

And all that you have accomplished in a year of convalescence.

Thanks for the magazines. I always enjoy the poems, the either emotional or humorous moods—deftly expressed. Wish you could have a *rest* between jobs—a sabbatical. Is that impossible to manage?

Bonne chance
Amicalement
Anaïs

[California]
[June 29, 1959; postmark]

Dear Felix:

Please don't feel impatient now—Jean has told me twice he was using one (or two) of your poems in No. 2 and I wrote you this some time ago. I know he should write you himself but he is overworked—and think of it, he turned down 5 writers I sent him and kept only you—so at least the waiting was not in vain. He did not know what he was getting into—has a job all day at hospital. Do forgive him,
Anaïs

Chapter 8: April 1959–September 1961

[Paris]

[July 30, 1959; postmark]

Dear Felix:

Your poems are out in *Two Cities* but I was keenly disappointed that after I wrote you to explain Fanchette's reasons for not writing you, birth of his child, all the work of magazine, his exams for medicine, his day of work at Hospital, you sent him a pedantic letter so unlike the tactful European I knew you to be, the kind that is not customary in Europe among writers and artists and only right for tough American magazine editors. I'm afraid it made Fanchette feel you to be intolerant—and I blushed thinking life in America and in the University, curt, business-like precise, etc. is so far from the life of St. Germain des Prés in Paris—I do think this is your accumulated irritation from years of dealing with little magazines in U.S.A. I know waiting 5 months *is* long but you also knew from me what the reasons were—and you knew I was doing all I could—Long ago when I realized this typical situation irritated you I suggested you print your poems and avoid loss of time, frustration, irritation—As I understand it, all magazines are about the same.

Well, you were justified in your impatience, but I am to blame for seeking to situate you among bohemians.

I'll be back in Los Angeles August 3—not well enough to keep travelling and eager to work. By now you must have magazine. I'm helping to mail some out today. I'm glad you like your new job.

Amitié from Paris

Anaïs

[Madison, Wisconsin]

August 5, 1959

Dear Anaïs—

I was very surprised and sorry about your letter. In this issue we just don't see eye to eye. If treading on a person's nerves is Bohemianism, then I simply am not a Bohemian, nor care to be. Fanchette ignored for 5 months my pleas to send me at least a post card. For an editor, this is a gross inconsiderateness to a contributor and very insensitive. Neither "Bohemianism," nor his having a job and his wife's getting a baby is an excuse for that. Particularly since all he had to do was what I asked him to do: to write 3 lines on a postal card, saying, "I have accepted those and those of your poems," period. You knew and told me that he had accepted some (3, or 2, or 1) so it wasn't a case of pressing him to make a decision—just to let me know about the decision he had made.

When I wrote a piece in *Trace* about the treatment some (not all) editors inflict on authors, you applauded it, calling it a service to writers. I recall your hurt—sending letters to Mr. Titus, pleading for at least an answer. When Djuna Barnes never replied to your letter, you resolved you wouldn't inflict that treatment on others and to answer every letter you received. You know quite well how torturous it is not to get a line from someone from whom one wants—or needs—to hear. Yet in this case it is all my fault because Mr. Fanchette didn't realize what he was letting himself in for, because he has many other things to do, because his wife is having a baby, and because he's a Bohemian and I am not. But I assure you it was not America nor my job that prompted my "pedantic" letter to him. In fact, I mailed you a carbon of it, thus showing you that I did not intend to act behind your back and against your advice to be patient; I thought I was doing Jean a favor in designing a form that would save him time and effort and at the same time give me the information I so badly wanted. I don't think you are quite just in reproaching me for this the way you did. As a proof that Jean himself does not seem to feel that I am to blame in the matter, I enclose a photo-copy of his note to me. . . .

As for publishing poems in book form—it is not at all a matter of getting them published and having it over with so I won't feel so anxious and impatient with editors henceforth. You seem to imply that. I won't try to explain what I assume you understood. When I think that I have written enough poems that warrant publication in a book according to my own standards and judgment, I'll try to have them published, and not sooner—even if I never do. Every amateur is publishing books today—that proves nothing.

I hope this won't spoil our friendship. Little emotional spats are natural and healthy among friends, I trust you won't consider this affair as anything more.

Amitié,

Felix

[California]
[August 10, 1959; postmark]

Dear Felix:

I know friends have spats. The difference between the little magazines who never answered, and *Two Cities*, was that I am one of the editors and that I answered you even while I was in hospital and kept you informed as well as I could. Also kept you informed of what was going on and you were not kept 5 months without contact and a disregard of your sensibilities. It is not at all similar to what you complained of in *Trace*.

Anaïs

I was going to bring back your unpublished poems but Fanchette had a breakdown the last two days and I could not get the manuscripts. He finally collapsed—We spent a day in Paris distributing Review ourselves to bookshops—going to the Post Office.

New York
[October 2, 1959; postmark]

Dear Felix:

Just as I was about to write you: as you said all friends have tiffs and I hope ours is over. I get your card! Of course you have a right to contributor's copies. It was an oversight on my part. You will continue to get your subscribed copies. If you need more than four, let me know. I am sorry that overwork, fatigue, inexperience, etc. has aroused your criticalness once more. I can't work any harder but something always gets left undone. I suppose one expects indulgence from friends—

Anaïs

[California]
[November 16, 1959; postmark]

Dear Felix:

Work for *Two Cities* has been such a burden that it has destroyed my letter-writing. That, and trying to work on a new novel—and diminishing energy. When magazine is on its feet, I will slowly detach myself from it—Hope you had some pleasure from it. Hope you are

happy in your new environment and have not missed Northwestern
—Have never been in Madison so cannot imagine it. Isn't it the
home of Frank Lloyd Wright's school in the summer?

Gave a reading in New York's Living Theatre—adaptation of the
Party as an abstract play *(Ladders to Fire)*. Do you know Daisy
Aldan's *Folder?*[1] She is now poetry editor of *Two Cities*. Imagine this
to be a long letter. Your tired friend,

A

[New York]
[December 26, 1959; postmark]

Dear Sara and Felix—

Wanted to surprise you for Xmas with more copies of *Two Cities*
to give to your friends but was snowed under by my brother's concert,
nursing a sick friend, a million duties so all will arrive late, even my
wishes for happiness and health and creativity from your affectionate
friend

Anaïs

[New York]
[January 14, 1960; postmark]

Dear Felix:

Please tell me quite frankly if you approve of this idea: my friend
Caresse Crosby (Black Sun Press) and head of Citizens of the World,
has bought a castle for an Art Center near Rome on the way to Spoleto.
She wants to build up a library and I have offered many of my own
books, many out of print duplicates of good writers, etc. She is particularly interested in poetry. I thought it might be interesting for me
to send her the magazines including your poems because so many
people will read and enjoy them—not just me—all the artists, visitors, guests, etc. If you like the idea I will send yours with my other
gifts. But if not, I won't. I thought of it as a way of sharing with the
world—But I will wait for your permission. . . .

Affectionately

Anaïs

[Madison]
January 17, 1960

Dear Anaïs—

Thank you so much for your letter and your wonderful offer. Yes, certainly, I would be happy and flattered to be represented in Caresse's castle library—I always wanted to reside in a European castle anyway, and I admire Caresse and the Black Sun Press, she must be a fabulous person. Glad to know she has enough money to buy a castle—will she live there too? It was very good of you to think of me in that connection, too bad I can't be the librarian there too! . . .

Our correspondence has been so intermittent lately, and brief to boot, that I never had a chance to comment on your pieces in the magazine ["The Writer and the Symbols" and "The Synthetic Alchemist"].[2] I like both of them very much, the second one even better than the first. There are brilliant passages in the first, nothing unexpected in content for those who know your work but lucidly and succinctly condensed and expressed, and certainly endowed with much truth and insight. Reworked in some spots and transitions, this essay would make a fine booklet in itself—or could be combined with "On Writing" and "Realism and Reality" as another step in your contribution to the understanding of the artistic process, temperament, and your view of the theory and aim of art. I particularly liked the concrete examples you gave and think they could be extended to add both weight and color and drama to what you are saying. But your real forte is the imaginative writing itself, the practice of your art, even beyond its theory. Your poetic prose is superb and one feels infused and infected by your description, undulating in your own contagious rhythm, hearing the sounds of colors, seeing the colors of sounds. There is an intoxicating power of suggestion in your sentences, and the ordered way in which you form the chaotic, the artistic intelligence and skill at work after the initial inspiration has taken place, the expedition into the depths has been accomplished and the raw material of art brought to the surface—this exemplifies in itself most convincingly what you're saying in your essay on theory. Too many surrealists have given us only the raw material of art—as today the members of the so called Beat Generation are doing—without having either the patient will for the hard labor of forming the chaos, or the artistic power of doing so. An artist without chaos is no artist, he has no material on which to exercise his skill. But an artist with only chaos, with only the raw materials, is no artist either if he can't give it form. The first is like a sculptor without a stone; the second like a sculptor standing before a stone without a chisel in his hand. The artist is like the oyster: he has to produce out of himself, the pearl around the stone within himself. There is intelligence in the idea of a pearl around a disturbing stone, but without the presence of the disturbing stone the intelligence can't manifest itself. I hope I interpret you correctly.

Knowing the *House of Incest* and the artist you are, the word artist you are, I wouldn't even bet that you actually took the drug, though you probably have. But you could have written this piece even without it, I believe, even without having as much as a martini. It is your world of vision and sensitivity, as you yourself say in the beginning: "Nothing unfamiliar about this final mobile world." You have lived long enough in it to know it by heart, by visions and imagination, the drug could only reinforce, recreate, reemphasize it. I vaguely remember a sentence from the Paris edition of *Winter of Artifice*. I believe, when a girl, that stripteaser wife of Henry's, was trying to seduce you into taking drugs, describing its erotic sensations and sensual effects, and you answered, "I have known all this without drugs"—or words to that effect. I was quite impressed with that passage always. (I still think it is your best book, that unexpurgated version—a magic, entrancing piece of writing.) I wonder whether today, when taboos have receded even in this country, when *Lolita* can be published and all the "forbidden words" for which Miller was (and still is) banned here can appear, incongruously and ludicrously, in [Allen] Ginsberg's *Howl*, in magazines like *The Big Table, Chicago Review, Yugen, Hearse* and, I believe, *Evergreen Review*—I wonder whether you should not consider republishing now the original version of *Winter*— if someone like Grove Press would bring it out. It may make the stir it ought to make and bring financial rewards besides. Have you ever thought of it? Or portions of the diary? . . .

Affectionately,

Felix

P.S. Was very shocked and saddened by the death of Albert Camus. What a tragic, senseless death!* He was an outstandingly honest, outstandingly gifted man, so young so much yet to give! To think of all the works we lost—Thomas Wolfe dead in his forties, Dylan Thomas in his thirties (Ruth Diamant said, you and he didn't click, but he was a great poet!), now Camus. Not even to speak of Mozart, Schubert, etc!

*Camus died in an automobile accident on January 4, 1960.

[New York]
[January 20, 1960; postmark]

Dear Felix:

Yes, it is true I am no longer a letter writer. It is the first year I surrendered all the activities I have no strength for—(*Two Cities* was the excess)—so I stopped. It is hard on friendship, I realize, but I guess it is harder on friends if one gets ill. So please understand if I write less, and less often.

Caresse's Castle only cost $15,000! She just had the imagination to get it, to persuade the Italian government to repair roof, and her friends and relatives to share in the cost of making wings habitable. She is no longer wealthy but has a genius for life as [Jean] Varda has with even less. But this is why we are all giving books—I will send you her address soon, as soon as I hear she is there. It is very generous of you to send her magazines with your poetry. She is particularly fond of poetry and that was why I offered my poetry library. . . .

Thank you for all you say about "On Writing"—I know it needs reworking but I prefer to write novels and not ideological writing—I have enough for a book. I particularly like all you say about the imaginative writing—very proud in fact. I am glad we agree on organization of chaos. Yes your interpretation is true to my meaning.

I also agree with you about the drug not being necessary. I took it once to prove to myself that it only opened the same realms which I have a natural access to, and you are very right to observe the similarity between *Synthetic Alchemist* and *House of Incest*. I could have written extensively on this as Huxley actually states the opposite, that these realms can only be opened with the drug. I still feel as I always did that the effort made to live, love, or create without artificial stimulants is part of the enrichment, strengthening the active will, whereas those who are passive, helped, and fond of short cuts never become such vigorous creators. [Henri] Michaux is an exception. He was always, and still is after ten years of drugs, the greatest poet of today. About Dylan [Thomas] I feel that compared with Michaux he was one dimensional, just a folk singer, a bar entertainer, a village band— Michaux, [Blaise] Cendrars, [Jean] Genet, are the real alchemist poets, [Jean] Giraudoux and Pierre Jean Jouve* — they *alchemize* — into gold—Hugo and I walked out of *Under Milkwood*—I feel he [Dylan Thomas] has been enormously over-estimated, but I attribute this again to the phenomenon of suggestion and contagion.

Grove Press would never publish me—My literary agent, Gunther Stuhlmann (who is a most *literary* agent, a German), tried to get them to do *Solar Barque*. It is primarily a homosexual clique.

I am writing now *Seduction of the Minotaur* which I hope Obelisk will take, Olympia Press, as in spite of loosening of taboos, American publishers are intensely distasteful to me.

Two Cities III will be here soon. It has Durrell's Preface to *Black Book*, a section of it, and a study of Miller by [Karl] Shapiro.** But Fanchette's disorganization has caused me to work three times harder and to lose friends, so I am losing interest in it.

I hope you will have a good inspired year of writing, good health and much publication. Amicalement,

Anaïs

*Pierre Jean Jouve (1882–1972), French poet and novelist, whose writings reflect his interest in Freudian psychology, eroticism, and Catholicism.

**"The Greatest Living Author," by Karl Jay Shapiro (b. 1913), American poet, critic, and editor of *Poetry* magazine (1950–56).

[In flight, New York–California]
[March 27, 1960; postmark]

Dear Felix:

I wanted to make sure I gave you our new address, 3 Washington Square Village, New York City 12. I spent the whole month making a new home. Now flying to L.A. Harvard gave me a warm wild welcome. *[Harvard] Advocate* writing me up May 15. We go on a tour with films and reading to London, Stockholm, Brussels and Rome— home end of June—This is our story. And you? Where will you be this summer? Are you and Ruth [*sic*] well? Contented? Is the new library interesting? Would they buy a manuscript of e.e. cummings? Everybody teasing about Penny Card Club—but adopting it. Better than silence, isn't it? Must finish new novel [*Seduction of the Minotaur*]. My love to you both,

Anaïs

[Madison]
April 7, 1960

Dear Anaïs—

. . . So glad to hear about your Harvard reception, have tried unsuccessfully to see the respective issue of the *Harvard Advocate*—have you got an extra copy? Or one you could lend me? And your summer plans sound exciting and enviable again. Hope the new film (films?) will win a prize in Brussels, and wish very much that I could see them! What is the new novel you're working on? You're such a productive and hard worker, wonderful. And on top of all your travels, moving, etc.! Am glad to hear you're all installed in the new apartment. Maybe, someday when we both are in New York at the same time, I can see it. I'd love to. (There's nothing like inviting oneself, is there?)

Yes, penny cards are better than silence, though letters are better than penny cards; but I know only too well how difficult it is to keep up a correspondence on top of all the other activities and one's real writing. I've curtailed my letter writing considerably too, with a tinge of regret within a great feeling of relief. It's a chore, though I love it; if I had time for it, I'd be a great letter writer. Sara (not Ruth, as you called her—she'd never forgive you if she knew, but I can see how it could easily happen) and I are all right, like Madison, job, and some of the people here. Someday, on occasion, I'll tell you more. . . .

Enough for now, all good wishes and affection to you,

Felix

[New York]
[July 25, 1960; postmark]

Dear Felix:

When prima donnas keep saying they will "retire" no one believes
them—When I kept saying I would have to "retire" from letter writing I didn't believe it myself but it seems to be true—I wanted to
write you as soon as I received the wonderful pile of magazines
which I forwarded to Caresse. A million thanks! As she is having
trouble with her eyes (cataracts) she may not thank you personally
but all those who will sit in the Castle Library will thank you! Trip to
Europe was marvelous—a love affair with Stockholm—met all the
writers, critics, poets, was fêted and treated like a movie star, they
loved Hugo's films, I loved them, their depth and their basic melan-
choly—Brussels official (Embassy evening, much chichi, etc.) Paris
as always a life-drug for me—all so intense, so charged, so rich, like
years of living in 5 weeks—that I collapsed on the plane and was
given oxygen—so I spent a peaceful month in L.A.—I resigned from
Two Cities (gladly) and here I am in New York, looking down on
Washington Square—helping Hugo cut his film on Venice, and at
last answering letters!

The consequences of not writing are so serious—I don't want to
pay the price of not knowing how your friends are! So—how are you?
How is your life there? Are you happy? Are you well? Are you publishing enough to be content? . . .

Avec amitié
Anaïs

[Madison]
August 22, 1960

Dear Anaïs—

Forgive me for being so late in answering your letters; things have
been hectic here until now when I am starting my vacation, two
weeks late, as it is. I was so glad to hear from you again, it is a distressing feeling when one wonders if one is losing touch with a
friend, with you, in particular. . . .

. . . We like it here. Sara and I are still having our ups and downs,
am at present recovering from a down in the course of which I came

only a hair's breadth from leaving her. After ten years of marriage one finds it difficult to live alone, despite everything. It is as if one couldn't stand and walk any longer without a crutch. . . . Things are mixed up and confused, and none of it is any good for my health. This last consideration poses continually the question to me of what is worse for me—to stay with Sara or to leave her. I can't answer it at this writing.

You may wonder what the disagreements are all about. . . . Mostly it is small petty unimportant things: my turning the car into the wrong street, or going too fast, etc.; or being late in getting ready for a party because I am working till the last minute. Things like that. . . . Tired. This was supposed to be . . . a bread and butter letter, like it fine here, etc. Doesn't seem to work with you, though I can write such letters to other people. With you my pen runneth over of what my heart is heavy with. I hope I am not burdening you by that method. You are wiser and more reticent about your life to me. But I feel your understanding and sympathy and it helps me and I'm grateful to you for it. For being here, for being what you are.

And again, I hope you are well again! Write me.

Affectionately,

Felix

. . .

[In flight California–New York]
[late 1960]

Dear Felix:

It seems as if to take up with my correspondence I have to take an airplane—so here I am with time for myself—5½ hours (time off for lunch). I'm glad you gave me library address. I did not feel free to comment on your last letter in which you unburdened yourself of so many discords—If I console you, dear Felix, all marriages have these dissonances—suffer them—and the real question is whether solitude would not be worse. Long ago, I made my choices. Relationship is the most difficult thing in the world but I always bring myself up short of disaster by reminding myself that what one really wants is *impossible* (and in this the romantic and neurotic are similar). So, unless you find someone closer to your needs and wants, be patient.

Hugo has jaundice so I'm on my way to a repetition of my last stay in New York—days at the hospital—but it is not serious. Your *Library Journal* probably awaits me in New York. R.'s house is such a work of art that I can only compare it to a Japanese house, full of beauty, and views of the lake and the mountains so varied and entrancing, it makes one contemplative.

Amicalement,

Anaïs

Are you receiving *Two Cities* as you should? Fanchette is impossible.

[Madison]
January 3, 1961

Dear Anaïs,

Just received and read your letter to the library, am moved and shamed by it, forgive me. I did of course give you the benefit of the doubt, more than that, but I felt I was inflicting my troubles on you who no doubt have some of your own—and Hugo's deplorable relapse is one of your worries—and I wondered whether I was not really tiresome. Yet it means a very great deal to have someone to talk to about what I really feel and think and the things that really affect me and my life. I know I am very lucky to have at least one person I can write to about this, though I would much rather talk to you.

More upset and drama in the meantime, relations always on again and off again, I feel like a fish on the hook, can't get off without tearing my flesh, can't stay on without those dismal quarrels, discussions, upsets, scenes, frozen silences, hurts, blocks, irritations. . . . The irony of it is that I do love Sara in many respects; but to love someone doesn't mean that one can also live with him. Another even greater irony is that most, practically all, of our acquaintances think ours is a perfect marriage.

You say these things happen in most, even in all, marriages. More or less so, possibly. I do know, I think, of a couple of exceptions. But those are more friendships than marriages. A compromise. Yet sometimes I think I'd settle for friendship and peace in favor of the wounds inflicted in the name of love.

. . . Of course, difficulties are just that, not impossibilities, and one has to weigh, always, loss against gain, and decide what one wants most. Life is not an insurance policy where everything is certain, and where all risks can be calculated. It wouldn't be worth living if it were. Above all, the question comes down to how much living one wants out of life and how much one can attain in the eternal compromise that seems to be, alas, inevitable. I took to heart what you said about marriage in general because it is so poignantly true: too often one tries to attain the unattainable, and the more one tries this, the more one must become disappointed and disillusioned. I talked with Sara about this on a long walk in the snow yesterday and we came—it seems, I hope it's true—to some agreement here.

Problems, problems, I've come to believe, are unsolvable. Whatever can be solved is, by definition, not a problem. . . .

I do hope that Hugo will fully recover soon and stay well! Is everything all right with Rupert? And your dream house? And I very much hope you are and will stay well, and your life rich, manifesting itself in your work. Please let me know what you are working on and whether you're continuing to print. And forgive me for my vague doubts.

Very affectionately,

Felix

P.S. I just went across the hall from my office into the art exhibit room and heard a professor tell his class: "Perhaps we ought to concentrate more on creating new art than on becoming a nation of collectors of old art. I remember a piece of modern sculpture exhibited in New York which moved by a built in motor, moved ceaselessly, and in moving gradually disintegrated, destroying itself. This was, and was meant to be, a symbol." Indeed. And of more than art. I was quite struck by that story.

It is good in actual and potential loneliness, to know that someone cares about one, has sympathy and concern. I am more than grateful to you, Anaïs; sometimes, when I learn of other people's troubles, I realize despite everything, how lucky I am, how much worse, not only how much better, things could be. . . .

[California]

[August 13, 1961; approx.]

Dear Felix:

You must not think that it was the fullness of your last letter which caused me to write less. It is true the overwhelming troubles of human beings sometimes seem beyond help, but it was not that. It is a lessening of energy which is reflected not only in fewer letters, but less writing, less diary writing, less activities.

Believe me, there is nothing tiresome about revelations on one's life. . . .

Los Angeles State College offered me a visiting professorship—four hours a week, $10,000 a year and alas—I couldn't take it! It has been my year, at last, Swallow doing all books Sept. 15—a story in *Vogue*[3] August 1, an offer from State, and now an actress [Tracey Roberts] took an option on *Spy in the House of Love*. . . .

R. is very happy in his house—a real work of art by Eric Wright*—view of Silver Lake—a pool—eight glass windows. He is very proud of it. We work all day at it! Few visitors. Varda came when he had a big exhibition, sold many paintings—One of his will be on the cover of *Seduction of the Minotaur*—in color. . . .

Your friend,

Anaïs

*Architect Eric Wright, Rupert Pole's stepbrother, son of Lloyd Wright and grandson of Frank Lloyd Wright.

[Madison]

Sept. 17, 1961

Dear Anaïs—

So glad to hear from you, and such a variety of good news! I'm very happy for and with you. Swallow had sent me the list, too, and I wrote him congratulating him also. Will get new *Solar Barque* (*Seduction of the Minotaur* is a good title!) as soon as I see it in the book stores. Am curious about the new section.

Too bad you couldn't take the position Ruth Diamant (I presume) offered you (or helped in being offered to you). It would have been good for the college and the students and probably also for you, apart from the fabulous salary even. Things work out strangely that way. If one worked oneself to the bone to get such an offer, one wouldn't get it. But it must have buoyed you up, nevertheless. Shabby treatment from Grove Press, I'd say. Is it true that Henry went back to Paris to live? I wrote him a note when *Tropic* came out, but no answer. Heard the above rumor. . . .

Will look up your story in *Vogue* right away; just came back from vacation. First ten days with my brother and mother, discovering anew that the expression "family problems" is a tautology. . . .

Now back in the groove again—on my new schedule of working only every second day so I can spend some time on preparatory work on the book. Otherwise, yes, I like my library work here better than at Northwestern on the whole. No tyrant like Nyholm over me, much better salary ($8,500), better and bigger rooms, light, air-conditioned, quite friendly colleagues. . . .

We hope to go to Europe next year, or to Japan. Does Japan tempt you at all? It does me. . . .

Shall we write each other only short letters but in not too long intervals? I'd like that. All the best (some of my past wishes for you came true!) As ever,

Felix

9

October 1961–June 1962

A QUARREL AND A BREAK

IN LATE 1961, POLLAK DISAPPOINTS Nin by entering another argument, this time with her new publisher, Alan Swallow, concerning an article by Pollak on little magazines. This exchange evidently puts Pollak in a combative mood, which carries over into his correspondence with Nin.

It is a considerable irony that a quarrel over a review of *Seduction of the Minotaur* that Felix Pollak undertook only reluctantly, and at Anaïs Nin's request, should have brought about a ten-year silence between the two. In the draft of his review, Pollak casually refers to "Lillian's life in Paris with the painter Jay—transparent disguises for Anaïs Nin's own pre-war days with Henry Miller." Nin, with her "horror of personal publicity," sees Pollak as ready to break the carefully guarded secret of her affair with Miller, about which even Miller himself will keep an honorable silence until after Nin's death.

Two further ironies: first, the formerly argumentative Alan Swallow also reads Pollak's review and finds it to be "a very good job indeed"; second, the projected review which causes so much grief is never published.

[California]

[October 19, 1961; postmark]

Dear Felix:

This time I could not be lavish in giving books as I have to pay for them—forgive me. Forgive me! But here is the *Vogue* story. You can keep it.

You ask about Tambimuttu. Every now and then he turns up at a party in New York, always terribly drunk and half-mad, bitter, megalomaniac. He was the lover of a friend of mine and almost dangerously violent. For a while in London he was privileged, an Editor—but whatever forces destroyed him, now he feels only bitterness because according to him he "discovered" all the poets, and yet cannot legally assert they are his writers. He depends on women to finance his *Poetry* magazine—but he lives now in a time harsh and cruel to mad poets. With what longing I read the *Banquet Years* by Roger Shattuck[1]—a marvelous recreation of that period, [Henri] Rousseau, [Erik] Satie, [Guillaume] Apollinaire, [Alfred] Jarry—what an atmosphere! Do read it if you haven't already. You will exist for a few hours in a world that is *breathable*. That is the time I would have liked to live in. He really knows about music and French literature, Mr. Shattuck.

I don't know anything about Miller. Don't you get the monthly letters from Friends of Henry Miller Society? . . .

About Japan—it is only aesthetically interesting to me. I can sit for hours at Japanese films, but I'm not attracted to it because I have no relation to them individually. As relationship, talk, exchange, creative friendship is what I can't get in America—what I hunger for is Europe where I can talk with a taxi driver on the advantages and disadvantages of experimental theater and philosophy of [Jean] Genet. Japan is an exterior for me—I have enough externals in American life—the friends I have in Europe are endlessly interesting. . . .

Stock will publish me in French and wants an option on the Diary, but alas introduction came through Fanchette and André Bay wants to give him translation and knowing his irresponsiblity it would amount to suicide.

Could you review *Seduction* for *Library Journal* or a poetry magazine? I could ask Swallow to send you a review copy.

This year has been difficult because I'm deeply in debt because of R.'s house.

Yes short and oftener letters! For they are too pleasant to write and we write them instead of working!

Anaïs

Nice description in Diary of my visit to Evanston and your charming behavior, arriving through a flood!

[Madison]
October 25, 1961

Dear Anaïs—

Here is the first of the "new-look" short letters. Loved yours. Enjoyed the *Vogue* story, *beautifully* written, as always. Thanks so much.

As for the review of *Seduction*—I am so swamped that I feel panicky and kind of desperate, sometimes, but you are my no. 1 friend, you're a wonderful writer and a beautiful and indeed bewitching woman, and I am only a poor male, and can't say no to you. So I'll say, *yes*, I'll *try*. Have Swallow send me the book and I will see what I can come up with (and when). Where to send it is another question. . . . But once it's written, I'll find a good place.

Would *love* to read your Diary description of Evanston arrival, etc. Any chance at all? (Swear to return everything.)

Affectionately,

Felix

[Postscript written along sides of page]

. . . I think you're very right about Fanchette and about refusing to give the diary translation to him! But it's the first straw in a wind that will gain force in time—*I'm convinced.*

[California]
[November 3, 1961; postmark]

Dear Felix:

Short letters are working well! I'm glad you sent your poems to Swallow. He seems very decent and responsible but I don't know his taste in poetry and like everyone we know he may not be consistent or predictable. . . .

Was interested in your opinion of [Karl] Shapiro—corresponded with him. Erratic. Desperate at his imprisonment—that was why he became so hysterical over Miller—asked if I could preserve a truthful novel—I offered my vault with diaries—Said he wept over my work. When I asked him for a comment for Swallow he could only write a line! He's in Europe now I believe. Did your aphorisms ever appear in Europe? Found copy you had given me and enjoyed them.

Complete silence from reviewers. . . .

Your friend

Anaïs

[California]

[December 14, 1961; postmark]

Dear Felix:

Forgive me for not reading about quarrels, literary or domestic. They sadden me. I always have the feeling that there is another reason for our quarrels—we do so when we're unhappy. Particularly between you and Swallow² who have both been good to me—There's so little time for writing, friendship, etc.

This is to wish you happy holidays—I'm in Los Angeles concerning the film—N.Y. was wonderful. Party at the Gotham—Publishers asking for the Diary. Saw 200 persons at least. Much work. Many burdens (invasion of Cuban relatives to be helped)—

I hope you and Alan get reconciled—I hope your book of poems comes out—Have you tried the Doubleday's Poet Series—And England? I still feel it is best to do poems one's self quietly and beautifully —publishers do so little for it—it should be an objet de luxe— Couldn't the University do it—Then you'd have pleasure—no pain or frustration—Collect all the published ones—For instance do you know anyone with a beautiful writing? Done in handwriting then offset, bound as Japanese do, by sewing—

I would never be published today if I hadn't done it myself for years. Try.

Warm wishes to you and your wife.

Anaïs

. . .

[Madison]
Sunday, January 28, 1962

Dear Anaïs—

Here, finally, it [draft of his review of *Seduction of the Minotaur*] is. I hope you'll write me your reactions, correct mistakes, etc. I also hope you will, on the whole, approve. . . .

Incidentally, I must confess that I'm not altogether clear on the title. *Solar Barque* was beautifully explained, but *Seduction of the Minotaur* has to do with the labyrinth, of course, but is the beast's seduction the alternative of its being killed? If I understood it, I might have commented on it in the review.

While I was writing the piece last night, I kept thinking about a few things that have intermittently come to my mind. I know your wonderful and dreadful story *Birth,* and had wondered whether it is your own experience you recreate there. It would be almost inconceivable that anyone could write this who *hasn't* experienced it; though an artist's imagination is the most potent thing in the world. Still, I couldn't picture any *men* writing this, not even an obstetrician! Now in *S. of the M.* you refer repeatedly to Lillian's children. I don't think this means that you actually have—or had—other children, but it may. Did you? Do you? I always thought you didn't, but I know really so little about your life, apart from the outlines on the surface. You no doubt want it that way and you needn't answer my questions, needless to say, but I would be curious.

Am I right about different names for the same people in your books?

You said too you've corrected so many printing errors Swallow's printer had made to the proofs. They must indeed have been plentiful, for I am still finding some, and also some occasional passages that could bear revision in another printing. If you care, I can point them out. They are like tiny marks on the skin of a beautiful woman and they bother me. The use of the fragmentary and the imperfect which I mentioned notwithstanding. (A too wide mouth can be sorely tempting; a mole seldom is.) . . .

H. M. [Henry Miller] is living it up in Europe, it seems, after Eve left him (or he her?); he is now living, I hear, with a young widow in Hamburg whose poet-husband, a former Nazi, killed himself after the war. Is he forever young and potent??? Ageless? Or does he just think he is—or want others to think so? Eve, I heard, was quite bitter and disillusioned about him—in many respects. That at least is the story Jonathan Williams, a poet, told me when he was here. He is also (or mainly) a publisher and book designer—Jargon Books in North Carolina, but publishes only a very special clique of authors, Robert Creeley, Charles Olson, Ariel Corman, Irving Layton, etc. His books are quite strikingly done. He knows of Renate G[erhardt] because she was his girlfriend in the last months of the war and after, when he was stationed in Hamburg as a soldier. He knows about H. M., I don't think he has met you, I believe I asked him, knows your work, of course, and likes it.

Must close, work is piling up all around and on top of me. Hope all is well with you.

Affectionately,

Felix

. . .

[California]
February 4, 1962

Dear Felix:

First let me say when I asked you to write a review for library journals I only meant a *few lines* and had not meant you to take so much time and care over a fulsome review. Then I will say that I am grateful and fully appreciative for all the parts concerning the interpretation of the book, which are most accurate and understanding—I will certainly try to interest Shapiro for his review. When you focused on *Seduction* your résumé was perfect—I have a few details to discuss, minor ones. First a personal favor, I don't know what the critics' ethics are, but when a writer fictionalizes it is I think better for the critic even if he knows the personal sources of the roman à clef not to use such a knowledge. In this case as you know, mention of my life with Miller would do my life a great damage—and aside from this, it is not accurate—For it is not a portrait of Miller, it is not a portrait of my relationship and I am not Lillian—too I think it is delicate and may one day be disproved when you assert that these passages are no doubt lifted from Miss Nin's diary. For both our sakes, do you mind if we eliminate this?

I only object to an erroneous statement—All the rest are opinions, and these are *your* right. When you say I have introduced the same characters by different names is another error. Lillian does not bear the features of Sabina, she is a musician, rather masculine, violent, aggressive, not seductive, a Puritan, slowly softening and finding her femininity.

If you are thinking of characters in *Winter of Artifice* these were my first attempt to deal with a set of characters—they are in no way part of *Cities*—they were a preliminary sketch—like Proust's first version of *Remembrance*—a try-out. Once having found my direction I did a full portrait, and gave them new names. The "resemblances" are the kind of resemblances one finds in life, between similar types, and as soon as you go below the surface—I am sorry that an "overall organization and unification of the work" is felt by you because this is exactly what I have so often explained which is false in the novel. There is no such unity or organization in our life, it is a flow of impressions, a difference similar to the arrival of Debussy after Wagner, Bach or Beethoven etc.—Evidently you expect what others do, impressionism and abstraction to have the resolution or finality of a classical piece indicating end—Being a poet I thought you would have understood that I was being faithful only to moods, states of being—You see, this *is* the crux of why I have not, as you regret, received recognition. Because of this—and your saying it only adds to the study made in *Harvard Advocate* and many others . . .

Now all this is purely theoretical and I will never tamper with or ask you to change an "opinion," but personal references damaging to my life I will ask you to leave out. After I read this review I realized why you asked me about children. You certainly confused me with Lillian only because I was in Mexico! No, I have no children!

Having mentioned negative, let me say I liked your words on style: uses words the way a painter uses color and a composer tones, etc. a fine passage—When you write as a poet enjoying another poet (And by the way is it fair to compare a novel to a prose poem, and expect a novel to be as poetic as a short prose poem?) Being yourself a poet, I wonder why you could not throw overboard more easily than others the idea of a formal development of a novel? Or artificial unity?

Before I write to Shapiro will you allow me to remove references to Miller and Diary?

Yes, by the way, I do expect readers to have read the other books—why not? I have always made it clear that this was a roman fleuve—Nobody reads just one volume of Proust or Durrell? . . .

I know how busy you are and thank you again for giving this more time and care than I ever meant to ask for! What did you think of German magazine?

I would answer question about *Birth* story except that after your reference to Miller and Diary I fear your use of facts about my life! One writes fiction because one does not wish to publicize one's life. Unless a painter says it is a portrait it is dangerous to say this is so and so—Proust made composites and denied portraiture. Rightly.

What did you think of German magazine? If my letter alters any of your feelings and opinions let me know. As you know my motto is Realism is not Reality.

I would love to pay you a visit and give a reading but schedule is difficult just now, perhaps in the Spring. I'll be in N.Y. Feb. 24 to work on filming of *Under a Glass Bell* at New York University.

Thank you again

Anaïs

[Madison]
February 7, 1962

Dear Anaïs,

I am sorry to realize that you seem to be disappointed and on the whole displeased with my review. I felt that it was a very favorable review, despite small reservations and criticisms here and there. I didn't want to make it sound as a review written by a friend about the book of a personal friend; pure eulogies will be dismissed by readers as such, and not unjustly so.

Of course I will delete the personal reference to your association with Henry, since this seems to disturb you the most. I thought this was all an open secret, if a secret at all. It has come out in so many ways, his books, your books, articles about him and you, etc., that I felt free to make the remark I did. But by all means, if you feel it can damage your life or reputation, or cause whatever complications or harm, let's eliminate the reference. It really is not important in the context. I remember your objection of being mentioned in the Perlès volume,[3] but I thought it concerned the way the matter was handled there rather than the fact itself. However, you are the best and only judge on how much of your private life you want to reveal, and you, as everybody else have the right to your privacy against any invasions. My personal, as well as my critical ethics are embodied in that statement.

I'll send you a corrected version of the review—corrected also in regard to factual errors (whose possibility I admitted, saying "I have the impression"—not having the time to go carefully through your books to investigate the matter of names and persons); to make it possible for you to correct such errors was my purpose in sending you the carbon in the first place, and saying I would hold the original back until I heard from you. In fact, my whole aim in writing the review was to help you, if possible, and not to harm you; in accordance with that principle I am going to change also a few of the other things you object to. I *am* your friend, Anaïs, you really ought to know this by now, and an admirer of your art.

I *was* hurt, I admit, by your sentence, "I would answer question about *Birth* story except that after your reference to Miller and Diary I fear your use of facts about my life! One writes fiction because one does not want to publicize one's life." Well, well. I won't comment on the first sentence. But is the second sentence really true? Is that the only, or even the main, reason why one writes fiction? And isn't that, if so, an admission that fiction writing is a very autobiographical business for you? You also say, "Proust made composites and denied portraiture. Rightly." Of course, rightly. Please do re-read what I said in my review about composite pictures within an autobiographical frame.

Past bad experiences may have made you particularly sensitive and (unnecessarily so, as far as your artistry is concerned) vulnerable to any criticism. I was amazed and grieved about the signs of upset in your letter. You say two or three times that there is nothing of you in Lillian, you even say to me straight-on, "You certainly confused me with Lillian only because I was in Mexico!" If you think me that primitive, you certainly cannot consider me qualified at all to write a

Chapter 9: October 1961–June 1962

review about your books, only a booknote for the library journals at best, seeing that I am a librarian. (I am still willing to shelve the whole review and to write a 10 line booknote for the *Library Journal,* if you prefer—I mean that.) You even ask me twice, on the same page, what I thought about the German magazine. (Not much, to be frank, but that's another subject).

I am bringing this up only because those are signs of distress which I am sorry about. To cause you distress was about the farthest thing from my mind. Even my saying that you may have lifted something from your diary is due to a sentence of yours, in a letter to me, in answer to the first letter I ever wrote you, after having read the unex-purgated version of *Winter* which is kept in the vault at Northwest-ern. I quoted a marvelous passage to you, and you replied, "This was lifted verbatim from the diary." I made an—apparently erroneous—analogy here. (I still feel as strongly as ever about the merits of that unexpurgated version of your book. Your outlook on it may be col-ored by your later feelings about Miller, by your judgment that you were, stylistically or in outlook, too much under his influence then, or by the few four letter words that occur in it—and which are found today in countless books and even a number of magazines like *Ever-green Review.* Well, this, too, is merely my opinion, and really none of my business. Having associated yourself publicly, through your preface, with *Tropic of Cancer,* I personally can't imagine why any of those reasons should cause you qualms, but, again maybe it is a mat-ter of your association with him, per se, that embarrasses you today. You can't prevent people from thinking, even though they—and at least I—am only too happy to respect your wish to refrain from saying). . . .

I realize how you try, throughout your letter, to say something nice to me and stress your gratitude, but it never comes quite off. Nor do I want you to be grateful to me; I only said what I felt—both in the praise and the small reservations; I always admit the possibility of being wrong. . . .

And I do hope that what I wanted to be an act of friendship didn't spoil our friendship. That would be sadly ironical!

As ever,

Felix

P.S. The magazine—and thanks for sending it, even though I

wasn't too enthused with it—was sent from 2335 Hidalgo Avenue. . . . Can you be reached there too?

As for structure and organization—there is the anecdote of the actor who went on the stage drunk every night—except when he had to play a drunk. Then he had to be dead sober and to know what he was doing every moment, to give the impression of drunkenness and disorganization and flow and haphazardness. Organization is the core of art. The function of art is to make logos, order out of chaos. If you want to picture the unorganized, un-formed flow of life, you have to do it through order and organization, otherwise you must fail. To look casual, one has to be precise. Some women work for hours before a mirror to achieve that windblown look. That's art. The artist does the same with his words, his sentences, his poems, his novels, his colors and canvasses, his musical instrumentations. There is no stricter requirement than that of poets. The music of [Anton von] Webern, [Arnold] Schönberg, [Béla] Bartók, etc. is organized, even if it does not sound it—in order not to sound it. That's where the beat poets fail and even Ginsberg ascribes to some kind of prosody in his rhythms and supposedly breath-length lines. Your reaction that anybody who insists on organization and appears to miss it in your work is not a poet but a kind of pedantic unartistic Philistine, is as feminine (lovely so) as it is feeble. It misses the point. And why fight so hard to make a virtue out of one's fault? No writer is perfect. This is not your forte, but it's a flaw, nevertheless. There is organization also in your work, of course, or it wouldn't be art, but there is not enough, and occasionally it fails. If this is the reason for your difficulty to be accepted, and if so many people have pointed it out, why not consider the possibility that it might be true, and if you can, do something about it. And if you can't, at least face it as your Achilles' heel, and take comfort in the knowledge that other artists have other Achilles' heels and that you have so many plusses to compensate for that minus that you're superior to the bulk of them, even so!!??

Structured spontaneity, even the tossed-off must be prepared—especially the tossed-off. Improvisation succeeds only within a frame—even in jazz. After a theme has been planned, spontaneity can take it from there, in conversation and otherwise. Henry Miller has that organization and structure, even if it doesn't seem so. A Machiavellian, crafty man having, unlike Anaïs, the craft of his art, knowing every moment what he is about and what he is doing, calculating timing and effects. Anaïs, you said to me: "I can't play chess because because I can't plan ahead." Actually, the idea that "life is that way" unstructured and unformed, that is, is realism. The unkempt lair is realism. The woman who works before the mirror does what art does: create reality. Form makes reality out of realism.

[California]
[February 8, 1962; postmark]

Dear Felix:

   ... Would you mind if shortened version were published in Glendale newspaper? It would not prevent it appearing elsewhere—I have not heard Swallow's reaction yet—I hope you understood mine. What do you think of *Echo*?

   Anaïs

[California]
[February 9, 1962; approx.]

Dear Felix:

   A Glendale paper asked me to send in anything I wanted about the book but short, I made this selection and will wait for your approval before giving it to Eva Thompson. I hated to give up beautiful description of theme of the book Page 3 (on the moon and enumeration of characters beginning: "organization of the book is rather loose")—You did some fine poetic writing yourself when dealing descriptively with the book. What I felt I can better explain now after retyping section: there is a contradiction between response of the poet, and that of the critic, like two different men speaking, one enjoying, the other feeling grave responsibility of detecting weakness—when you write about style like an artist, and when you write like the rational man who demands directness and 'resolution'! If you think about your life I am sure you experience an impressionistic series of fragments, never an organized synthesis—A synthesis is only an ideal state, impossible to reach when you live by true unconscious—What do you think? Like Alban Berg in contrast to classic construction.

   A bientôt
   Anaïs

A Quarrel and a Break   173

[California]
February 10, 1962

Dear Felix:

We're both hypersensitive! I mentioned what I *admired* about your review, and what I felt to be *less* understanding, you mentioned what you admired and what you didn't! And then we try to persuade each other. . . .

I did not mean to hurt your feelings but to tease you when you asked me if I had children. *Birth* story is the one I told you was taken from the Diary. But I do have a horror of personal publicity. (I could not prevent my preface from being published, it was in public domain. Or I would have. My association with Miller has done me only harm). . . .

Dear Felix, I am harassed enough on every side (you seemed to be aware of this when you opened your review with my need of an introduction), ignored enough, and enough Achilles' heels have been hurled at me! I am over-saturated with misinterpretations. So please let us just be friends and forget literary discussions. In my case the negative statements have so far surpassed the positive that I felt the need of being championed. But that belongs to the Middle Ages. I needed to be defended!

Perhaps my second letter dissolved your feeling that I did not appreciate your review properly.

Anaïs

[Madison]
February 12, 1962

Dear Anaïs—

I can't say I'm too enthusiastic about newspaper reviews or about this condensation of my review—a kind of pearl fishing expedition— but if it helps you and it really doesn't militate against a magazine publication of the whole piece, all right. . . .

. . . One last word on "organization": Rudolf Kolisch, head of Pro Arte Quartet here, a Viennese and friend of mine, earliest fighter for Schönberg, Berg, Webern and others, and a personal friend of them, tells me that there is a very strict construction, structure, organization in all of these composers, different from the classical pattern, but actually a development of it rather than a break, and equally precise, only more complex. I was actually talking about an overall unification of your work as a whole, not just the organization of *Seduction*. And you do have organization, form, selectivity, inter-relation, structure and synthesis even in your series of fragments—and also in your sentences which are anything but "automatic writing," or else it wouldn't be art. The unconscious and subconscious may be the source and the beginning (Goethe's "mothers"), but then the conscious will of the artist has to take over and form the raw material. I am sure you do agree with this, at least I hope so. I don't believe in the artist's being only a tool for higher or lower forces, a kind of conveyor belt, with no formative influence on what it is he conveys. All right. So it's only a matter of degree, or of the type organization and structure. As I pointed out, even in order to give the impression of improvisation and spontaneity, you have to plan and work and arrange. Art is deliberate spontaneity. Even jazz exists within a frame, within a theme. Freedom can exert itself only within the boundaries of freedom. If you are really true to your motto that realism is not reality, you must ascribe to my theory. For to try to duplicate the impressionistic formlessness of life would be realism. Reality is the meaning behind the unordered. As Nietzsche called it, "die Sinngebung des Sinnlosen"— the giving sense to the senseless. The imitation of the senseless is, at best, reportage, a poor kind of photography, not art. Art, form, makes reality out of realism. And it does this by structuring, ordering, forming, synthesizing it. You can put a life story into a book, abbreviating it, finding its meaning, its interpretation, making it understandable. To duplicate the life story, it would have to take as long as the life itself, and would be chaotic.

I am sorry I sound dogmatic, or lecturing. But I feel dogmatic about this and I know you need no lecture on it, for you actually practice what you dispute doing. It's a matter of degree, perhaps of semantics. What gets my (non-existent) Irish up is when you resort to the defensive counter-attack of calling me a pedant, a rationalist, a Philistine, etc. (not expressly but implicitly) or saying I am a split personality, half poet, half "critic"; as if they couldn't form a synthesis (speaking of synthesis). Every artist has to be a critic, a self-critic. Self-criticism is part of the creative act. Woe to the artist who lacks it. To the degree he lacks it, to that degree he is not an artist. You did the same to me, when I complained to—and about—M. Fanchette, when he didn't report on my poems for 8 months. You wrote me then I wasn't a Bohemian, understanding of the ways of the artists in Paris, but just an old picayunish bourgeois, or something to that effect. Only after you yourself got fed up with Fanchette's irresponsibility, you called him impossible, sloppy, unreliable, etc. Enough. *Sapienti sat.*[4]

I enclose Swallow's reaction. Also a new version of the review. I'd like to try either Shapiro or the *Chicago Review*, whichever you think is best. Let me send the original; if you want to write in support, so much the better. I hope you like the revision. Upon the slight bit of criticism and reservation I'll have to insist. I don't want to write a pure fan's eulogy. We may have more letters crossing each other in the mail, but they'll even themselves out I believe, anticipating questions or assertions or replies. (Incidentally, I never called for a "resolution" or "finality" of ending, or "definite answer," etc. To me, as to you, there is no such thing in human affairs. At least, we as humans can't see the absolute. All I insist on is form, structure, an artistic will and attempt to convert *chaos* into *logos*) . . . .

One other thing that puzzles me re the now eliminated reference to Henry Miller. What about the publication of your diaries in that respect? Wouldn't that disclose what you say would be too damaging to you? It is true you told me once you want the diaries to be published after your death, to protect people still living who are mentioned in them. But only recently you wrote me that a Paris publisher wants to bring them out in French and that Fanchette wants to translate them, but that I, knowing him, could imagine how impossible this would be. But you seemed to indicate that otherwise you'd be quite willing to have them appear. And Henry wrote many years ago "let them be published, all of them, the whole damn thing" or some such phrase, remember? Are you ambivalent about this? . . .

All the best,

Felix

. . . Incidentally, I did not feel "the grave responsibility of detecting weaknesses." I was aware of those weaknesses all along. Do you, on your part, feel that there really are no weaknesses in your work? That all is strength and perfection? That every critic criticizing you—and most I assume won't first submit their ms. to you—is just misunderstanding and maligning you? Some may, but some may not.

Some criticism *could* be right and just. To realize that you seem to feel the opposite, is—frankly—somewhat disillusioning to me. Why are you *so* insecure? Vanity is insecurity.

[California]

[February 15, 1962; approx.]

Dear Felix:

We have gotten on a treadmill. If I said anything that hurt your feelings, I never meant to. I have never liked arguments. I thought I could make you understand certain things. Arguments are never creative. They are a great waste of energy. Even as a child, I left rooms where people argued. I will merely answer your factual questions.

When I mentioned publication of the Diary I forgot to add: plans are subject to a condition: they cannot be published until after the death of Hugo. French publisher has accepted condition. He is young, and can wait. I will not use your review in the Glendale newspaper, as it does not seem to please you to have it quoted.

I have never said my work had *no* weaknesses. I have said that American reviewers have been either silent or prejudiced, and that I wanted my friends (read history of writers, critics, friends in the time of surrealism) to put them straight. If this does not appeal to you, this role, I mean, you are in your right. I will try to get your review published as it is, your revised one.

Personal references to a writer's life are *always unethical.* Coming from strangers there is nothing I can do. Coming from friends, I have a right to object. It is as if I inserted in my criticism of Tennessee Williams the fact known to me that he is a homosexual. This to me is journalism, not criticism. At least wait until I am dead!

Form and organization are too big a subject for us to tackle. I do feel one's energy should go into creation, not trying to persuade others of what you believe. I have not implied anything about your being pedantic, a rationalist, a Philistine. These are *your* misinterpretations.

Please reread my letter. . . .

As for advising me to listen to my critics, dear Felix, no writing, no art would exist in the world if artists listened to critics! Critics are impotent to create. Some are very good, like some of the French critics.

Most of them are reactionary and static. They stand defending old forms. They make historically famous errors. The rare critics I respect are men who were objective and thorough. (Léon Pierre-Quint on Proust, for instance, or Roger Shattuck on Satie, Rousseau, and Apollinaire). Most of what passes for criticism in America particularly, is a personal reaction dressed up as criticism. The weaknesses in my work are in every work, one faculty developed at the expense of another. But it is not the critic who will help me develop, you can be sure of that. The people I most respect in the world, I had to work against *their* opinions, and twenty years later (one a painter, and the other Hugo), when they became, one a famous painter, and the other a first class poet of the film, they acknowledged that they had been wrong. I am sorry that you have to call vanity my efforts to make you understand. And keep your disillusion. We are all disillusioned. I am disillusioned in your understanding!

Anaïs

[Madison]
February 24, 1962

Dear Anaïs,

Treadmill and cul-de-sac, indeed. I hope we find our way out of it. . . .

When you reacted to my review by objecting (a) to my personal references and (b) to my few and mild reservations, you said in a following letter, "And then we try to persuade each other." Now you call the same thing "arguments," saying that even as a child you left the room where people argued. But my remarks on composition, our discussion of form, were not at all what I would call "arguments" and a waste of energy. There is a difference between discussing things, e.g. artistic principles, and quarrelling. I wasn't aware that we engaged in the latter.

Yes, we both have emotions and we showed them. I don't blame you for your temper, for I have one myself. But I didn't ever intend to hurt your feelings—or hurt you in any way—any more than you say, and I believe you, that you wanted to hurt me. On the contrary. The absurd thing is that if someone would just read your letters without having read my review, he would have to think that I panned hell out

Chapter 9: October 1961–June 1962

of your book. While in actuality I praised it very highly. I showed my (revised) review to some people here and the reaction invariably was, "I want to read that book." What else can you expect of a review than to have such an effect on its readers?

I did get angry when you charged me with looking for weaknesses, out of a critic's "grave responsibility." While it was the other way around: I just didn't want to gloss over completely all the weaknesses I was aware of, just because you are a friend of mine. I wanted to write an honest, though kind, review of a writer I very much admire and whose faults I have not failed to notice. I never, for instance, mentioned, even in our correspondence, the matter of characterization, of creating living blood and flesh persons, rather than abstractions who have something to say you want said, spokesmen in a scheme of things, delineations of various types of love and loneliness, as I said in the review, etc. This, too, is not one of your fortes, I feel; but I didn't point it out, first because I wanted to concentrate on the positive, second, because the creation of three-dimensional human beings, seen from the inside as well as the outside, is probably not even your intention. You are more interested in moods and colors, psychological insights beyond individual persons, fragments and fleeting impulses and sensations. All right, so I didn't speak about it. But then, in the face of this, your accusation (however mildly expressed) angered me.

When I spoke about disillusionment, I meant mainly your attitude of wanting to be "defended," as you say, and of defending yourself against any criticism. Whatever is not pure praise, it seemed, you rejected as "misunderstanding." The critics misunderstand you, and I, wherever I voiced a reservation or objection, misunderstood you, too. But this formula of "Praise is understanding, and criticism is misunderstanding" seems too simple a formula to me. You may say you didn't say this, or mean this; but that's, really, what your reaction implied. And *that* I found disillusioning. Perhaps I shouldn't have said so, for it did hurt your feelings. I am sorry. Your ending of the letter, "Keep your disillusion. We all are disillusioned. I am disillusioned in your understanding!" sounds both furious and sad. Could we possibly strike both our references from the record?

What you say about critics in general, is partly true, but greatly overstated, I feel. Too broad a generalization. There are good critics as well as bad ones. And the good ones have their function and have furthered, by their criticism, many an artist. Uncritical acceptance and adulation can be as bad, if not worse, for an artist than stringent criticism. It depends upon the artist's reaction.

Nor can I agree with your saying that "personal references to a writer's life are *always* unethical." A writer's life is one of the most potent factors in his work and any good criticism—the New Criticism notwithstanding—has to take all factors into account. [Charles] Baudelaire, [Paul] Verlaine, [Arthur] Rimbaud, [Marcel] Proust, [D. H.] Lawrence, etc, etc. cannot be truly understood without a knowledge of their lives, their neuroses, addictions, associations, phobias, idiosyncrasies, fear, hopes, etc. Nor can [Feodor] Dostoevsky or [Vincent] Van Gogh—or any artist of consequence, for that matter. Many made art of their very autobiographies—[Thomas] De Quincey; [Benvenuto] Cellini; Augustine; [Jean-Jacques] Rousseau; [André] Gide; Frank Harris (with lots of grains of salt); Henry Miller, after all; and you, yourself, in your diary. What is the use of writing a diary, and contemplating its publication, with whatever provisions, if it isn't the intention to make personal references to a writer's life? To make, it would seem obvious, the reader understand him and his work better, learn from his life. All biographies of great people are "personal references" to their lives, aren't they? And many appear— biographies, as well as autobiographies ([Conrad] Aiken, Margaret Anderson, thousands and thousands)—while the subject is still alive. So why sound so bitter and violent out of all proportion in saying to me (to me, of all people, who isn't writing a thesis on you, nor plans to write a biography of you, or even any contemplated future criticism of your work)—to say, "*At least wait until I am dead!*" You're not talking to *me* when you say that, Anaïs. No, I think the sentence, "Personal references to a writer's life are *always* unethical" is also a broad generalization, an over-statement, a half-truth at best; whether it applies to biography, memoirs, or criticism. The allusions of a gossip columnist or of pornographic trash rags like *Confidential* and *Whispers*, etc. are in a different category. These can, and should, be taken before the courts, and thus be put out of business; as they were. I believe my remark about your association with Miller was not quite in that category. And all you needed to have done to make me delete it, is to say quietly that you wished I did. To fly off the handle as you did, and jump all over me, and make remarks about "the use I am making of your life," the betrayal of your confidence, the unworthiness of learning about the story *Birth*, etc., etc.—all that stunned me in its uncalled-for violence. I assure you I didn't commit a crime, nor intended to do you harm, and would have, at the slightest hint, respected your wishes. I said what I did because I didn't consider it a secret at all nor anything you needed to be ashamed of. It was you who, for reasons far beyond my half-sentence, blew the thing up out of all proportions. Enough, no point in going on with that. (The fact, incidentally, that Tennessee Williams is a homosexual is not just known to you, either, it is also an open secret, if any, and probably one to which a serious study of his work might well refer; for it does shed light on many aspects of that work. It all depends how, in what spirit, for what purpose, with what intention and skill and tact and taste it is done. It *needn't* be journalism; it *can* be criticism.)

Well, where do we go from here? If I could meet you, person to person again, I trust we would be able to straighten out our ruffled feelings quickly and easily enough. This way, I can only hope we get out of this maze and on an even keel again. At least we know that both of us are saying to each other what we think instead of lying or beating around the bush. That, too, is reassuring in a relationship, isn't it? Particularly when there is no malice on either side, but (as far as I am concerned) respect and admiration for all the many admirable qualities. I have sent the (revised) ms. off to Shapiro, saying in an accompanying note that you told me you would write him about it. . . .

Will you smoke a peace pipe with me? And accept my hand stretched over the continent? I hope so.

Your *friend*,
Felix

[California]
May 15, 1962

Dear Felix:

Peace pipes are best smoked in silence! I do not wish to go back into painful discussions. I have done all I could to get your review printed in its entirety. *The Village Voice* had already given the book to Adam Margoshes. *Prairie Schooner* is publishing a critique by Oliver Evans. I sent it to *Between Worlds*. No answer yet. . . .

Time not words heals up troubles.

Anaïs

[Madison]
June 9, 1962

Dear Anaïs:

Thank you for your note. The reason I didn't write sooner is that I was waiting for a report from Robert Hatch, book review editor of *The Nation*. For I had never expected you to take over the job of the author of sending his work out, and thus had sent it myself, after querying various places. Hatch expressed interest and promised me a quick answer, but it took him from April 17 till yesterday to reply. I'll send you his letter if you want to see it. I don't want to do so without your asking for it, for it is critical of both of us. Nevertheless, he still expresses interest if I can make some of the revisions he requests, and comply with some of his suggestions. I don't think I want to do so, for several reasons. Time is one of them. I received another positive reply to my query and so want to try the magazine in question first before I make up my mind about *The Nation*. Please don't send the piece out any more, and in fact withdraw it from *Between Worlds* in the unlikely case that [Gilbert] Neimann wants it. If he does, I have to clear with the other people first who are considering the ms. or may by then have accepted it—one of them, that is. But Neimann stated in the first issue very unequivocally and indeed belligerently that he will not print any criticism whatsoever. So I don't believe he was a good choice for the review in the first place. Also, I made a few changes in the ms., so that the copy you have is obsolete.

Thank you for sending me the essay in *The Village Voice*. I am sure you liked what Mr. Margoshes had to say. I did so in part. But I don't want to disturb the silence of peace pipe smoking by commenting in detail.

I'll keep you posted on the fate of the review.

Sincerely,

Felix

[California]

[June 15, 1962; postmark]

Dear Felix—

No, don't bother to give me opinions of *Nation*. It is a political magazine, not a literary one—Positive criticism is appearing now, a long, real, profound study by Oliver Evans in *Prairie Schooner* in the Fall, 2 theses by students being printed. I think the end of shabby treatment is over—I could not take any more after 20 years of negativity—(contradicted every day by letters from people, who sustained the work).

Yes. Peace is best. I'm busy on a 7-hour [Antonin] Artaud program on FM, reading from [Henri] Michaux for FM station, talking at L.A. State College—and selling copy of diary to Kinsey Institute[5] where secrecy will be preserved as long as necessary. . . .

Hope you are well and working on your poetry—Why don't you try *City Lights* for publication?

Anaïs

10

November 1972–April 1976

RECONCILIATION AND

THE FINAL YEARS

IN NOVEMBER 1972, AFTER A SILENCE of ten years between the two writers, Anaïs Nin offers Felix Pollak an olive branch. In the intervening years, a great deal has changed in the lives of both writers. Nin has published four volumes of her Diary with great success and is working on volume 5. She has become a figure with an international reputation who draws packed halls wherever she lectures, a guru for a rising generation of feminists. Pollak has published two volumes of his poetry and has consolidated a reputation as a regional poet.

Further changes will ensue in the next five years. In 1974, Felix Pollak is forced to retire from his position as curator of rare books at Madison when he becomes legally blind. Nevertheless he continues to write, publishing four more volumes of poetry, including some deeply moving reflections on his own blindness (see Appendix B).

Anaïs Nin oversees the publication of volumes 5 and 6 of her Diary and receives numerous accolades: France's Prix Sévigné for the first two volumes of her Diary, honorary doctorates from Philadelphia College of Art and Dartmouth College, election to the National Institute of Arts and Letters, and selection by the *Los Angeles Times* as 1976 "Woman of the Year." Curiously, her letters to Pollak, which earlier were almost never dated, are now dated without fail. As a celebrity with a punishing schedule of appearances, she laments: "FAME IS WORK."

At the same time, Nin's health declines sharply. She loses her battle with cancer, her suffering increases, and her death comes finally as a release.

In this final section, the energy of the earlier letters is gone, but it is replaced by a glow of warm and wistful affection. These two romantics now long as much for who they were as for who they were unable to become. Felix Pollak's letter of consolation to Rupert Pole provides a fitting coda.

[California]
November 4, 1972

Dear Felix:

A long time ago we were friends. You now appear in Volume 5 and as always, I show what I write to the person I portray, in case there should be, unknown to me, any cause for distress. I suggest you take a red pencil and mark what you wish out. If too much is taken out, I withdraw the portrait but I know in your case it won't be because your letters were very beautiful and for years you sustained me by your understanding of the work. I have not yet reached the part where something intervened and interrupted the friendship but my memories are warm and friendly. I did not know where you were or I would have asked about you when I visited Madison, Wisconsin, and gave a lecture there.[1] I obtained your address from Richard Centing, librarian, who edits the newsletter.[2] As you probably know, my efforts were finally rewarded in full as soon as the diaries came out. Late, of course, so I do not have all the energy I would like to respond to the love and appreciation, but that is so often the case with writers. I hope you are well. I see your poems in magazines now and then. Please, when you have read these pages, return them to me signed by you and saying "O.K. *Lu et approuvé* [Read and approved]."

I send you and your wife my love, hoping for a renewal of the old friendship.

Anaïs

[California]
December 8, 1972

Dear Felix:

It was well worth while writing again to receive such a package of delights, the witty poems, as spirited as always, the intelligent and wise essay on pornography[3] (what nonsense the others wrote compared with you, specially Susan Sontag and her cerebrations. Bataille,* the best erotic writer she says, and I threw his book into the waste basket barely read, for its sheer grotesquerie and perversion). Your writing has not grown old, so you cannot either. Poor Henry [Miller] has not escaped, because of a limp and painful hip, he does not sleep well, and the drugs make him less alive, but he has good moments, as when we went to show him the documentary on me made by Robert Snyder, the same one who made the *Odyssey of Henry Miller*[4]. . . .

Naturally I don't feel only the young understand me, but they have in far greater quantity that their elders. At one time, when I knew you, I could count my believers on my fingers. Yes, I am glad to have received the love I gave. Just before Diary One was coming out I had surgery. If I had disappeared then I would have left persuaded I was a failure. Now I seem to have inspired thousands. In America it is mainly the life giving qualities. In France they read it as a work of art.

I am sending you the latest newsletter [*Under the Sign of Pisces*]. If it interests you I have some duplicates in New York which I can send you, not the complete collection.

Or any book you don't have. Just let me know.

I am getting ready to go to Fez, Morocco, on a magazine assignment so I cannot write in detail about the poems but I truly enjoyed them all.

So eat lots of vitamins and certain foods, and keep your youthfulness which is in the writing.

Anaïs

* Georges Bataille (1897–1962), French librarian, journal editor, and writer of essays, novels, and poetry, whose focus was on eroticism, mysticism, and the irrational.

[California]

April 2, 1973

Dear Felix,

How are your eyes? Can you help me with the date of the Evanston lecture from your diary? I don't have the exact date.

I'm working on Volume 5—will write you later when ordeal of lecture is over May 10.

Love,

Anaïs

[Madison]

April 9, 1973

Dear Anaïs,

Just a hasty note to answer your question. I don't have a diary, alas, but I keep things compulsively, and especially things connected with you. So I am glad that I can tell you that you were at Northwestern on Wednesday, May 25 and on Thursday, May 26th, 1955. The first evening you showed three prize-winning films of Ian Hugo's, the second was your talk on writing. . . .

My eyes are slightly better, but they keep changing, the vision that is, so I'm in need of a new pair of glasses again. Reading is still troublesome and tiring, and the world in general looks hazy, but somewhat lighter than before, due to new drops. One never knows the preciousness of one's possessions, particularly one's health, until one loses them. . . .

Felix

[California]
April 20, 1973

Dear Felix:

. . . And now the beautiful *Ginkgo*[5]—which really asserts your value as a valuable poet. I love to see the poems in one book, not scattered in magazines. They form a world. The poems now are like gems, so clear and transparent. They will answer many moods. The familiar humor is there. The sadness of "8½." The little poem "Vienna 1967" touched me particularly, of course. And "Vienna Revisited." The "Kandinsky" is perfect, enchanting. "Ginkgo," which gave the book its name, is beautiful. I will read them again. Delight in them. Send them (only while they visit me and sit in the garden) as a treat. The quality and inner meaning, the skill of language is the best I have read in years.

Love,
Anaïs

To think we could have seen each other in Madison. How could they not notify the library of my coming?

Is the library buying any ms. (H. Miller letters unpublished—a huge amount)?

[California]
[May, 1973; approx.]

Dear Felix,

Do you want me to mention the pseudonym you used for your poetry [Felix Anselm]? Would it be good for you or bad?

Anaïs

[Madison]
May 2, 1973

Dear Anaïs—

Thank you for your beautiful letter and all the heartwarming things you said about *Ginkgo*. Your praise makes me happy.

I just returned from my annual visit to Gloversville to help celebrate my mother's 87th birthday. Except for her eyes, she is in remarkable shape. The day before we arrived, my niece had a baby girl—lots of family and commotion, I was rather worn out upon our return. Am now swamped with mail and work. So just this note for now. As for mentioning my pen name, it's all right, I think it will be neither harmful or useful for me, it's just a fact, if not a very important one. I used it in Vienna where Pollak was a name as common as Smith (almost) and sounded less romantic to me, the aspiring writer and stage director than Anselm, which was inspired by my favorite author, Jakob Wassermann. I kept it in this country for a while to perpetuate my persona, my real I, and to bridge the gap from one world into another. But the dualism began to get burdensome and sound insincere, with all kinds of ulterior motives being insinuated by people —like a desire on my part to disguise my Jewishness, so I discarded the nom de plume with the publication of my first book *(Castle and Flaw)* in 1963 and have appeared with my real name ever since.

I hope you get the copies of the *Library Bulletin* from Northwestern, concerning your appearance there and our past purchases and collection activities of your work while I was there. We have no money here right now but I'll broach the question of Henry's letters—and possibly your own ms., if available and not promised to Northwestern—at the end of June, when our new budget begins. I see black about this, the funds at a state university being what they are—but it's worth a try. Perhaps you can tell me in the meantime how many letters, etc., are involved, and at what price, if you have any idea. More soon. Again—thank you.

Love,

Felix

My eyes are still cloudy and far from satisfactory, sorry to say.

[California]
June 18, 1974

Dear Felix:

You must forgive me. Because I did not want to answer your letter hastily, I carried it with me waiting for a peaceful moment. I took it to N.Y. I wanted to acknowledge all the news, the praise you received, your life's work—and the moment never came. Because of publication of Vol. 5, I was submerged in interviews, by visitors, by correspondence and public appearances. You cannot imagine the pressures, the needs and demands of friends, 3 prefaces to write in one week, plans for an assignment to visit and write about Bali in August, work with my editor on a supplement of photographs. Work. FAME IS WORK. I felt very badly when I returned to Los Angeles and in a carton one yard wide and one yard deep of mail and books, your wistful letter. Of course you would not offend me. Of course I will sign your book. My unlisted secret phone is 213 665 5017. I disagree. Your poetry will remain and nourish others. Think of a world without writers! Think what writers, poets meant to us! We do learn from others' lives. You are receiving appreciation. I do understand that for you to lose eyesight is a form of death but even that can be transcended—The poet remains.

    Love,
    Anaïs

[Madison]
July 9, 1974

Dear Anaïs,

Thank you so very much for the lovely and generous inscription, and your letter.[6] And for your phone number—a sign of trust which I will not misuse.

Fame must be both sweet and bitter. You have wanted it and worked for it all your life, and I am happy for you that it came to you in your lifetime, not, as in so many instances, when it is too late for the artist. At the same time, what a burden to face those boxes of letters, and answer to all the tuggings and urgings and pullings and demands to give, give, give. Especially for one as kind and conscientious as you, who is determined to answer everybody, I imagine, and slight nobody, and be personal to all, the deserving as well as the leeches who are out to suck your blood and sap your strength. And do you have that much strength? I suppose you have more of it than your seeming fragility would indicate—you have proven that in your life, in your perseverance, in your faith in yourself and your truths. Still, when it comes to the chores, the trivia, the small talk, the required empty gestures, the meaningless parties, like the one Wally Douglas gave after your Evanston performance—that must be wearing. I, far from famous, cannot cope with my own correspondence, as it is, quite apart from the misery and tragedy of my eyes (yes, a kind of death), and I sometimes think back with nostalgia to the time when we both still had time for long letter conversations. I still, occasionally, write letters of 10 or more pages, but rarely. So, for today, only this note of thanks. I'm sending you by separate mail the current issue (a women's issue) of *Arts in Society* whose poetry editor I am. I hope you like the poems I picked, and some other things in the issue.

Stay well and take care.

Much love,

Felix

I retired the end of June (big party with flattering speeches and gifts), but am still finishing an exhibit of significant 20th Century English and American (stretching the term) authors. You are, of course, included in a prominent spot!

Excellent essay by [Robert] Kirsch.* And *congratulations on your honorary Doctorate!*

*Robert Kirsch (1923–1980) was book review editor of the *Los Angeles Times*.

[California]

January 4, 1974 [*sic*—properly 1975]

Dear Felix:

What a revolting story.* One forgets that there are such narrow-minded people in the world. Strange country, swinging between crime and puritanism—perhaps crime as a consequence of withered hearts.

I hope the fracas will call attention to your poetry—sometimes evil accidentally does good.

I hope 1975 will be kind to your eyes, will bring you full appreciation of your work in increased demonstrations.

I send you and your wife affection and heartfelt wishes for whatever *you* want.

Anaïs

*The letter in which he relates this story, apparently concerning an incident of censorship involving his poetry, is missing from the record.[7]

[Vienna?]
Tuesday, September 2, 1975

Vienna, not since 1967. Still (again) beautiful—as far as I can see (not far). Would you consider living in Paris again? Rupert? You're like a cat (or a snake) soaking up the heat.

Does Henry still live with his young Japanese wife? Hard to picture him incapacitated.

Felix

[California]
September 9, 1975

Dear Felix:

What moving poems you fashion out of your sadness.[8] Beautiful, wistful poems of deep feeling. You have not lost your gift. What a pair we are. I have been fighting cancer for 6 months. May be well in August. I will read your poems to my students.

Love,

Anaïs

[California]
September 16, 1975

Dear Felix:

It is beautiful to see how you continue to write marvelous poetry in spite of your handicap and I know how much courage that takes. . . .

Please give my warmest greetings to Sara, and believe me your most faithful fan,

Anaïs

Felix Pollak
3907 Winnemac Avenue
Madison, Wis. 53711
March 16, 1976

Dear Anaïs,

I was so glad to hear your voice a little while ago! It was very good of you to call to alleviate my worry, though I am very sorry to have my fear that you're in the hospital again, confirmed. It is terrible that you are so ill. At least not another operation! You must have been in the hospital for close to two weeks—but it is good to hear that you will be back home in another two, hopefully much improved. I do hope your doctors are optimistic and you are not too depressed.

You sound very brave and uncomplaining, and it doesn't do much good to complain, that is true, but I myself am getting a little impatient with the Anglo-Saxon virtue of putting up a front and the social requirement that one "keep smiling" in the face of great adversity and grief. I don't mean *you*, who surely could never be accused of Anglo-Saxon virtues, but I, who doesn't have the WASP ethics either, am myself rebelling against the expectation of pretending that all is well when it isn't, just to live up to the expectation that one will not, under any circumstances, disturb the conventions and comforts of one's neighbors who refuse to acknowledge tragedy (except on TV, where it isn't real and does not involve *them*). I attended a funeral recently and was appalled by the sterility and propriety (so-called) of it all; I almost yearned for the oriental grief-women, keening women, wailing women, *Klageweiber*, lamenting, singing, family members throwing themselves across a coffin, or the emotional choruses of Greek tragedy. Those things can be repulsive, but almost anything, I felt, would be preferable to that fake "dignity" which, at bottom, probably bespoke an inability of feeling anything at all. I know that silent and private grief can go deeper than outward displays but I believe this civilization has been emotionally emasculated and made afraid to acknowledge the basic things that are common to our humanity. We seem terrified by the stigma and label of "self-pity," afraid to let out an elemental howl of pain and protest. I have only yesterday heard a poet inveigh against "daydreaming" and "self-pity" with which he charged not only Sylvia Plath and Anne Sexton and John Berryman, but even Dylan Thomas, who had written, "Do not go gentle into that good night . . ." Yet the same man (Robert Bly) praised Allen Ginsberg, who, after all, had written a poem called "Howl" and a poem full of protest and self-pity, called "Kaddish." There is, it's true, self-pity and self-pity, and one brand of it *can* be egotistical and tiresome and repulsive—the kind that assumes misfortune befalls only the complainer, that no one's misfortune is and ever has been as unique and grievous and *unfair* as his, and who keeps searching for reasons why the bad thing has happened to *him*, of all people. But the existential self-pity that includes all living creatures, that *knows* about la condition humaine, that does not *expect* lasting happiness and *yet* experiences pain and helplessness and the senselessness of it all deeply and unflinchingly, is another thing again. And the attempt to look the other way, trivialize it all, and pretend forever to "feel fine" is as distasteful to me, as it is common. Among friends, at least, one should be open and honest, and cry and rage if one feels like it. I've done this in my poems about my eyes, addressed to no one in particular, to the anonymous reader, and if I succeeded to make art out of a personal and private affliction, to give it a sort of universal validity, I am not ashamed of it and don't care if someone calls it "self-pity," as is undoubtedly the case in some quarters. My friends know better. I firmly believe that the inability to feel self-pity precludes any feeling of pity for anyone else, man or beast, and is paramount with being inhuman. Pity, like love, is a basic *human* emotion, almost by definition. The same is true for love: if one cannot love himself, he cannot love anyone else either. (I find it cumbersome to say "he/she all the time; when I use "he" I use it as a generic term that includes both sexes, needless (?) to say.)

I know that you have stressed many of these things and outlooks in your books and that they are akin also to *your* basic philosophy of life. I hope you will know and trust me enough to feel free to speak unguardedly with me, with no brave mask needed. Bravery, which I *know* you have in the face of your affliction, can also consist in the willingness to discard the mask of bravery.

I will call you the end of the month. I was so startled to hear you suddenly on the phone that I didn't say, or ask, most of the things I really should have said and asked. For example, I didn't even ask how Joaquín is? Well, I hope. Or if he is staying with you as long as you are in the hospital. Please give him my best regards. I hope he is well. I also wanted to ask you whether you have chemo-therapy or radiation treatments. I know of two cases where they were very successful. And I meant to ask when the 6th volume will be out—I believe you mentioned May the last time we talked. I look forward to it, and so must you. That is probably the best therapy for you—for any artist. I wonder if you can work, or at least read, in the hospital—hard to do with intravenous feeding gear in one's arm. I do hope everything possible is done to alleviate the "little" pain you mentioned. I met Diane Wakoski,* and we talked about you. She is in Eastern Europe now, said she would call you before she left. Wonder if she did.

Anaïs, concerned as I am, your call has eased some of my distress — it was most thoughtful of you, utterly in style. And most of what you said on the phone was about *me*, not *you*, also most characteristic. I wish now I had asked you which hospital you're in. I have my best ideas afterwards, always. If I can send you a book or a tape, or can do anything at all, please *don't hesitate* to tell me. It would be a pleasure for me to do anything that may help or please or comfort you. Your voice sounded frail, I hope you're not too exhausted and run down and get enough sleep. Hard to do in a hospital, I know. As someone remarked, "hospitals are no places for sick people." I hope and trust the time until you can go back to your home will be short and not too difficult, and improvement will take place and continue. Sara, too, sends her very best wishes.

Your friend,

Felix [handwritten addendum] who personally lacks the wisdom (?) of getting resigned and reconciled to the indignity of getting old and ill.

Wonder how Henry is and if you hear from him. He, in contrast to you, is the egotist par excellence — Wonder if Djuna Barnes is still alive.** Perhaps the Library knows.

Those times in Paris — and you forever young . . . it is as if I had been there. I can't get away from those visions . . . all one ever dreams about. It should be enough for one life, but *is* it??

*Diane Wakoski (b. 1937), Polish-American poet who published a "Tribute to Anaïs Nin" in the Jan.–Feb. 1973 issue of the *American Poetry Review.*
**Djuna Barnes (1892–1982), avant-garde American writer well known in Parisian literary circles in the 1920s and '30s. Pollak visited her in New York City early in January 1957; see his letter of January 8, 1957.

Felix Pollak
3907 Winnemac Ave
Madison, Wis. 53711
April 25, 1976

Dear Anaïs,

I am near Albany, N.Y., visiting my mother. She will be 90 tomorrow.

I am sorry you never called back. I must conclude from that, and from the few words you said on the phone (I had difficulty making them out) that my letter must have distressed and upset you. It seems needless for me to tell you that such was the farthest thing from my mind. I was hoping it would have just the opposite effect. To think that the reason for your silence is due to your state of health and that you are having a difficult time (Rupert intimated problems since your return from the hospital), would be much worse, of course. I would be sad to think that you don't want to talk with me, but I would be infinitely sadder to think that you *can't.*

In any case, I hope very much for your improvement and recovery. Please give my best regards to Rupert.

As always,

Felix

[HANDWRITTEN ADDENDUM]

In any case, I find it difficult to write conventional cliché-ridden, say-nothing letters.

I was encouraged by Rupert's report of your weight gain in the hospital. Also, congratulations on the Woman of the Year Award by the *L.A. Times!*

[California]
April 30, 1976

Dear Felix:

I do not understand what happened with the telephone. Your letter did not disturb me. Did I promise to call back and didn't? If so, I must tell you that the painkillers, opium, and other drugs they give me have affected my memory. The only thing I can imagine is forgetting, which causes me much distress. You may have called me when I had taken sleeping pills and painkillers and was not very clear.

I love you as much as ever so please don't fret. I spend so much on my illness (a nurse has to come every day) that I sometimes hesitate to telephone as much as I would like to.

Anaïs

Rupert reminded me of what happened. When you phoned me the nurse was there changing the bag of the fistula which makes my life miserable (a hole in the stomach). I talked and then the pain was too much so I said: I will call you back.

I was given a painkiller and I fell asleep. My memory is bad these days. I simply forgot I said I would call you back.

Felix Pollak
3907 Winnemac Avenue
Madison, Wis. 53711
January 29, 1977

Dear Rupert,

I heard the terrible news only belatedly, after returning from a trip to a small town in New York State, where my mother and brother live. After that, I was too shaken to write.

I knew things had gotten very bad when I couldn't talk to Anaïs the last time I called and when you even had to cut our conversation short, remember?, saying there was "a crisis" right then. I asked myself then, why anyone should have to suffer that way, particularly one as sensitive and exquisite and aesthetically conscious of her body as Anaïs. But it was a question not to be asked out loud, it seems, with no practical answer, and certainly with no cosmic answer. We are still in the Middle Ages, where we can be humane only to animals. Sigmund Freud, at least, was helped across — but how many have such courageous friends? In any case, while the thought, "she is dying" sent shivers through me after I had hung up the phone, I still couldn't quite believe it — as perhaps she and you didn't quite either — and I did not expect the imminence of it, even though I half wished it, for her sake. And when Sara told me upon my return and showed me the brief notice in our local paper, it hit me badly, nevertheless. Need I do anything as formal as express condolences? Hardly. It is my loss too—and the loss of many. I saw from the *New York Times* clipping that Ian Hugo is still alive. Has Anaïs been in touch with him lately?

There are of course questions in my mind. Was there a funeral, or was Anaïs cremated? How much was she able to do on her last projected volume? What will you do?—remain in the house?

If there is one comfort at all—apart from the fact that she is released from pain now—it is that she really completed her life's work and at the end, for quite a few years, lived to see herself attain the stature and recognition in literature which she had been striving for for so long and of which she had already begun to despair. And most gratifying must have been her knowledge in facing death—and I must assume that she must have been aware of it to some degree and at some times, no matter how optimistically and fervently she clung to life—that it was her very *life* that was extraordinary enough and full enough to enthrall tens or hundreds of thousands and make her famous. In that sense, she survives and will continue to live on for a long time, and that she must have known and drawn comfort and sustenance from. How many people have *lived* enough, have lived so much that their life's story will remain after they're gone? That is a cause for envy. The hardest thing about dying, I imagine, must be the feeling that one hasn't lived enough, and the easiest death must be with the feeling, "I've had my fill", even if that is not identical with "enough." Anaïs was among the few who had a right to feel that way. Henry Miller, Artur Rubinstein, [Pablo] Picasso, [Pablo] Casals, a few others, very few, come to mind who could say, or could have said, the same.

I am terribly sad. But I am happy I once met Anaïs and became her friend.

I would be pleased if you would write me a few lines, Rupert.

Cordially,

Felix

. . .

Appendices

Notes

Index

APPENDIX A

Samples of Handwritten Letters
by Anaïs Nin and Felix Pollak

Dear Felix: I was about to write you at length about Fromm when this powerful current I call living carried me far into urgent activities: consoling Hugo for the death of his mother, taking care of my brother Joaquin another orphan — for 10 days, enter Tammy Ruth Witt Diamant — the teacher of English and manager of Poetry Center at San Francisco I wrote you about — who is alone etc... Five weeks passed. Now I am at Sierra Madre again, my first hour of leisure. Did I express my delight that a poem of yours is being published?

The most important question now is that I remember you said you and Tara would spend your vacation

Excerpt from letter of Anaïs Nin, September 26, 1955
(Courtesy of the Department of Special Collections, General Library System, University of Wisconsin-Madison)

Appendix A

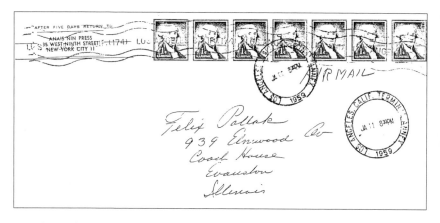

Envelope addressed by Anaïs Nin to Felix Pollak, January 11, 1959
*(Courtesy of the Department of Special Collections, General Library
System, University of Wisconsin-Madison)*

Samples of Handwritten Letters

January 12, 1956

Dear Annis — I am sure your intuition is seldom wrong, and it isn't in my case. But these things are awfully hard to discuss in letters. It is not a matter of candidness — I feel I could be utterly truthful and open with you, without reservations and inhibitions, but it is almost impossible to analyze one's inner life, and the way it is connected to external circumstances and to other persons and their lives and backgrounds, short of writing a book — and you're the last I have to tell that to. You have written — you are writing — books (maybe one book, all together) on just that theme. Only, to make it literature, it has to be taken out of the realm of the private (while still remaining personal) — and what you're asking me to talk about is private, involved, requiring a psychoanalyst's couch rather than letter paper. (Notwithstanding the fact that you, I realize, could be an ideal analyst for me — except for the acute danger of personal involvement ((as far as I am concerned!)) and added complications rather than their dissolvement; though sometimes added complications are solutions, are may be just what the doctor ordered"....) And so one faces two dangers: trying to tell too much — which, in a letter, would still be too little, even though it might become a monstrously long one — or to be glib and surface-skimming, which is really to evade the issues. Added to this is the matter of clarity (difficult to attain,

Excerpt from letter of Felix Pollak, January 12, 1956

(Courtesy of the Department of Special Collections, University Research Library, University of California at Los Angeles)

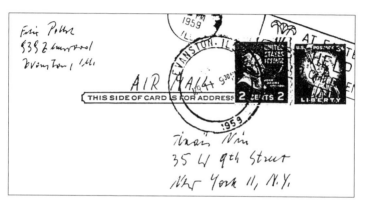

Postcard addressed by Felix Pollak to Anaïs Nin, March 11, 1959
(*Courtesy of the Department of Special Collections, University Research
Library, University of California at Los Angeles*)

APPENDIX B

Poems by Felix Pollak

A Living

From the time we go to school
to the time we go to the grave
we buy our tomorrows
with our todays.

We purchase time on time
with time for money
we trade our life
for our living,
we barter ends
for means
we must not live, so that we may
exist.

Nor do we die. Our ending
interferes not with any end pursued.
When we run out . . .
when we run out of the small currency of hours,
a small change occurs: we don't meet death

(not what is called the majesty of death, its
bitterness, its
darkness, its
release
—for meeting Death would be
—at last—
Life's birth . . . !)

no. We just cease making
what we have been making
and what is all we know to make

—a living.

[Handwritten Dedication: "For Anaïs from Felix"]
[Mailed to Anaïs Nin on April 14, 1955; *Inferno,* no. 11 (1955): 24.]

A Passing Visit

When you arrived the key
abruptly changed and I reappeared
—a chord, a theme, a melody,
half hoped half feared
forgotten. When I tried to unlock
the familiar door, the key changed, wouldn't fit.
Of course we recognized the symbol though not admitting
our shock. We joked
about it—but we knew the key had changed.
Then the brief interlude—looking too old
for feeling too young, all doors unhinged,
the trembling ecstasy of seeing the mold
breaking . . . and now feeling it slowly closing I again,
                                        since you left.
Will I be seized again and sound
in the old clef?
Will my text fade again, my refound
script again be lost? Only a hyphen
now between you and me:
two words—separated or linked?—waiting for the key
that would decipher them . . .

[Handwritten dedication: "For Anaïs from Felix. Evanston, June 1955"]
[Unpublished. Mailed to Anaïs Nin on June 3, 1955]

What It Always Comes Down To

Whether you're in the center
or on the periphery,
ride the subway
or the metro,
live in a via
or an avenue
—what it always comes down to is
a bed,
a pattern of light on the wall,
a fragment of sky, blocked
by a roof, crossed
by a bird, toned
by the hours
. . . and the spaciousness of your heart

the hunger
for being elsewhere
from where.

[Mailed to Anaïs Nin, January, 1956]
[*The Castle and the Flaw*, 1]

Think of the Planes Flying

— For William Carlos Williams

Think of the planes flying
into the morning sun
while I was my face
in the bathroom sink

Think of the ships sailing
across the trembling noon
while I eat my lunch
at the cafeteria counter

Think of the trains climbing
toward the first stars
while I help my wife
with the dinner dishes

Feel this summer-evening hour filled with
— what regret?
— what promise?
— what longing?
— what loss?

Is this why houses have windows . . . ?

[*The Castle and the Flaw*, 29]

Poems by Felix Pollak

Vienna Revisited

Here I am Antaeus, drawing life
from cobblestones: moon, roof, and leaves
cease being tentative, the air is feminine,
again a big clock shines, chimes the right time.

Yet: these streets grew fear: flags waved like fists
from windows; doors lurked—black caves
to death: hate occupied the benches in the park:
the cobblestones were rows of murderous stares.

Ghosts, misty shapes of blood, charge me with living:
to walk amidst the dead is guilt: am I worth having
what they lost? The wind blows frozen cries. My shadow stalks,
shrinking, across the obsolete stage.

And yet again: this afternoon in the garden
a tree still bore a code carved by an ardent
knife—a rune I could not read. I saw the slope
down which the ball had rolled, where it got lost.

And I returned the exiled pebble to the pond
in which the swans still swam.

[*The Castle and the Flaw,* 4]

Appendix B

Vienna 1967

Though my
roots are
cut off
here, they
hurt like
an old
scar when
it rains.

[*Ginkgo*, 50]

Speaking: The Hero

I did not want to go.
They inducted me.

I did not want to die.
They called me yellow.

I tried to run away.
They courtmartialed me.

I did not shoot.
They said I had no guts.

They ordered the attack.
A shrapnel tore my guts.

I cried in pain.
They carried me to safety.

In safety I died.
They blew taps over me.

They crossed out my name
and buried me under a cross.

They made a speech in my hometown.
I was unable to call them liars.

They said I gave my life.
I had struggled to keep it.

They said I set an example.
I had tried to run.

They said they were proud of me.
I had been ashamed of them.

They said my mother should also be proud.
My mother cried.

I wanted to live.
They called me a coward.

I died a coward.
They call me a hero.

[*Ginkgo*, 54–55]

Galileo

*Is it not ironic that I, who expanded the universe a thousandfold,
am now reduced to the dimensions of my own body?*
— Galilei Galileo, upon becoming blind

Here are my fingers, my arms, my knees.
Here is my face. These empty caverns
are my eyes. I trace the throbbing worm
across my temple. I touch my useless sex.
I listen to the garbled murmurs
of my heart. These monotonous explorations
yield the definition of my prison
My prison is smaller than my jail.

Beyond my body is the world. I thought
I had memorized it, but I am beginning
to forget. My friends (who may not visit
me anymore) used to say the world is in
my skull. Perhaps they're right. It would
explain why—though I'm not afraid
to die—the world in me dreads
to go under.

The dark slits in my face have seen
the stars, the moving planets and
the immobile sun. There are unseen stars
above the stars I saw. The sky leads
into skies that never heard of heaven.
Even the hell beneath circles around the sun,
pointing sometimes north and sometimes south.
This makes me laugh. Poor devil!

I shall recant my recantations yet, before
I die. When I'll be half across. Meanwhile
there is hot food, cool drink, the comfort
of the bed, the pail. How quickly one reverts
to animal! My universe now is a windowless

and doorless room, no breeze, no flickering
of candles. I need not close my eyes
to have it dark.

Here is my blotchy skin, my grizzled hair, my
straggly beard. Hairs are growing from
my nostrils and my ears. I have become a
prune, shrunk tight around its pit. I'm cold.
I will crawl back into my bed. Lord, how
much longer this rehash of yesterdays?
Here is my stomach and here is my arse.
Each day I'm bending closer to my shadow.

My daydreams won't let me sleep, I dream
of gliding on a moonbeam into space, lost
on the the Milky Way to even the strongest
telescope I built—my eyes—wide open
and filled with light—watching the clumsy
earth in its fixed arc around the sun, my ears
hearing the music of the spheres pierced
by my shout of triumph.

And yet it moves!

[*Tunnel Visions*, 4–5]

APPENDIX C

Felix Pollak's Introduction
of Anaïs Nin

EVANSTON, MAY 25, 1955

THERE ARE FEW THINGS I would rather do than to introduce Anaïs Nin. I've known and admired her work for many years, and when I say that it is a pleasure and a privilege to welcome her here, then this is not a stock phrase—I mean it!

You've heard, I'm sure, introducers begin by saying that so-and-so does not need an introduction, whereupon they invariably proceed to introduce him. With Anaïs Nin this is different—she needs an introduction. That this is so, is still so, after she has published more than a dozen books, is, I'm afraid, something of an indictment of our thoroughly commercialized practices of book publishing, book reviewing, book selling, and the standardized tastes of a reading public that is accustomed to letting others choose their books for them, evaluate, abridge, digest, and interpret their books for them and send them as book club selections into their homes, wrapped in cellophane, every first of the month. Such a system has, of course, manifold reasons and ramifications going deep into our whole social, political, and economic structure—ramifications too complex and vague to discuss here. But it stands to reason that such a system is not prone to bring to the fore authors who go their own ways, off the public highways (or low-ways). Anaïs Nin is such a writer. Which is only another way of saying that she has only herself to blame. That is what the publishers tell her. If she wants to be read and make money writing and get up to the summit of achievement where she can step out on a lecture platform and hear her introducer say, "Miss Nin, as you all know, needs no introduction, Metro Goldwyn Meyer has just bought her latest novel for $500,000"—if she wants that, the publishers tell her, why, then she has to write what the public wants, which, say the publishers, is the same that they, the publishers, want. But judging from the books Anaïs Nin keeps on writing, that is *not* what she wants. Judging from the books she keeps on writing, she is a very stubborn person. In fact, the suspicion arises that she considers writing an art and not a business. And so, of course, she needs an introduction.

To be sure, there are *degrees* of stubbornness and intransigence. Many writers may not be willing to re-write their whole book, but they have no scruples about re-writing a few chapters, changing a few characters, avoiding certain subject matters, observing certain taboos, etc. When Anaïs Nin encountered these suggestions, she did something very few writers have, to my knowledge, ever done: she borrowed enough money to buy a small foot-powered printing press, learned how to set type and to print, and began to print her books herself. Then she bound them herself, sent copies to friends and reviewers, and distributed the rest to bookstores in New York, carrying them there and leaving them on consignment. Now this sounds very interesting and romantic in retrospect, but you will agree that it is the hard way of being a writer. Anyone with a little imagination must shudder to think of the loneliness this must entail, the disappointments and abuse that must follow in the wake of such a procedure, the inevitable heartbreaks, the bitterness, the self-deprivations. And anyone with some imagination must be awed by the courage and strength and belief in oneself and in what one is doing, that must be at the core of such decisions—a will power and inner strength and a driven-ness not apparent in all of Miss Nin's charm and gentleness and gentility. That it did not end in abysmal failure and despair, that it all was actually pulled off and came to something, will be very ob-

　　　　　　　　　　　　　　Appendix C

vious to anybody who reads Anaïs Nin's books, whether he likes them or not. For there is something here which cannot be ignored, which one has to react to, either positively or negatively, and sometimes both simultaneously. I'm trying not to use big words, but to me this comes as close to a definition of greatness as any criterion I know. Even reviewers noticed that eventually, particularly good reviewers, like Edmund Wilson, who called her "a very good artist, as perhaps none of the literary surrealists is," and Rebecca West who is more than a professional reviewer anyway, and who spoke of Anaïs Nin's "real and unmistakable genius," or Paul Rosenfeld who ranked her musical and yet very precise prose with the "most admirable" of contemporary writing. To me, her feeling for words, their various simultaneous levels of meaning as well as their sound and rhythm in a sentence, is one of the most exquisite features of her art.

I have mentioned Anaïs Nin's intransigence and her refusal to compromise and conform to the standards and demands of the market. But in giving credit to her artistic integrity, it is possible that the choice I intimated was misleading. For it is possible, indeed probable, that the choice for Anaïs Nin has never really been to write either the way she wanted to, or the way the publishers wanted her to—to write either so, or so; but her choice, I am sure, was really only to write the way she *had* to write—or not to write at all. For Anaïs Nin must write the way she does, simply because she is the way she is. Simply because she is genuine. And that is the rarest quality of all. The non-personality has always more choices than the personality, the merely skillful and versatile and clever. The frauds and the phonies can please everybody and be and do thisaway and thataway; those whom you can recognize by their style without their signature—they experience forever anew Luther's "Here I stand, God help me, I cannot do otherwise." Their choice is only to be or not to be, to do or not to do, never to be or do one way or another. Which , of course, makes their choice not easier, but harder.

The world of Anaïs Nin's books, in consequence, is not a wide world—horizontally. Her horizons, if one can express it that way, are not horizontal but vertical horizons, her world expands into the depths rather than in width. And so, into depth rather than width will the horizons of her readers be enlarged. There are no social problems here, no political, economic, ideological issues. Her domain is the domain of psychology, of introspection, the eternal search for the self—or the selves that compose the self. And particularly in the psychology of women she is unexcelled—

The whole subject of sex in Anaïs Nin's books is of basic importance for an understanding of her underlying philosophy of life. S-E-X in this country is the trademark of the number one seller; the advertising industry, the movies, the pocket book designers, the newspapers, radio and TV—they all live on the promotion of sex, just as the censors of advertising, of pocket book covers, of newspapers, radio, movies and TV, all the various leagues of decency and guardians of public and private morality live on the denouncement of sex and sin, which they consider synonymous. Now, what they all have in common is that they isolate sex as something in itself, something separate and apart from other human phenomena and aspects of life; they put it into a show case and make it sensational. Anaïs Nin's books display a quite different attitude. In them sex is an all-pervading, ever-present force, an unceasing quality rather than an intermittent activity, an essence that manifests itself in the most varied forms and appearances. This seems closer to the European concept, for in Europe sex is something less headline-making and more taken for granted. (Maybe a few hundred years more practice—I wouldn't know.)

In this country, when a girl meets a boy, one can always sense how she is wondering whether his intentions are honorable or dishonorable. In Europe she *knows* that his intentions are dishonorable—so she's prepared (and not necessarily for defense either)! Anaïs Nin, in other words, spurns the thinking in dualisms and dichotomies, in Manichean antagonisms of flesh and spirit, love and sex, body and soul, pure emotions and impure emotions, and all the other dogmas of those who labor under the Puritan strain. She refuses, if I understand her correctly, to create or continue the artificial cleavages and contrasts, to split natural wholes into civilized halves; on the contrary, she is striving to unite again what scholastic and rationalistic thinking has for centuries torn apart—to man's misery. She would re-unite instinct and reason, restore the synthesis of thought and emotion, fuse again the sensual and the spiritual. It is not surprising that she has written a book on D. H. Lawrence, by whom she has been influenced, but with whom she also takes issue. She believes in Eros, which includes both sex and love inseparably welded together.

It has been observed—rightly, I believe—that most serious writers have only one basic theme, of which their works are but maturing variations. In her essay "On Writing," Anaïs Nin defines her fundamental topic: the depiction of a "collective neurosis," as she calls it, which is a form of protest against the suppression of our natural instincts by the demands and taboos of civilization. "Today," she writes, "a novelist's preoccupation with inner psychological distortions does not stem from a morbid love of illness, but from a knowledge that this is the *theme* of our new reality."

Like Thomas Wolfe, she is in reality writing only *one* book, of which all her novels and stories are mere parts. She is weaving a large tapestry with intricate recurrences and variations. Her characters appear and reappear over and over, under the same names, under different names, acting out parts of their lives, probing their relationships with each other in ever new mutations; and if you look through her manuscripts (which Deering Library is fortunate enough to have under its care and which are at present exhibited there)—if you look through her manuscripts, you'll find that the heroes' names often change from version to version: Sabina, Djuna, Lilith, Alraune, Mandra, Stella, Jay, Hans, Rab—forever the same cast in different settings, with different costumes. What does this mean? I believe it means that Anaïs Nin's novels, like the works of every creative writer worth his salt, are primarily autobiographical—but autobiographical in a peculiar way, not on the flat, one-dimensional level of "realism" but in an exalted metamorphosed second and third dimension of artistic insight, where the often actually or seemingly senseless happenings of our daily lives take on meanings, are meaningfully rearranged by the creative urge and skill of the author, become symbols out of facts. In the manuscript of *Winter of Artifice* I found this passage: "Literature was a race with life, sometimes surpassing it, sometimes falling below. Anita would raise inferior experiences to a superior plane by writing. But when she meets superior experience (tenderness), it silences literature." Only a wide personality can create as many women characters as Anaïs Nin, for example, who are all *she*, yet none of them fully she, all but aspects of her, blendings of her self with other subconscious selves, and with outside selves too. This is different from the schizophrenic's split personality in that all the various selves form a unity at the core, are only the multicolored rays of a single sun. Actually, this is peculiar to the artist in merely a higher degree than to the rest of us. It is something we all experience when we try to understand and describe something. We have first, as the very deep word says, to *assimilate* it, to make it part of ourselves, for we can never understand anything outside of us. To describe and bring to life the character of, say, a thief or a murderer, one does not have to be a thief or a murderer, but one surely must have the *potential* of a thief or a murderer in oneself, or one could never create him. That is the reason why the Philistine cannot be a creative artist—he is too narrow and limited inside, he has too few potentials.

I have not given you many external biographical data of Anaïs Nin, apart from intimating that she was born in Europe—in Paris, to be exact, of Spanish ancestry on her father's side. Ever since she came to this country at eleven years of age and learned English in the public schools, she has kept her by now fabulous diary, which at present, I learned today, comprises 90 handwritten volumes. This diary is an awesome thing to me and I won't say a word about it, because that could get me started, and I'm supposed to get finished, not started, I know. And with that, I'm most happy to turn the program over to— Anaïs Nin.

APPENDIX D

Aphorisms by Felix Pollak

From "Mental Reservations"

It is the margin of imperfection that makes a work of art effective, for it transforms passive observers into active participants. The flawless pleases perfectionists; the flawed makes prefectures.

I'd never suspect some of my ignoble capacities, were it not for the fact that I am capable of suspecting them in others.

Life sharpens me as the pencil sharpener the pencil. I am becoming more pointed, but less.

My sense of humor prevents me from laughing more often, just as my aesthetic sense keeps me from enjoying more sights. Only the tasteless live in the land of plenty.

Marriage: She chanced to fall into the searchlight of his love and was run over. She didn't leave the scene of the accident (from which he never fully recovered) but took her seat beside him, in charge of dimming his headlights to safeguard him against future accidents.

Happiness: The thought of the cinder that failed to fly into your eye.

Technical progress can be measured by the degree to which machines become humanized, and humans mechanized.

Many people mistake their inhibitions, that is, their cowardliness, for their morality.

How characteristic of our civilization the expressions " a house of joy" and "a house of ill repute" are used as synonyms.

When your whiskers are long, you're unshaven. But when they are still longer, you're wearing a beard. Thus many of our faults develop into virtues simply by growing bigger.

When people speak of "unnatural acts," the chances are that their standards, rather than these acts, have become alienated from nature. Morality can divide human behavior into "proper and "improper," but it cannot divide nature into "natural" and "unnatural."

["Mental Reservations: A Group of Aphorisms," *Chicago Review* (Summer 1957): 77–79]

From *Lebenszeichen*

To write an aphorism means to miss the target with meticulous precision.

There is nothing new under the sun. But everything is unprecedented.

Appendix D

To create a work of art is to create a disturbance.

It is just because life is potentially satisfactory, that one feels its unsatisfactoriness so strongly. If it *couldn't* be better, it wouldn't be so bad.

The Bible is the source book of atheism for the unbeliever, while a believer will draw religious conversion from an atheistic tract.

"I'd love to become an introvert," said the extrovert, "if I could only be sure that people will learn of my conversion."

America's staff of life is not bread but dough.

People bent on putting their best foot forward must needs develop a limping gait through life.

Original sin: man's belief in original sin.

I write the way I shave, going over and over the same territory, cutting, scraping, smoothing—and forever finding rough spots right under my nose.

[*Lebenszeichen*, 123–50]

APPENDIX E

Selected Bibliography
of Felix Pollak

Poetry

The Castle and the Flaw. New Rochelle, N.Y.: The Elizabeth Press, 1963.

Say When. Temple, Maine: Juniper, 1969.

Ginkgo. New Rochelle, N.Y.: The Elizabeth Press, 1973.

Subject to Change. La Crosse, Wisc.: Juniper, 1978.

Tunnel Visions. Peoria, Ill.: Spoon River Poetry Press, 1984.

Benefits of Doubt. Peoria, Ill.: Spoon River Poetry Press, 1988.

Vom Nutzen des Zweifels [*The Uses of Doubt*] [bilingual edition in German and English]. Frankfurt am Main: Fischer, 1989.

Aphorisms

"Mental Reservations: A Group of Aphorisms." *Chicago Review* 2 (Summer 1957): 77–79.

Lebenszeichen: Aphorismen und Marginalien [*Vital Signs: Aphorisms and Marginal Notations*] [bilingual edition in German and English]. Ed.

Reinhold Grimm and Sara Pollak. Vienna: Verlag für Gesellschaftskritik, 1992.

Prose Writings

"Reflections on Political Opinion." *The Humanist* 14 (1954): 259–64

(Under the name Felix Anselm) "Utopia." *Trace*, no. 20 (February 1957):
31–34.

(Under the name Felix Anselm) "Through the Gripevine." *Trace*, no. 25
(February 1958): 21.

"Alfred Polgar: An Introduction." *Tri-Quarterly* 2 (Fall 1959): 35–39.

"Pornography: A Trip around the Halfworld." *Tri-Quarterly* 12 (Spring 1968).
Reprinted in *Perspectives on Pornography*, ed. Douglas A. Hughes,
170–96. New York: St. Martin's Press, 1970.

"New York: Ein Schiff, ein Emigrant," *Akzente* 3 (June 1979): 314–20.

Prose and Cons [Essays]. La Crosse, Wisc.: Juniper, 1983.

Autobiography

"Felix Pollak: An Autobiographical Sketch." *Northeast*, series 5, vol. 5
(Winter 1991–92).

Writings about Felix Pollak

Grimm, Reinhold. "'So Much to Praise': On Felix Pollak and His Poetry."
Wisconsin Academy Review 37 (Spring 1991): 6–8.

———. "'My Stepmother Town': Felix Pollak and Vienna." In *Turn-of-the-
Century Vienna and Its Legacy: Essays in Honor of Donald G.
Daviau*, ed. Jeffrey B. Berlin, 507–28. Boulder: Atelier, 1993.

Grünzweig, Walter, "Der Exilautor und sein Publikum: Über den Lyriker
Felix Pollak." *Das Jüdische Echo* 1.29 (October 1990): 164–68.

Mason, Gregory. "Felix Pollak: An Austro-American Poet." *Austrian
Studies* 6 (1955): 120–33.

Smoller, Sanford et al. "A Tribute to Felix Pollak." *Pembroke Magazine* 22
(1990): 7–36.

Appendix E

NOTES

Introduction

1. In 1980, Pollak explained his pen name, Felix Anselm, as follows: "Why did I have a pen name? you'll ask. First, because the Viennese phone book was full of Pollaks, all spelled that way, and I felt I couldn't possibly become famous, needless to say. Second, it was the fashion in Vienna, for writers, actors, instrumental virtuosos, artists in general, they all, or their majority, had beautiful, euphonic names, like today's film stars still. And thirdly, I had fallen in love with one of the characters in a novel by a marvelous, if now forgotten novelist, who was called Anselmus. Felix Anselm sounded intoxicating to me." "Felix Pollak: An Autobiographical Sketch," *Northeast*, series 5, vol. 5 (Winter 1991–92): 21–22.

2. Felix Pollak's major publications, all under the name of Felix Pollak, are as follows: *The Castle and the Flaw* (New Rochelle, N.Y.: The Elizabeth Press, 1963); *Say When* (Temple, Maine: Juniper, 1969); *Ginkgo* (New Rochelle, N.Y.: The Elizabeth Press, 1973); *Subject to Change* (La Crosse, Wisc.: Juniper, 1978); *Prose and Cons* [essays] (La Crosse, Wisc.: Juniper, 1983); *Tunnel Visions* (Peoria, Ill.: Spoon River Poetry Press, 1984); *Benefits of Doubt* (Peoria, Ill.: Spoon River Poetry Press, 1988); *Vom Nutzen des Zweifels* [*The Uses of Doubt*] [bilingual edition in German and English] (Frankfurt am Main: Fischer, 1989); *Lebenszeichen: Aphorismen und Marginalien* [*Vital Signs: Aphorisms and Marginal Notations*] [bilingual edition in German and English], ed. Reinhold Grimm and Sara Pollak (Vienna: Verlag für Gesellschaftskritik, 1992).

3. The Felix Pollak Prize in Poetry carries with it a cash prize and the publication of the award-winning volume. The Prize for 1997 was awarded to Libby Thurston for her manuscript entitled *To Move Forward*.

4. In this later period, Nin maintained an active exchange of letters with a host of correspondents, to whom she wrote faithfully over a period of twelve years. She also nursed her husband Hugo and her companion Rupert Pole when they were sick, as well as various friends. The generous side of Anaïs Nin's personality remains under-acknowledged.

5. The term "existential exile" was aptly coined by Reinhold Grimm in "'My Stepmother Town': Felix Pollak and Vienna," in *Turn-of-the-Century*

Vienna and Its Legacy: Essays in Honor of Donald G. Daviau, ed. Jeffrey B. Berlin (Boulder, Colo.: Atelier, 1993), 507–28 (518).

6. William Carlos Williams read Pollak's poem "Think of the Planes Flying" (Appendix B) and wrote him: "May I congratulate you on [that] piece of verse. . . . It is a man's duty, as it should be his pleasure in this desert we inhabit, to salute every poet of whom he can find anything to approve. Particularly, there is so much to praise in this short verse." Quoted in Reinhold Grimm, "'So Much to Praise': On Felix Pollak and His Poetry," *Wisconsin Academy Review* 37 (Spring 1991): 6–8.

7. *The Diary of Anaïs Nin*, ed. Gunther Stuhlmann, vol. 5, *1947–1955* (New York: Harcourt Brace Jovanovich, 1974), 163.

8. *Diary*, 5:228.

Chapter 1: *July 1952–February 1953*

1. *Diary*, 5:83.

2. In fact, Pollak's "enclosed note" was a carefully researched, nine-hundred-word introductory essay on Nin with biographical background, comments from prominent critics, and a description of her working methods and aesthetic philosophy. See Felix Pollak, "Significant Acquisitions: Anaïs Nin Manuscripts," *Northwestern Library News* 6 (July 18, 1952): 1–2.

3. Through the extended mediation of Chicago gallery-cum-bookstore owner Kathryn Winslow, Jens Nyholm, the director of the library at Northwestern University, assisted by Felix Pollak and the James Joyce scholar Richard Ellmann, eventually acquired thirty-nine folders of Anaïs Nin's original manuscripts for $500. When the negotiations seemed endless, Nin wrote to Kathryn Winslow: "Don't worry about time and don't worry if nothing happens. All of it is due to the fact that I have no established commercial value, and people with money want names, as they want famous painters only. Those who read me are poor and unable to buy even books. Only friends showed up loyally to my reading from new manuscripts in New York, and we sold only 3 books and 2 records. Later—too late, the ms. will increase in value, I know."

4. This refers to the original edition of *The Winter of Artifice*, and the later left-out section "Djuna," also known as the "Hans and Johanna" novella. Part of this novella was published for the first time in the United States in *ANAIS: An International Journal* Vol. 7/1989.

5. *Under a Glass Bell* (New York: Gemor Press, 1944; New York: E. P. Dutton, 1948).

6. *This Hunger* (New York: Gemor Press, 1945 [Part I of *Ladders to Fire*, 1946]); *Ladders to Fire* (New York: E. P. Dutton, 1946; Denver: Swallow Press, 1966).

7. *Children of the Albatross* (New York: E. P. Dutton, 1947; Denver: Swallow Press, 1966).

8. "Realism and Reality" and "On Writing" are both collected in *Anaïs Nin, The Mystic of Sex: Uncollected Writings 1930–1974*, edited and with a preface by Gunther Stuhlmann (Santa Barbara, Calif.: Capra Press, 1995).

9. Jakob Wassermann (1873–1934) was Pollak's favorite German novelist after Hesse. Pollak took his pen name, Anselm, after a character in one of Wassermann's novels. A Jewish liberal intellectual, Wassermann was influenced by both Feodor Dostoevsky and Leo Tolstoy. His novels blend social criticism with the search for a new, socially uniting spirituality. The artist figure is initially criticized for self-absorption, but ultimately assigned a prophetic role of inspiration and leadership. His novels include *Die Juden von Zirndorf* (1897), translated as *The Jews of Zirndorf* (1933), and *Das Gänsemännchen* (1915), translated as *The Goose Man* (1922).

10. Hermann Hesse (1877–1962) was German-born but, after a visit to India, he moved permanently to Switzerland in 1911 and became a citizen in 1923. Pollak's sensibility resonated to Hesse's novels, which portrayed artist-dreamer figures such as *Peter Camenzind* (1915) stifled by conventional morality and groping for deeper understanding. Hence the importance of Hesse's novels *Siddhartha* (1922) and *Steppenwolf* (1927), which Pollak urges Nin to read in this correspondence. Hesse was a symbol for Pollak of his lost homeland. When Pollak received a letter from Hesse in 1949, he replied: "It awoke a feeling of homesickness in me and calmed it at the same time, because my homeland, the only one left to me, and probably the only true one that there ever was, was in this envelope." (Felix Pollak Collection, December 17, 1949.) Clearly thinking also of himself, in a 1947 essay on Hesse, Pollak wrote: "Hesse's fundamental fable is the endless struggle of the individual for self-recognition and self-realization, and the resulting conflict with the equalizing forces, the temptations and taboos of a given environment." Felix Anselm, "Herman Hesse," *Poet Lore* [Boston, Mass.] 53 (Winter 1947): 353–60.

11. Ian Hugo's film based on *House of Incest* was *Bells of Atlantis* (1952). He screened it with great success at the 1952 Venice Film Festival.

12. Anaïs Nin had written the preface to the original edition of *Tropic of Cancer* in 1934, and praised the novel as "a vitalizing current of blood."

Chapter 2: March 1954–February 1955

1. *A Spy in the House of Love* (New York: British Book Centre, 1954; Denver: Swallow Press, 1966).

2. Films by Ian Hugo (Hugo Guiler) include *Ai-Ye* (Mankind), 1949; *Bells of Atlantis*, 1952; *Jazz of Lights*, 1954; *Melodic Inversion* (1958); *Venice*

Etude No. I (1962); *The Gondola Eye* (1963); *Through the Magiscope* (1968); *Apertura* (1970); *Afrodisiac 1* (1971); *Afrodisiac 2* and *Levitation* (1972); *Transmigration* (1973); and *Transcending* (1974). According to film historian Sheldon Renan, "Ian Hugo made brilliantly colored works in which the action is suffused with many superimpositions that yield abstract compositions"; *An Introduction to the American Underground Film* (New York: Dutton, 1967), 90. Ian Hugo's films are collected in the Museum of Modern Art, New York City.

3. Pollak wrote: "The four manuscript versions are particularly interesting because of the numerous changes from state to state—changes that range from alterations of words and sentences to additions and deletions of whole episodes. In an accompanying letter Miss Nin notes the curious fact that she corrected the last proof sheets without reference to the manuscript from which it was set up, because the Dutch printers who mailed her the galleys from Holland had forgotten to enclose the manuscript. Pressed for time, Miss Nin had to proof-read without her original at hand and never compared the two—which, of course, led to very interesting, if small discrepancies between the book and the final manuscript version of the book." In "Significant Acquisitions: *A Spy in the House of Love* Manuscript," *Northwestern Library News* 9 (December 3, 1954): 11.

4. Felix Pollak writing under the pseudonym Felix Anselm, "Reflections on Political Opinion," *The Humanist* [Yellow Springs, Ohio] 14, no. 6 (1954): 259–64. In this essay, Pollak argued "it is surprising how little political substance is actually contained in most utterances of so-called political opinion. These utterances are in the great majority of cases merely the manifestations (in political terminology) of basic mental attitudes . . . using seemingly rational arguments to express personal and group fears, hates and hopes."

5. Pollak had always considered himself an aphorist, having published two sets of aphorisms in German under the name Felix Anselm in *Die Glocke* in 1935 and 1936 before he fled Austria. His work with aphorisms in English was a further part of his attempt to make the transition to becoming a word artist in a new language. See Appendix D.

6. *Spy* received four reviews in prominent national journals: Jerome Stone, "Fiction Note: The Psyche of the Huntress," *Saturday Review*, 15 May 1954, 32; Charles Rollo, "Pot-Pourri," *Atlantic* 194 (Aug. 1954): 86; Maxwell Geismar, "Temperament versus Conscience.," *Nation*, July 24, 1954, 75–76; Marvin Mudrick, "Humanity is the Principle," *Hudson Review* 7 (Winter 1955): 610–19.

7. In 1931 Anaïs Nin had tried to interest Edward Titus, the editor of the literary magazine *This Quarter*, who also operated an English-language press, At the Sign of the Black Manikin, from his bookstore in Montparnasse, in some of her early fiction. Instead, she had ended up writing for

him her first book, *D. H. Lawrence: An Unprofessional Study*. Shortly after its publication the press collapsed when its backer, the cosmetics entrepreneur Helena Rubinstein, divorced Edward Titus. Nin apparently had difficulties collecting royalties due her. See Gunther Stuhlmann, "Edward Titus et al.," in *ANAIS: An International Journal* Vol. 7/1989: 113–18.

8. Nin must here be referring to her brother Thorvald, who spent considerable time in Mexico. However, given the somewhat distant relations between the two, it is odd for her to claim she "can and must visit [him] once a year." This remark may have been to mislead Pollak about her intention to vacation in Mexico with Rupert, since it precedes her confiding in Pollak about her double life.

9. Maxwell Geismar taught at Sarah Lawrence College and was a reviewer for *The Nation*. He and his wife Anne became friends with Anaïs and Hugo, and he arranged for Hugo to show his films at Sarah Lawrence College. Geismar later reviewed *A Spy in the House of Love* for *The Nation*, a review that did not entirely please Nin. Eventually their friendship cooled, due in large part to the incompatibility of Geismar's left-wing sociological approach to literature with Nin's depth-psychological, aesthetic interests.

Chapter 3: February 1955–June 1955

1. This reference to a two-week teaching assignment at the University of Mexico (presumably in Mexico City) cannot be verified in any other correspondence or records of Anaïs Nin. Similarly, there is no verification of the later report that Felix Pollak receives from Hugo (mentioned in Pollak's January 8, 1957 letter) that Nin has been working in Hollywood on a film script of Jean Christophe. It is possible that Nin fabricated both these activities as alibis to cover her tracks while living "on the trapeze."

2. "A Living" (see Appendix B), published under the pen name Felix Anselm in the International Issue of the San Francisco literary magazine *Inferno*, no. 11 (1955): 24.

3. Pollak was somewhat smitten by Nin, as she recalls in her diary: "Lecture at Evanston. Felix Pollak was at the station, after driving through flooded roads in a taxi, poor Felix, an extravagance for his modest budget. He looked like his handwriting, small, delicate, with big, sad Spanish eyes, a gentle smile, the hands of a violinist. In the taxi he kissed my hand like a true Viennese, and during the drive we had a long talk. He had been nervous, he was not nervous anymore. As I found out later he was being metamorphosed from a man of 40 to a man of 18. A metamorphosis not without inconvenience, for with it were reawakened his adolescent romantic longings for other lives" (*Diary*, 5:228).

Obviously, Pollak and Nin exchanged no letters during Nin's time in

Evanston, but Pollak's introductory address for Nin's lecture on May 25 (Appendix C) belongs here chronologically.

4. Karl Kraus was a dominant figure in the cultural scene in Vienna when Pollak was coming of age in the late 1920s and early 1930s. Another figure who reminded Pollak acutely of his cut-off roots, Kraus was a brilliant, idiosyncratic character who could hold audiences spellbound with his solo recitations and play readings. Like Pollak, Kraus was passionately interested in language and a master of the aphorism, such as "Psychoanalysis is the disease of which it purports to be the cure." Pollak collected the entire series of *Die Fackel* (The Torch), the satirical journal that Kraus edited and mostly wrote from 1899–1936, but his family destroyed them all when Pollak fled, as social satire had come to be considered subversive. Pollak still retained a large collection of Kraus's writings and recordings, and in 1985 he bequeathed it to the University of Connecticut.

5. Djuna Barnes, the American-born novelist, spent much of her life in Europe. Her fame rests on her novel *Nightwood* (1936), a macabre tale of five psychopathic characters horrifyingly linked together as they move toward their mutual destruction. T. S. Eliot praised *Nightwood* as "so good a novel that only sensibilities trained on poetry can truly appreciate it." Anaïs Nin admired Barnes's work also and wrote to her. Barnes failed to reply, for which Nin never forgave her, vowing never to leave a letter unanswered, a promise she appears largely to have kept. Early in 1957 Felix Pollak visited Barnes at her apartment in New York City, and he wrote about it in his letter to Nin of January 8 that year.

6. Alfred Polgar was famous for his sharp insights, wit, and anti-bourgeois attitudes. In one of his brief, aphoristic takes, "Social Disorder," for instance, a prison chief asks the wretched culprit to be hanged early next morning: "What would you like for dinner? You may eat and drink anything and as much as you want." To which the condemned man replies: "Too bad, if you had asked me that three months ago, this whole robbery-murder would not have happened" (in *Kleine Zeit*, Berlin, 1919). Like Pollak, Polgar was a Jewish refugee from Vienna to the United States. Pollak admired Polgar greatly, and particularly cherished his dictum: "The foreign land has not become home, but home a foreign land." See Felix Pollak, "Alfred Polgar: An Introduction," *Tri-Quarterly* 2 (Fall 1959): 35–39.

The article on Egon Friedell by Alfred Polgar to which Pollak refers is "A Great Dilettante," *Antioch Review* (Summer 1950).

Chapter 4: July 1955–December 1955

1. *Lebenszeichen*, 200.

2. Erich Fromm (1900–1980), born in Frankfurt and trained as a psychoanalyst at the Berlin Psychoanalytic Institute, emigrated in 1934 to the

United States where he eventually became professor of psychiatry at New York University. Differing with Freud, Fromm stressed the role of culture in the formation of personality. Fromm's analysis of the authoritarian personality has gained wide currency as a concept in the psychological study of personality. The interpretation of fairy tales, to which Pollak refers, comes from *The Forgotten Language: An Introduction to the Understanding of Dreams, Fairy Tales and Myths* (New York: Holt, Rinehart and Winston, 1951). Fromm authored numerous other books on psychology, sociology, ethics, and religion, including *Escape from Freedom* (1941) and *The Sane Society* (1955).

3. Anaïs Nin was undergoing psychoanalysis in New York with Dr. Inge Bogner.

4. John Burk, *The Life and Work of Beethoven* (New York: Random House, 1943).

5. *Ladders to Fire* was eventually published in France in 1962 by Editions Stock. Somewhat ironically, it was translated (and promoted) as *Les Miroirs dans le Jardin: Romain Americain* [lit. *Mirrors in the Garden: An American Novel*].

Chapter 5: January 1956–October 1956

1. Alfred Perlès, *My Friend Henry Miller: An Intimate Biography* (London: N. Spearman; New York: John Day, 1956). Perlès had lived with Miller in his apartment in Clichy at the time when Anaïs Nin spent much time there as Miller's lover. Nin was enraged and distraught that Perlès intended to make their affair public and tried to stop the book's publication. Finally, Perlès agreed to rewrite the book, with Nin's character being split in two. A new character, an imaginary courtesan named Liane de Champsur, was invented to serve the role of Miller's lover in the narrative.

2. James Thurber's story "The Secret Life of Walter Mitty," first published in the *New Yorker* in 1939, was later anthologized in *The Thurber Carnival* (New York: Harper Brothers, 1945). This humorous short story, a kind of miniature, comic analogue to *Steppenwolf*, involves a timid schlemiel, Walter Mitty, who retreats periodically into a glamorous, fantasy life of his imagining. *The Secret Life of Walter Mitty* was also the title of a successful film version starring Danny Kaye (1947) and a Broadway musical.

3. These poems first appeared in the following journals, all under the name Felix Anselm: "On Listening to a Dead Poet's Recording," *Fiddlehead* [Fredericton, New Brunswick] no. 28 (May 1956): 17; "Zoo," *Fiddlehead* no. 29 (August 1956): 17; "What It Always Comes Down To," *Whetstone* [Philadelphia] 1 (Winter–Spring 1956): 173; "Trees through a Window," *Hawk & Whippoorwill* [Sauk City, Wisc.] 4 (Spring 1963): 30.

4. The artist Jean "Janko" Varda was introduced to Anaïs Nin by Henry Miller. Nin admired Varda's bohemian lifestyle, and the two became good friends. Varda presented Rupert Pole and Anaïs Nin with a collage as a housewarming gift, and Nin subsequently named her volume of collected character sketches *Collages* (Denver: Swallow, 1964) in Varda's honor.

5. Felix Anselm, "Utopia," *Trace* [Hollywood] no. 20 (February 1957): 31–34. This amusing and possibly prophetic piece anticipates a time when electronic means of communication have entirely replaced books, and books with all their portable and tactile elegance are rediscovered.

6. Henry Miller, *A Devil in Paradise* (New York: New American Library, 1956).

Chapter 6: October 1956–April 1958

1. Anaïs Nin met the Viennese painter Renate Druks in Los Angeles in 1953 and the two became close friends, confiding often in each other till around 1964. Druks hosted the now legendary "Come as Your Madness" masquerade party and introduced Nin to filmmaker Kenneth Anger. Nin made Druks the central figure in her last work of fiction, *Collages* (1964).

2. Christopher Isherwood's sketches, *Good-Bye to Berlin* (1939), were adapted for the stage by John van Druten as *I am a Camera* (1951). One of the stories, "Sally Bowles," served as the basis for the stage musical *Cabaret* (1968) and its subsequent film version (1974). As mentioned in note 1 to chapter 3, there is no evidence that Nin was working on a film project, and it is possible that she used this as an alibi to explain her California visits to Hugo.

3. These poems first appeared in the following journals, all under the pseudonym of Felix Anselm: "Primeval Sin," *Humanist* 17 (1957): 82; "Just Asking," *Houyhnhnm's Scrapbook* [New Orleans] no. 2 (February 1957): 22; "The Dream," *Flame* [Alpine, Texas] (Winter 1956): 20; "White Lines on Blue," *Whimsy* [Wakefield, Mass.] 2 (December 1956); "The Bomb," *Bridge Anthology* (1957), 12; "They Are the Pitchmen of the Lord," *Epos* [Lake Como, Fla.] (Winter 1956): 12.

4. Kenneth Anger, *The Inauguration of the Pleasure Dome* (1957).

5. The books Nin mentions by Erich Fromm (1900–1980) are *The Art of Loving*, vol. 9 of the World Perspectives series, ed. Ruth Nanda Anshen (New York: Harper and Row, 1956); and *Escape from Freedom* (New York: Farrar and Rinehart, 1941).

6. The biography of Byron by André Maurois (1885–1957) was published in French as *Don Juan; ou, La vie de Byron* (Paris: Editions Bernard Grasset, 1930) and in an English translation by Hamish Miles as *Byron*

(New York: D. Appleton and Company, 1930); Maurois's *Lélia; ou, La vie de George Sand* (Paris: Hachette, 1953) appeared in English as *Lélia: The Life of George Sand* (New York: Harper, 1953).

7. *Justine* (New York: E. P. Dutton, 1957) is the first volume of the series of four novels that constitute *The Alexandria Quartet* by Lawrence Durrell (1912–1990). *The Black Book: An Agon*, also by Durrell (Paris: Obelisk Press, 1938), did not become available in an American edition until 1960 (New York: E. P. Dutton), which partly accounts for Nin's query about buying books in Paris.

8. Pollak did not succeed in placing any aphorisms in *New World Writing*, but he was successful with *Chicago Review*. See, under the name of Felix Anselm, "Mental Reservations: A Group of Aphorisms," *Chicago Review* 2 (Summer 1957): 77–79.

9. "Pornography: A Trip around the Halfworld," *Tri-Quarterly* 12 (Spring 1968). Reprinted in Douglas A. Hughes, ed., *Perspectives on Pornography* (New York: St. Martins Press, 1970), 170–96.

10. Nin had not here revived her Gemor printing press but was having her work printed privately and attempting to distribute it in person. The modest amounts of money involved even by 1950's standards, 50 cents per copy, 50 copies to break even, again underscore both the economic pressure Nin was under and her totally unflagging determination to bring her work to a public readership.

11. In her introduction to *Under a Glass Bell*, first published by Gemor Press in New York in 1944, Nin was persuaded by the left-leaning Gonzalo Moré (the book designer who was Nin's partner in Gemor Press) to excuse herself to her wartime readership for offering a collection of stories far removed from the horrors of the war that the world was then experiencing. She wrote then of these stories she had written earlier: "the fact that I describe the adult fairy tales, the fantasy, the decadent poet's world, does not mean I remained one with it and permanently identified with it." Quoted in Deirdre Bair, *Anaïs Nin: A Biography* (New York: G. P. Putnam's Sons, 1995), 294. This preface was never again used, and here she recants her recantation.

12. For a brief time Anaïs Nin had a "distributor"—a bookseller on East 34th Street in New York—but the arrangement did not amount to anything worthwhile, and their relationship is not documented. She affixed a label in the back of the first edition of *Cities of the Interior* that listed no publisher or printer.

13. Under the name of Felix Anselm, "Through the Gripevine," *Trace*, no. 25 (February 1958): 21.

14. The article by Rebecca West appeared in a British publication; Stanley Kunitz supplied the entry on Nin in *Twentieth Century Authors: A*

Biographical Dictionary of Modern Literature, ed. Stanley Kunitz and Howard Haycraft (New York: H. W. Wilson, 1955).

15. It is unclear which of Hugo's films Nin means. *Melodic Inversion* was a nine-minute film Hugo finished in 1958, but he was also working on and showing different versions of his film on Venice—*Venice, Etude One* and *Venice, Etude Two*—which eventually became *The Gondola Eye*.

Chapter 7: *May 1958–April 1959*

1. *Two Cities: La Revue bilingue de Paris* was initiated and first published by Jean Fanchette in April 1959. The "two cities" of the title were Paris and New York. Nin was introduced to Fanchette, a medical intern, by Lawrence Durrell when she was in Paris. She subsequently served for a short time as New York editor of the journal.

2. Claude Mauriac, *L'Alittérature contemporaine: Artaud, Bataille, Beckett, Kafka, Leiris, Michaud, Miller, Robbe-Grillet, Nathalie Sarraute* . . . (Paris: A. Michel, 1958).

3. The short-lived literary journal *The Booster* (September 1937–Easter 1939) began as the house publication of the American Country Club of Paris. Fred Perlès, who became its editor and was initially given complete freedom so long as he published the club's golf scores, used *The Booster* to publish his own writings and those of his friends, including Henry Miller and Lawrence Durrell. Miller and Durrell were joint literary editors. In the December 1937/January 1938 "Womb" issue, Anaïs Nin's short story "The Paper Womb" was published alongside "womb"-themed submissions by Durrell, Miller, and Dylan Thomas. Durrell's *Zero, and Asylum in the Snow: Two Excursions into Reality* was first published privately on the island of Rhodes in 1946.

4. *Lolita* (1958) is undoubtedly the best-known work by Vladimir Nabokov (1899–1977), the Russian-born writer who moved to the United States in 1940. The story of a middle-aged intellectual's infatuation with a twelve-year-old American "nymphet," *Lolita* was considered scandalous when it was first published in Paris by Maurice Girodias's Olympia Press; it was subjected to widespread censorship before finally being published in the United States in 1958.

5. René Clair's sentimental, romantic early musical *Sous les Toits de Paris* (1930) was released with the English title *Under the Roofs of Paris*. Albert Lamorisse's *Le Ballon Rouge* (1956), a childhood fantasy set in the Menilmontant district of Paris, was released with the English title *The Red Balloon*.

6. Anaïs Nin had used copies of earlier editions of her out-of-print novels to offset the first edition (1959) of *Cities of the Interior*, which gave no im-

print or printer. (The first Swallow Press edition was apparently offset from this version, which was later re-edited and reset with new front matter.).

7. This privately printed edition of *Solar Barque* contained illustrations by Peter Loomer, the young son of Anaïs Nin's artist friend, Renate Druks.

8. "Seeing Double" and "Manichean" both appeared in Pollak's first book of poems, *The Castle and the Flaw* (1963).

9. The two poems chosen by Jean Fanchette for inclusion in *Two Cities* (the third poem was not used) were "Vienna Revisited" (see Appendix B) and "Street Walk." They appeared in *Two Cities* 2 (15 July 1959) under the name Felix Anselm.

Chapter 8: April 1959–September 1961

1. Poet Daisy Aldan (b. 1923) co-edited *Folder*, published by Tiber Press of New York from 1953–56, with Richard Miller; issues 1–4 have been reprinted as *Folder* (New York: Kraus Reprint Company, 1970).

2. Anaïs Nin contributed to numbers 1 and 2 of *Two Cities* the essays "The Writer and the Symbols" and "The Synthetic Alchemist," respectively; the former was reprinted in *The Mystic of Sex*, and the latter in *ANAIS*.

3. Nin's story in *Vogue*, August 1, 1961, was entitled "The Seal Friends." It was later included, with slight changes, in *Collages* (Denver: Alan Swallow, 1964).

Chapter 9: October 1961–June 1962

1. Roger Shattuck, *The Banquet Years: The Arts in France, 1885-1918: Alfred Jarry, Henri Rousseau, Erik Satie, Guillaume Apollinaire* (New York: Harcourt, Brace, 1958).

2. On November 14, 1961 Alan Swallow wrote Pollak a letter objecting to an article that Pollak had written concerning the relationship of little magazines to major literary figures and currents. He found Pollak's article "basically obscure" and considered that Pollak had "written badly." In Pollak's reply of November 22, 1961, he defended himself at length against what he called "your [Swallow's] strange, agitated and deeply provoked letter." For all this, Swallow signed his pillorying letter "Cordially," and Pollak concluded his rebuttal with "With best wishes." Original correspondence in Felix Pollak Archive, Madison, Wisconsin.

3. Alfred Perlès, *My Friend Henry Miller: An Intimate Biography*; see note 1 to chapter 5.

4. The Latin quote is from Pliny: "Dictum sapienti sat est" (These words are enough for the wise).

5. This projected sale did not materialize. The Institute for Sex Research, Inc., was founded in 1947 at Indiana University in Bloomington by Alfred C. Kinsey (1894–1956).

Chapter 10: November 1972–April 1976

1. Nin visited Madison to read in the 1960s. It was perhaps disingenuous of her to claim "I did not know where you were or I would have asked about you when I visited Madison." On the other hand, it also seems odd that Pollak, as involved as he was in the literary scene in Madison, would not have been aware of the visit of someone as famous as Nin had now become. Perhaps he intentionally stayed away.

2. *Under the Sign of Pisces: Anaïs Nin and Her Circle*, edited by Richard R. Centing and Benjamin Franklin V, published at the State University Libraries in Columbus, Ohio.

3. "Pornography: A Trip around the Halfworld," *Tri-Quarterly* 12 (Spring 1968). Reprinted in Douglas A. Hughes, ed., *Perspectives on Pornography* (New York: St. Martins Press, 1970), 170–96.

4. Robert Snyder's film *Anaïs Observed* premiered in 1973; from it he developed the book *Anaïs Nin Observed: From a Film Portrait of a Woman as Artist* (Chicago: Swallow Press, 1976). His earlier film on Henry Miller, *The Henry Miller Odyssey*, led to the book project *This Is Henry, Henry Miller from Brooklyn* (Los Angeles: Nash, 1974).

5. Felix Pollak, *Ginkgo* (New Rochelle, N. Y.: The Elizabeth Press, 1973).

6. Anaïs Nin's inscription, on a loose piece of paper apparently originally inserted in Felix Pollak's copy of volume 5 of her *Diary*, reads as follows: "For Felix, whose poetry has illumined the paths of many, whose loving care of books taught others to read and appreciate, whom I appreciate as poet and longtime friend. With love, Anaïs."

7. According to Sara Pollak, the "revolting story" refers to an occasion when Felix had been prevented from reprinting or reading his poem "Speaking: The Hero" (see Appendix B) in some public forum, because of its anti-war sentiments. The letter that recounts this story is missing, and it seems likely that other Pollak letters from the later correspondence are still undiscovered.

8. Pollak composed poetry right up to his death in 1987. His last two anthologies, *Tunnel Visions* (1984) and *Subject to Change* (1988), both concern his blindness and contain some of his most powerful and moving verse (see "Galileo" in Appendix B).

INDEX

Frequently mentioned names are abbreviated in the subentries as follows: Hugh Guiler (HG); Henry Miller (HM); Anaïs Nin (AN); Rupert Pole (RP); Felix Pollak (FP); and Sara Pollak (SP).

dream house, 102, 107, 128, 143,
  158–60, 164
as violist, 111
See also Pollak, Felix: and Rupert
  Pole
Polgar, Alfred, 45–46, 52, 236 n.6
Pollak, Felix (FP):
  life and career of, x–xiii, 49, 68, 76,
    91, 99, 120, 195
  bibliography of, 229–30, 237 ch.
    5 n.3, 238 n.3, 241 n.8
  as bilingual poet, xi
  censorship of his poetry, 191
  as existential exile, xii, 231 n.5
  eyesight problems, xi, 184, 187,
    189, 191–92, 242 n.8
  Fulbright grant, applied for, 99,
    118
  Karl Kraus, proposed study on,
    99–101
  as librarian at Northwestern
    University, xi, 3
  as librarian at the University of
    Wisconsin, xi, 143–44
  librarian, on life as a, 71–74, 80
  marriage with Sara Pollak,
    74–77, 156–59
  as political refugee from Hitler,
    xi, 3, 27–28
  pornography, article on, 110, 112,
    186
  poems by, reprinted, App. B:
    207–17
  recognition as poet, xi–xii, 184
  retirement, xi, 184, 191
  on security, 98, 145
  Swallow, argument with, 162, 241
    ch. 9 n.2
  as violinist, 24, 27
  Aphorisms of, 26, 49, 51–52, 55, 234
    n.5
  AN's critique of, 50–51, 53
  AN's interest in, 89, 95, 112, 116,
    165
  attempts to publish, 27, 66, 239
    n.8
  examples of, reprinted, App. D:
    225–27
  on art and artists, 28, 37–38, 83–84,
    147–48, 152, 172–73, 175–76,
    180
  on California, 54, 64–65
  on courage involved in decisions,
    98

on death, 124, 197
on fame, 190
on family problems as tautology, 161
Hugh Guiler, interest in, 46, 58,
  93, 104, 155
on hospitals, 126, 195
on individual-society relationships,
  28–29
on letters as magical, 33
and Henry Miller, 72, 98, 126, 128,
  198
  asking after, 161, 166, 192, 195
  pornography article on, 110
  visit to, at Big Sur, 60–61, 64–65
and Anaïs Nin, 104, 123–24, 177,
  179, 198
  critical writings, 151
  faith in as a writer, 6
  as his ideal confessor, 70–71, 82,
    110, 157, 159
  infatuation with , 44–45, 48
  introduction of in Evanston, 235
    n.3, App. C: 219–24
  meeting with, xiv, 78
  quarrel with, 162, 167–69, 172,
    174–81
  refusal to date her letters, xvi
  waning of friendship with, xv,
    242 n.1
  See also correspondence be-
    tween AN and FP
on passion, need for, 93
poetry prize in honor of, xii, 231 n.3
and Rupert Pole:
  letter to, 185, 197–98
  visit to, in California, 50, 63–64,
    66–67, 92–93
on psychoanalysis, 55, 57, 71–73, 83
on publishers, 6, 113, 166
self-pity, defense of, 194
on typewritten letters, xvi, 21
See also: Nin, Anaïs: and Felix Pollak; Pollak, Sara: and Felix Pollak
Pollak, Hans (FP's brother), 10, 114–15
Pollak, Sara (neé Sara Allen):
  life and career, xiii
  and Anaïs Nin:
    greetings to, 16, 62, 140
    letter to, 46
    letters from, 122–23
    AN's interest in and greetings to,
      35, 42–43, 59, 63, 79–81, 95,
      97, 103, 106, 108–9, 119, 192

Index